Scripture

BLOOMSBURY GUIDES FOR THE PERPLEXED

Bloomsbury's Guides for the Perplexed are clear, concise and accessible introductions to thinkers, writers and subjects that students and readers can find especially challenging. Concentrating specifically on what it is that makes the subject difficult to grasp, these books explain and explore key themes and ideas, guiding the reader towards a thorough understanding of demanding material.

GUIDES FOR THE PERPLEXED AVAILABLE FROM BLOOMSBURY INCLUDE:

Balthasar: A Guide for the Perplexed, Rodney Howsare
Benedict XVI: A Guide for the Perplexed, Tracey Rowland
Bonhoeffer: A Guide for the Perplexed, Joel Lawrence
Calvin: A Guide for the Perplexed, Paul Helm
De Lubac: A Guide for the Perplexed, David Grumett
Luther: A Guide for the Perplexed, David M. Whitford
Pannenberg: A Guide for the Perplexed, Timothy Bradshaw
Schleiermacher: A Guide for the Perplexed, Theodore Vial
Tillich: A Guide for the Perplexed, Andrew O'Neil
Wesley: A Guide for the Perplexed, Jason A. Vickers
Zizek: A Guide for the Perplexed, Sean Sheehan

A GUIDE FOR THE PERPLEXED

Scripture

WILLIAM LAMB

B L O O M S B U R Y

LONDON • NEW DELHI • NEW YORK • SYDNEY

Bloomsbury T&T Clark

An imprint of Bloomsbury Publishing Plc

50 Bedford Square	1385 Broadway
London	New York
WC1B 3DP	NY 10018
UK	USA

www.bloomsbury.com

Bloomsbury is a registered trade mark of Bloomsbury Publishing Plc

First published 2013

British Library Cataloguing-in-Publication Data
A catalogue record for this book is available from the British Library.

ISBN: HB: 978-0-567-14953-4
PB: 978-0-567-51409-7
ePub: 978-0-567-19035-2
ePDF: 978-0-567-56338-5

Library of Congress Cataloging-in-Publication Data
Lamb, William
Scripture: A Guide for the Perplexed/ William Lamb
Includes bibliographic references and index.
ISBN 978-0-567-14953-4 (hardcover) – ISBN 978-0-567-51409-7 (pbk.)

Typeset by Newgen Knowledge Works (P) Ltd., Chennai, India
Printed and bound in India

CONTENTS

Preface   vi

1 Reading Scripture   1
2 Making History   25
3 Telling Tales   67
4 Seeking Inspiration   95
5 Calling the Shots   151
6 Conclusion   175

Notes   181
Further Reading   195
Biblical References   203
Subject Index   205

PREFACE

This compact volume is about the art of reading scripture. It is a distillation of material used in teaching a number of courses to ordinands at two Theological Colleges in the Church of England, first at the College of the Resurrection, Mirfield, and more recently at Westcott House, Cambridge. It does not pretend to be a general introduction to biblical criticism. There are plenty of introductory guides to the conventions of historical criticism and explorations of the prospects for literary theory. Instead, this book offers an exploration of the *theological* interpretation of scripture. To understand what I have attempted to say in this book, it may help the reader to know that the experience of teaching in both of these institutions is informed not simply by interactions in the lecture room, but also by a deeper shared experience of reading the scriptures in the context of prayer and worship day by day. Both Mirfield and Westcott are communities which place enormous value on praying the Daily Office. This involves saying the psalms and listening to readings from the Old and New Testaments at Morning and Evening Prayer. These offices are part of the Anglican inheritance of faith. When Thomas Cranmer distilled the seven offices of medieval monasticism into two, he sought to make them the offering of the whole Church, and he invited clergy and laity to listen to the whole of the scriptures – the whole of the psalter in the space of a month, the whole of the Old Testament in the space of a year and the New Testament read twice in the course of the year. The systematic reading of scripture shapes the life of both these communities. They take scripture seriously. So before I acknowledge my thanks to particular individuals who have helped and guided me in writing this book, I want to acknowledge a considerable debt to two communities of faith for reminding me and showing me how to listen to the scriptures prayerfully and attentively.

While this 'spiritual exercise' has formed and shaped my own reflection and thinking about the reading of scripture, it is also important to acknowledge another point which emerges from this. One of the things that distinguishes the books of the Christian Bible from other ancient texts – indeed, the thing that makes them sacred scripture – is the fact that they are read in the context of Christian worship. I share the conviction that worship is the basic and fundamental activity of the Church of God. To write a book about the theological interpretation of scripture without acknowledging the significance of a worshipping community and the practices associated with the reading and interpretation of scripture would be very odd indeed. As Dom Jean Leclercq, the great Benedictine who produced one of the classic studies of *lectio divina*, wrote, 'just as there is no theology without moral life and asceticism, so there is no theology without prayer'.[1] Whatever the influence the Bible may have in the development of Western culture, the Bible is not simply a cultural artefact. It is also a religious text. The scriptures serve to animate the practice of Christian discipleship. They serve to transform and shape the theological imagination through prayer and worship. That is not to lay claim to the Christian scriptures as some kind of personal possession. It is simply to acknowledge that the reading of these texts in public worship and in private devotion continues to enliven Christian communities all over the world. This practice is a proper subject for theological reflection and scholarly inquiry.

I am grateful for the encouragement, help and advice of a number of friends and colleagues: Professor Loveday Alexander, Fr Peter Allan CR, Dr Tiffany Conlin, the Revd Gillian Cooper, Canon Simon Cowling, Professor James Crossley, Professor Philip Davies, Dr Andrew Davison, Professor William Horbury, the Revd Richard Jenkins, Dr Philip Jenson, the Revd Max Kramer, Dr Andrew Mein, Dr Elizabeth Phillips, Dr Jeff Phillips, Professor Hugh Pyper, Dr Vicky Raymer, the Revd Samantha Stayte and Dr Margie Tolstoy, the Archivist at Westcott House. I am also grateful to the students of the College of the Resurrection, Mirfield and the Cambridge Theological Federation for their provocative questions and helpful feedback.

The writer of Ecclesiasticus tells us that 'A scholar's wisdom comes of ample leisure' (Eccl. 38.24). Whether there is any evidence of wisdom or scholarship in this book I will leave the reader to decide, but I would like to record my thanks to the Rt Revd Stephen Conway, the Chair of Westcott Council, and the Revd Canon Martin Seeley, the Principal of Westcott House, for making me take time out in a busy schedule to devote time to writing this book. I am also grateful to Anna Turton and the staff at Bloomsbury for their careful assistance and gracious patience in allowing me a little more 'ample leisure' than they had perhaps anticipated at first.

CHAPTER ONE

Reading Scripture

In the gentle sunshine of a garden in Milan, a young man is sitting under a fig tree. Protected by its shade, he is burning with shame and remorse. Captivated by the drama of his own suffering, he weeps with a mixture of bitterness and despair. No one seems able to stir him from his listless introspection. And yet, suddenly and mysteriously, he is distracted by a sound, carried by the breeze from the open window of a neighbouring house. He hears the sound of a child singing over and over again, 'Take it and read it: *Tolle, lege*'. He picks up a copy of the first book which comes to hand, opens it and reads the first passage he finds: 'Not in revelry and drunkenness, not in debauchery and licentiousness, not in quarrelling and jealousy, but put on the Lord Jesus Christ, and make no provision for the flesh, to gratify its desires' (Rom. 13.13–14).

This is the rather startling way in which St Augustine of Hippo describes the moment of his conversion in the summer of AD 386. In his *Confessions*, he reveals the way in which he responds to this curious invitation to read a passage from scripture: 'I neither wished nor needed to read further. At once, with the last words of this sentence, it was as if a light of relief from all anxiety flooded into my heart. All the shadows of doubt were dispelled'.[1] In that instant, Augustine recognized that his conversion to true philosophy would only ever be satisfied when he had embraced the Christian faith. In the account of his conversion, he goes on to describe his experience to his friend, Alypius. His friend asks to see the text he has been reading. When Augustine shows him the

passage, Alypius, unconstrained by Augustine's decision to read
no further, is mesmerized by the passage which follows: 'Receive
the person who is weak in faith' (Rom. 14.1). Alypius applies these
words to himself. He interprets these words as a direct and personal
summons, and he resolves from that moment to join Augustine in
his newly found faith.

There is little doubt that Augustine's description of his
experience at this point was informed by his reading of the life
of St Antony of Egypt.[2] In fact, Augustine describes the call of
Antony almost in the same breath as he recounts the experience
of his own conversion. Antony, who lived between c. AD 251
and AD 356, had heard the words of Jesus Christ recorded in St
Matthew's Gospel: 'Go, sell all you have, give to the poor, and you
shall have treasure in heaven; and come, follow me' (Mt. 19.21).
Antony heard these words and took them to be words addressed
directly to him. Selling his possessions and gathering a small circle
of friends with him, he withdrew into the desert to establish a
monastic community. It is for this reason that Antony is often
acknowledged as the father of Christian monasticism.

These pivotal incidents in the lives of Augustine and Antony
share a common feature. Both these accounts appear to describe
moments of *clarity* when all doubt, anxiety, confusion and
perplexity are dispelled. Both Augustine and Antony see their lives
in a new light, and, in both cases, their lives are illuminated by the
words of scripture. But the words of scripture are also understood
in terms of divine address. Some kind of divine disclosure arises
in their engagement with the scriptures. In both cases, Augustine
and Antony give expression to their encounter with the mystery of
God. Their reading of these texts is grounded in a profound sense
of *trust* that God is speaking to them. Although we might baulk at
the rather curious form of Augustine's encounter with the sacred
text, the direct appropriation and application of these words of
Paul offer a moment of clarity and insight. It is a moment of intense
lucidity. He comes to see his whole life in a new perspective, a
perspective which is shaped by the language and imagery of the
Bible.

The conversion of St Augustine has enormous significance for the
intellectual history of Western Europe. This is not simply because
his *Confessions* remain one of the great masterpieces of Western
literature. The reason is that, from the time of late antiquity,

Augustine has exercised a profound influence over the development of Christian theology in the West. His theology represents an unwavering synthesis of faith and reason, drawing on the wisdom of the Christian tradition as well as preserving the insights of ancient philosophy. Henry Chadwick, one of the most perceptive and astute of recent commentators on Augustine's legacy, notes that 'Anselm, Aquinas, Petrarch . . ., Luther, Bellarmine, Pascal, and Kierkegaard all stand in the shade of his broad oak. His writings were among the favourite books of Wittgenstein. He was the *bête noire* of Nietzsche. His psychological analysis anticipated parts of Freud: he first discovered the existence of the "sub-conscious".'[3] In other words, Augustine has contributed in significant ways to the development of Western philosophy and thought. This extraordinary legacy stems from a distracted moment when he picked up a copy of the Christian scriptures and read words which he understood to be addressed directly to him.

One can respond to these observations about the influence of scripture in two rather different ways: first, one might conclude from these observations that the Christian scriptures constitute little more than a cultural artefact in the genealogy of Western thought and literature. Scripture is worthy of study simply because of the way in which it has continued to animate aspects of Western culture through the centuries. Indeed, the recent celebrations associated with the four hundredth anniversary of the King James Bible tended to underline the role of the Bible as a cultural artefact. As celebrities and politicians were invited to wax lyrical about the beauty of its language and the significance of its influence, many could express how reading the Bible had enriched their understanding of poetry and literature but few were as confident in articulating the way in which reading scripture might be construed as a spiritual exercise. In contrast to Augustine, commentators were rather more coy about speaking of reading the scriptures in terms of divine address. The second kind of response to these observations begins with the recognition that for Augustine the reading of scripture was intimately related to his understanding of God. There was a *theological* emphasis and a *religious* orientation in his reading of scripture, which needs to be taken seriously if we are to begin to do justice to its influence and legacy, not only for the history of Western thought and literature, but also for the Church's life and witness in the twenty-first century.

Nevertheless, such a *theological* emphasis in the reading of scripture is not as straightforward as it might appear. The sense that God speaks with clarity and directness through the scriptures may not seem so persuasive to the modern reader. And this is perhaps the reason why recent commentators have been so coy about speaking of scripture in a more theological or religious sense. While we might celebrate the King James Bible as one of the great gifts of the English Reformation and happily concede that Augustine exercised considerable influence over the Reformers, we might also want to acknowledge that we still live with the consequences of the considerable conflict and dispute which came to dominate the Reformation period. Much of that conflict centred on the interpretation of scripture. When one considers the way in which William Tyndale was persecuted and copies of his translation of the New Testament were burned, one is drawn inexorably to the conclusion that the Bible has sometimes generated more heat than light. Moreover, when this curious assortment of ancient texts in Hebrew and Greek is subjected to the criticisms and judgements inherited from some of the greatest thinkers of the Enlightenment, the writings of the Old and New Testaments appear to be rather more obscure and strange than the clarity and directness described by Augustine in his *Confessions* would suggest. The witness of scripture, with its account of creation and its description of miracles, angels and demons, appears to be at odds with modern scientific knowledge and discovery. Critics have also pointed out that the witness of scripture appears to be *inconsistent* at a number of points: for example, in 1 Sam. 21.1–6, there is an account of David and his men eating the bread of the Presence, which was reserved for priests, in the days when 'Ahimelech' was the priest. In Mk 2.26, Jesus says that this event occurred when 'Abiathar' was the high priest. Abiathar was in fact the son of Ahimelech. Mark's gospel begins with a quotation attributed to 'Isaiah the prophet', and yet the quotation is a combination of passages from Exod. 23.20, Mal. 3.1 and Isa. 40.3. Aware of this error, later scribes attempted to amend Mark's text so that it said: 'As it is written in the prophets . . .' Indeed, one of the greatest biblical scholars of the early Church, Origen of Alexandria (c. AD 185–254), suggested that the Evangelist had deliberately abridged a number of oracles to enable the reader to see that the entire prophetic witness pointed towards the coming of the Messiah. There is also a number of discrepancies between the gospels: for example, there is a discrepancy between the Synoptic gospels and John's Gospel with regard to the timing of the crucifixion. Mark's gospel places the crucifixion the day after the Passover (Mk 14.14–15 suggests that the Last Supper is a Passover meal), whereas Jn 19.14–16 and 19.31 suggest that the arrest, trial and crucifixion of Jesus had taken place before the Passover.

The texts contained within scripture were produced at different times and in different places, and the question of which texts were to be regarded as Christian scripture by virtue of their inclusion in the *canon* emerged over a period of time. In some respects, this is still a contested question: Anglican, Eastern Orthodox, Protestant and Roman Catholic Christians each have slightly different accounts of the precise canon of scripture: while there is common agreement between Christians about the contents of the New Testament, Protestants have 39 books in their Old Testament, while Roman Catholics have 46 and Eastern Orthodox Christians have 51. Anglicans share the 39 books of the Old Testament with Protestants, while also drawing on 14 additional books from the Septuagint, which are printed between the Old and New Testaments in the Apocrypha. Anglicans read these 'for example of life and instruction of manners'. In the absence of a division between the Old Testament and the Apocrypha, Roman Catholics and Eastern Orthodox Christians read these books in a different order. The emergence of these differences is in part due to some of the striking differences between the Masoretic text of the Hebrew Bible and the Septuagint (this Greek translation contains a number of additional books, such as Tobit, Judith and the Wisdom of Solomon). Moreover, just as these disagreements over the shape of the Christian canon stem from the reception of different translations of the biblical text, Christians have also discovered that the task of translation itself has not always been a straightforward exercise. At certain points, the translation of these Hebrew, Aramaic and Greek texts proves challenging, even perplexing: for example, 1 Sam. 13.1 describes the beginning of the reign of King Saul. The Hebrew reads literally, 'Saul's age was one when he became king and he reigned two years over Israel'. In the context of the story, this sentence simply does not make sense. To attempt to make sense of the passage, the King James Version follows medieval rabbinic interpretation and renders the verse as follows: 'Saul reigned one year; and when he had reigned two years over Israel, Saul chose him three thousand men of Israel'. The New International Version seeks to address the lacunae in the text by presenting the following translation: 'Saul was [thirty] years old when he became king, and he reigned over Israel [forty-] two years'. Although these are ingenious solutions, both are an approximation to the Hebrew. Similarly, in Mk 3.21, the evangelist uses a phrase *hoi par' autou* which most translators would now understand as a reference to the family of Jesus. Translated literally, the phrase means 'those beside him'. It is no accident that within the history of interpretation of this passage, some commentators understood this phrase to refer to the scribes and Pharisees surrounding Jesus at that particular moment in Mark's narrative.[4] There is an ambiguity about the language of scripture which means that the act of translation is almost always an unfinished business – hence the bewildering range of modern translations.

Questions of authorship are also controversial. When subjected to further scrutiny, many of the books within scripture appear to be *pseudepigraphal*, that is, they were not written by the author to which they have been ascribed. For example, tradition attributes the first five books of the Old Testament, the Pentateuch, to Moses, and yet with what appears to be an unusual degree of prescience, the Book of Deuteronomy records the death of Moses at Deuteronomy 34.5. A number of letters are attributed to St Paul in the New Testament, and yet their style and content suggest that they were written by others. The Fourth Gospel, ostensibly written by St John, appears to contain a reference to the testimony of the Beloved Disciple (Jn 21.24–25), which suggests that the gospel may have been subject to a series of editorial additions.

More secular critics have also questioned the moral integrity of scripture. Oblivious to the sophisticated and challenging reading offered by Søren Kierkegaard in *Fear and Trembling*, Richard Dawkins takes great exception to the indiscretions of Abraham in the Book of Genesis and particularly the infamous tale of the sacrifice of Isaac, his son (Genesis 22): 'By the standards of modern morality, this disgraceful story is an example simultaneously of child abuse, bullying . . . and the first recorded use of the Nuremberg defence: "I was only obeying orders".'[5] And although Dawkins is largely positive about the moral teaching of Jesus of Nazareth, such a perspective is not shared by other prominent atheists of the modern period: for example, in his essay *Why I am not a Christian*, Bertrand Russell teases out the story of Jesus' cursing of the fig tree (Mk 11.12–14) to question whether Christ was the best and wisest of men. Given the gratuitous and wilful destruction of a tree, he concludes: 'I cannot myself feel that either in the matter of wisdom or in the matter of virtue Christ stands quite as high as some other people known to history. I think I should put Buddha and Socrates above Him in those respects'.[6] The example presented by Russell seems rather flippant when one compares the criticisms of others who remind us that scripture has been used to justify different forms of oppression and violence: Christians have claimed the warrant of scripture to persecute Jews (Mt. 27.25), they have used scripture to justify slavery (Gen. 9.25; Eph. 6.5–9; Col. 3.22–4.1), to persecute homosexuals (Lev. 20.13; Rom. 1.27–28; 1 Cor. 6.9–10) and to subordinate women to men (Gen. 3.16; Eph. 5.22–33; 1 Tim. 2.11–15). Consequently, to the modern critic, much of the material contained within the scriptures appears to be at best, rather obscure, or at worst, simply erroneous and offensive.

In the light of these assaults on the integrity of scripture and the reliability of its testimony, it is perhaps remarkable that there are still nearly two billion people reading these texts in the modern world and bearing witness that in reading them they discover words of divine address. But, given the sophistication of contemporary accounts of hermeneutics and the art of interpretation, is it intellectually defensible to read these ancient texts as Augustine read them? How do contemporary Christians encounter God in their reading of scripture? If people expect God to speak with clarity and directness through the words of scripture, are they not likely to be disappointed, bewildered, even perplexed?

These are the questions that provoke the writing of this *Guide for the Perplexed*. This small volume provides an analysis and discussion of the *theological* interpretation of scripture. Its aim is to explore the ways in which theologians of the twentieth and twenty-first centuries continue to wrestle with the words of scripture in the light of contemporary biblical criticism and academic discourse. It is important to emphasize that its focus is the *theological* interpretation of scripture, and its principal interest is the Bible as a religious text rather than as a cultural artefact. But such an emphasis and orientation should not for a moment suggest that scripture is suddenly any less perplexing or difficult. If anything, I will argue, it makes it more so – for the simple reason that these fragile little words seek, sometimes haltingly and obliquely, to capture the almost unbearable weight of divine glory.

The Irreducible Strangeness of Scripture

Beginning with St Augustine of Hippo, the previous section might have led the reader to assume that there is a simple contrast to be made between the 'clarity' with which the ancient reader approached scripture and the 'perplexity' with which the modern reader approaches the same texts. Is the story of the interpretation of scripture simply the story of increasing confusion and perplexity? To pose the question in this way would be extremely misleading. It would disguise the fact that ancient readers were very much aware of the fact that the Christian scriptures were made up of obscure and perplexing passages. This is evident in the fact that Christian theologians of late antiquity put so much effort and energy into the task of biblical interpretation, compiling a vast collection of commentaries on books of the Old and the New Testaments. In spite of the self-evident and luminous acuity which marked the moment of his conversion, Augustine knew that the reading of scripture was not always characterized by clarity. There were passages within the scriptures which could be unrelentingly obscure. Moreover, what seemed obvious to one commentator could easily give rise to an alternative interpretation from another commentator.

Indeed, in his *Confessions*, Augustine goes on to recognize the ambiguity of scripture. In Books 11–13, he presents a brief commentary and exposition of Genesis 1. Although this section appears to sit uneasily with the more autobiographical focus of his writing in Books 1–9, Augustine is attempting to illustrate 'that the story of the soul wandering away from God and then in torment and tears finding it way home through conversion is also the story of the entire created order'.[7] Thus the account of creation in the Book of Genesis illuminates and is illuminated by the world of human experience. In offering this interpretation, Augustine makes two significant points: first, he acknowledges that there are a number of difficult and ambiguous passages in the scriptures. In Augustine's view, this ambiguity is intended by God: 'it is not for nothing that by your will so many pages of scripture are opaque and obscure'.[8] But then, in acknowledging the obscurity of scripture, he admits that there are a number of difficult passages, which have given rise to differing interpretations. While his exegesis of Genesis 1 takes issue with heterodox accounts of creation, Augustine is also conscious of the fact that fellow Catholics might have some misgivings about his own debt to the Neoplatonist and pagan philosopher, Plotinus, in giving an account of the doctrine of creation. He attempts to resolve potential dispute by offering the following observation:

> So when one person has said "Moses thought what I say" and another "No, what I say", I think it more religious in spirit to say "Why not rather say both, if both are true?" And if anyone sees a third or a fourth and a further truth in these words, why not believe that Moses discerned all these things? For through him the one God has tempered the sacred books to the interpretations of many, who could come to see a diversity of truths. Certainly, to make a bold declaration from my heart, if I myself were to be writing something at this supreme level of authority I would choose to write so that my words would sound out with whatever diverse truth in these matters each reader was able to grasp, rather than to give a quite explicit statement of a single true view of this question in such a way as to exclude other views – provided there was no false doctrine to offend me. Therefore, my God, I do not want to be so rash as not to believe that Moses obtained this gift from you. When he wrote this passage, he perfectly perceived and had in mind all the truth we have been able to find here, and all the truth that could be found in it, which we have not been able, or have not as yet been able, to discover.[9]

This passage is significant because it illustrates one of the fundamental insights which informed the emergence of biblical commentary in the ancient world. The obscurity, even the offensiveness, of the text was one of the things that alerted the reader to its special provenance. Augustine, who had himself been a professor of grammar and literary studies in Milan, is appealing here to a literary commonplace in the ancient world: the 'obscurities' of divine literature.[10]

Ancient readers found many of the texts, which populated the canon of classical literature, particularly in the fields of literature, philosophy, law and medicine, to be rather puzzling and obscure. Chief among these texts were the writings of Homer, the great epic poems of the *Iliad* and the *Odyssey*. Although Homer's poetry was part of the 'core' curriculum in the Hellenistic schools, many pagan readers found Homer's writings problematic because they betrayed a 'disrespect for the divine'[11]: for example, when Homer suggests that the gods attempted to bind Zeus in chains, the first century pagan grammarian, Heraclitus, writes: 'For these lines, Homer deserves to be banished not just from Plato's Republic but, as they say, beyond the furthest pillars of Heracles and the inaccessible sea of Ocean'.[12] For Heraclitus, the task was to rescue Homer from accusations of blasphemy by suggesting that such difficult or obscure comments should be read allegorically. The persuasiveness of this argument, however, depended on acknowledging that the obscurity of these texts was the result of a deliberate intention on the part of the author to hint at a great many things at once. As Robert Lamberton suggests, a 'canonical' author in the ancient world was incapable of an incoherent or unacceptable statement. For early commentators, 'an offensive surface was a hint that a secondary meaning lurks beyond'.[13] It was axiomatic that an authoritative source could not be mistaken or poorly argued . . . but it could be *enigmatic*: the Greek word *ainigma* and the corresponding verb *ainittomai* had been used from the time of Plato and before to describe the meanings hidden in a text. The task of the exegete was to explain the sense of the narrative and to elucidate unfamiliar vocabulary, but there was also the opportunity to uncover, within the hints and allusions of the writer, the truths which were also hidden beneath the surface of the text. The role of the commentator was to be attentive to the mysteries inherent within the text and to tease out their meaning. The text demanded a close and intensive reading, employing all the technical skill at the interpreter's disposal.

This perhaps illustrates that the search for truth in the ancient world was essentially an exegetical and interpretative exercise. There were a number of acknowledged authorities – for example, Homer in literature, Plato and Aristotle in philosophy, Hippocrates in medicine – and those who sought to master any of these fields were required to study these foundational texts, often with the help of a commentary. Sometimes comments involved little more than attending to unfamiliar place names and people, but where the text presented more significant difficulties, its obscurity served to indicate the density of its meaning: 'any potential meaning, as long as it was coherent with what was considered to be the master's doctrine, was consequently held to be true'.[14] This 'density of meaning' provoked the need for commentary. It is worth underlining that commentary arose specifically in a pedagogical context. A commentary was a tool for teaching and learning. But a commentary was also much more than that. When members of a particular school wrote commentaries on the writings of an acknowledged authority, they were using these writings 'to think with'. In other words, the act of reading invited them to probe further and to reflect with greater intensity. It provoked further thought. It excited the imagination. It served to illuminate the intellect.

We can see intimations of this strategy for reading scripture at work in St Paul's interpretation of the Old Testament. Paul believed that the Messiah, foretold by the prophets and awaited by Israel, had come in Jesus. He had been crucified and God had raised him from the dead. Through the death and resurrection of Jesus Christ, God was bringing about forgiveness, reconciliation and nothing less than the renewal of the whole of creation. This good news was to be shared with Jews and – shockingly – with Gentiles. Many of Paul's fellow Jews disagreed. So Paul sought to demonstrate the truth of his claims with reference to the interpretation and exegesis of scripture. Paul's writings abound with references to the Old Testament, and he employs a whole range of exegetical techniques in his reading of scripture, including his distinction between 'letter and spirit' (2 Cor. 3.6) and his appeal to allegory (Gal. 4.24). His purpose was not simply to use the scriptures to authorize his theological proposals (and anoint them with the authority of scripture), but to render them intelligible to his conversation partners. And although some of his interpretations might be regarded as tendentious by other Jewish commentators, Paul was convinced that the revelation to Moses, the oracles of the prophets and the wisdom of the sages, imparted their fuller meaning when they were illuminated by the light of the knowledge of the glory of God in the face of Jesus Christ (2 Cor. 4.6). In similar vein, subsequent commentators sought to read the

Old Testament christologically. In his *Exposition of the Psalms*, Augustine of Hippo would hear in the words of the psalms the voice of Christ himself.

At the same time as he was writing his *Confessions*, Augustine also penned a short treatise *On Christian Teaching*. His purpose was to provide his students with some guidance about the interpretation of scripture. He emphasizes the fact that his students needed to understand the languages in which the scriptures are written – or at least, when words such as 'Amen' or 'Alleluia' are transliterated, the student should have some sense of what these terms mean so that he or she might be protected from uncertainty over unfamiliar words or phrases. Much of his advice concentrates on the act of reading itself. In the ancient world, 'reading' involved the ability to decipher blocks of text without any gaps between the words and without almost any punctuation. So in Book 3, Augustine suggests that the reader needs to be alert to the 'ambiguity in scripture' caused by the reader's own inaccurate punctuation – or worse, the 'heretical punctuation' associated with the proponents of Arianism. The student also needs to be alert to the inaccuracies of scribes and the infelicities of translators. The collection and comparison of different translations was as invaluable in Augustine's day as it is in our own time.

But Augustine is also fascinated by the phenomenon of 'words' and how words relate to the things which they denote. Much of the material in this treatise reads like a gentle introduction to 'semiotics'. Augustine understands 'words' as 'signs': 'a sign is a thing which of itself makes some other thing come to mind'.[15] As 'smoke' relates to 'fire', or as a 'footprint' to the one who made the imprint, or a 'trumpet' announces an 'advance' in battle, so 'words' point beyond themselves to the thing for which the word was invented. But Augustine recognizes that signs can be either 'literal' or 'metaphorical'. Augustine gives as his own example the use of the term *bovis* 'ox' which Paul employs to describe a 'worker in the gospel'.[16] Augustine recognized that words may be signs, but these signs are not univocal. Where the language and imagery of the Bible is obscure, it must be illuminated by those passages which speak with greater clarity or with reference to the rule of faith. And yet, rather than lamenting the strangeness and obscurity of scripture, Augustine suggests that all of this is divinely predetermined 'so that pride may be subdued by hard work and intellects which tend to despise things that are easily discovered may be rescued from boredom and reinvigorated'.[17] The density of meaning contained within the scriptures is evidence of a divine pedagogy at work. The human mind is not a *tabula rasa*, a blank slate, on which divine revelation is inscribed. Human reason takes an active role in apprehending divine revelation, even when 'divine eloquence' speaks through the same words in different ways.

Until the schoolmen of the Middle ages went back to the original writings of Augustine, much of Augustine's teaching was conveyed in the writings and homilies of Pope Gregory the Great, who was the Bishop of Rome from AD 590 to AD 604. Often described as one of the great Latin Fathers, Gregory's teaching achieved prominence not because he was a great innovator in theological debate but because he had an unerring ability to summarize what had gone before, to identify the fundamental points of Christian doctrine and to do so in a way which rendered these things more accessible and intelligible. It is no accident that a large proportion of his writing has come down to us in the form of the homily or sermon. Gregory's *Homilies on the Book of the Prophet Ezekiel* provide a remarkable insight into the way in which he handles scripture. In Homily 6, Gregory betrays his debt to Augustine by acknowledging 'the very obscurity of divine speech'. He goes on to say that this obscurity 'is of great benefit because it schools perception to extend itself in weariness, and so exercises it to capture what it could not seize if idle'.[18] Gregory accounts for the obscurity of scripture by describing it in terms of a kind of divine pedagogy. But again, like Augustine, he recognizes that the scriptures have given rise to a variety of different interpretations. He continues by exploring these differences with reference to an intriguing interpretation of Ezek. 1.15: 'As I looked at the living creatures, I saw a wheel . . .' For Gregory, this wheel represents holy scripture, or more properly, its interpretation:

> For the circle of its precepts is now above, now below, those which are spoken spiritually to the more perfect, and accord with the letter for the feeble, and those which little children understand literally, learned men lift above through spiritual intelligence.[19]

In this allegorical interpretation of Ezekiel, Gregory fuses the image of Ezekiel's wheel with Paul's distinction between the 'letter' and the 'spirit' in 2 Cor. 3. As the wheel turns, the reader's perception expands and is drawn from the letter to the spirit, in Gregory's words, from 'history into mystery'. Margaret Mitchell has described Paul's observation that 'the letter kills, but the Spirit gives life' (2 Cor. 3.6) as 'the Magna Carta of allegorical interpretation'[20] in the development of early Christian hermeneutics. Even so, she emphasizes – rightly – that, in their original context, these words addressed a more specific issue, namely the fact that Paul's claim to be an apostle was not supported by a letter of recommendation. And yet the undeniable consequence of Paul's words is that the letter of the text is devalued and divine intent begins to take centre stage. This passage legitimates attempts to interpret Christian scripture by moving beyond the literal sense. In this respect, Paul not only provides an important and enduring precedent, he invites further commentary. Drawing on Kathy Eden's analysis of ancient rhetoric, Mitchell notes that Paul has appropriated the opposition between the letter of the law and the intention of the legislator, a common defence used in the law-courts, while at the same time drawing on the dualistic language between flesh and spirit employed in Ezek. 11.19 and 36.26. Thus, even in Gregory's appropriation of 2 Cor. 3, there is a further, if perhaps more tangential, reference to the prophet Ezekiel.

In Gregory's interpretation of Ezekiel, the wheel keeps turning, and as it turns, we discover some of the significant characteristics of his understanding of the interpretation of scripture: first, Ezekiel identifies 'a wheel within a wheel' (Ezek. 1.16). For Gregory, this wheel within the wheel represents the New Testament hidden by allegory in the letter of the Old Testament. The New Testament is encompassed by the Old: 'what the Old Testament promised the New showed forth, and what the one covertly announced the other openly proclaimed manifest'.[21] Thus Ezekiel's vision reveals the intricate relationship between the 'four faces' of scripture: the Law, the Prophets, the Gospels and the writings of the Apostles. Secondly, he betrays a considerable debt to Origen of Alexandria and the pioneers of Christian commentary in acknowledging the different levels of meaning to be found within scripture. He recognizes that there are literal and spiritual elements. Each reader

interprets the text according to their perspective: 'the one feeds
on the history alone, another seeks the figurative, another indeed
the understanding in the contemplative mode. And it very often
happens that . . . in this one and the same perception all three
can be found at once'.[22] Gregory's understanding of these different
levels of meaning draws on his own exegesis of Ezek. 1.20 which
describes the wheels of Ezekiel's vision following wherever the
spirit went:

> For whither the spirit of the reader aims, thither divine words
> too are lifted, because if you there seek something high by seeing
> and feeling, these same sacred things grow with you, and ascend
> with you to the heights. . . . For the reader's spirit, if he there
> seeks moral or historical understanding, the perception of moral
> history follows him. If he seeks figurative knowledge, allusive
> speech is soon recognized. If contemplative, the wheels forthwith
> almost take wing and are suspended in the air because heavenly
> understanding of Holy Scripture is laid bare in words.[23]

Finally, as this passage illustrates, Gregory attributes an active
role to the reader in the task of interpretation. He insists that
biblical interpretation demands of the reader a keen intellect and
the kind of disciplined reading which is informed by contemplative
prayer and a life of virtue. This capacity for faithful interpretation
increases and progresses with time and experience: 'divine words
grow with the reader, for the deeper each understands them the
deeper they penetrate into him'.[24] By using the image of a 'wheel',
Gregory accepts that there is a curious circularity about this
progress. If faithful interpretation of scripture depends on a life
of virtue, then the reader must discover how to plot the course
of a good life by reading scripture. Gregory simply notes that
the 'wheel keeps pace with him, because as you find increase in
divine speech you will yourself have progressed within it'.[25] But
the reader's use of reason is not to be considered apart from God.
Reason is a means of participating in the life of God himself for
'the wonderful and ineffable virtue of Holy Scripture is recognized
when the mind of the reader is pervaded by divine love'.[26]
    Inevitably, each of these elements of Gregory's interpretation of
scripture will be contested in the course of subsequent centuries.
Indeed, they remain contested. Gregory sought to uphold the unity

and consistency of God's address to humanity within the witness
of scripture, and yet as subsequent chapters will reveal, this
emphasis on the unity and consistency of scriptural witness has
not always been easy or straightforward to uphold. Some Christian
theologians will come to view the relationship between the Old and
New Testaments in terms of contrast rather than continuity. Jewish
scholars will criticize the 'supersessionism' of Christian readings of
the Hebrew Bible and the scant disregard of Christian theologians
for the integrity and legitimacy of Jewish interpretations of these
texts. Moreover, Gregory's insight that there are different levels of
meaning in scripture will also come under scrutiny. The schoolmen
of the medieval period will formalize the relationship between
literal, allegorical, moral and mystical readings by quoting the
following verse:

Littera gesta docet, quid credas allegoria,
Moralis quid agas, quo tendas anagogia.

The letter shows us what God and our fathers did;
The allegory shows where our faith is hid;
The moral meaning gives us rules of daily life;
The anagogy shows us where we end our strife.[27]

From the time of the Reformation onwards, this strategy for
interpreting Christian scripture will come under increasing
scrutiny. Reformers like Luther and Calvin will insist on the
priority of the *literal* sense and the plain meaning of the text,
while many biblical critics in the modern period will also question
the way in which patristic writers rely on allegory. In their use
of allegory, Augustine and Gregory – as well as their teachers
and their successors – will be dismissed as 'incompetent', 'ill-
prepared to expound' the scriptures and just 'plain wrong'. But
even as their interpretative strategies begin to unravel, their
fundamental insight that the critical contemplation of the text
is a means of participating in the life of God will also begin to
dissolve. Increasingly, in the minds of many thinkers, reason and
revelation will become strangers rather than friends.

The story of how this dissociation between reason and
revelation took place and how this dissociation has dominated
discussions of the *theological* interpretation of scripture will be
described in the following chapters. But the telling of this story

is overshadowed by the legacy of another writer who presented a treatise about the interpretation of scripture, including a discussion of the Biblical account of Creation and some of the more perplexing and esoteric passages in the Book of Ezekiel. He was also concerned about the apparent conflict between reason and religion. The writer was a Jewish philosopher and Biblical scholar called Rabbi Moshe ben Maimon. He lived in the twelfth century. Buried in Tiberias by the Sea of Galilee, one gains some sense of his importance from the Hebrew inscription on his tomb, 'From Moses to Moses, there arose none like Moses'. He is sometimes better known as Maimonides. His treatise was entitled *The Guide for the Perplexed*.

Maimonides wrote 'to enlighten a religious man who has been trained to believe in the truth of our holy Law, who conscientiously fulfils his moral and religious duties, and at the same time has been successful in his philosophical studies. Human reason has attracted him to abide within its sphere; and he finds it difficult to accept as correct the teaching based on the literal interpretation of the Law. . . . Hence he is lost in perplexity and anxiety'.[28] Should those who have embarked on philosophical studies follow their intellect and renounce the foundations of the Law, or should they turn their back on the demands of reason? Maimonides held that they should be taught to read the scriptures correctly in order to see the deeper truths beneath the surface of the text. Much of *The Guide* is devoted to a consideration of the language used to describe God in the Hebrew Bible. Maimonides understood that the prophets spoke in metaphors and parables, and he is quick to challenge crude anthropomorphisms. When the scriptures refer to God in human terms – with reference to the 'eye', the 'face', the 'hand', the 'feet' and a variety of different terms for movement and posture – Maimonides asserted that those who read the scriptures should not be led by this kind of language to think of God in corporeal terms. These words and phrases took on a specific and unique meaning when applied to God. They referred more properly to a metaphysical attribute or characteristic of God. Thus when the scriptures refer to God as 'seated in heaven', since 'a person can best remain motionless and at rest when sitting', this refers to the fact that God is everlasting, constant and unchanging. Maimonides' understanding of metaphysics, as well as his exposition of creation in the Book of Genesis, owes a considerable debt to the philosophy of Aristotle. Indeed, his synthesis of scriptural language and

Aristotelian metaphysics held a considerable fascination for the great Dominican theologian, Thomas Aquinas (AD 1225–1274). There are explicit references to Maimonides in the *Summa theologiae*, and we should not underestimate the extraordinary richness of the exchanges about the interpretation of scripture (including sometimes vigorous argument) between Jews and Christians over the centuries.

All these writings bear witness to the fact that early Christian commentators were attuned to the irreducible strangeness of scripture, just as much as their modern counterparts. For ancient commentators, the obscurities and difficulties encountered in the text reflected a density of meaning consonant with the divine message. Moreover, provoked by the sheer unfamiliarity of these words, the intellectual effort and energy expended in understanding these mysterious words constituted an appropriate response to what Augustine and Gregory regarded as a kind of divine pedagogy, which sought to arrest our attention and excite the imagination. But it was more than that. It was a way of participating in the life of the triune God.

And yet, for all their desire to make the scriptures more accessible and to lay bare the 'obscurities of divine literature', it would be fair to say that early commentators do not always succeed in rendering the words of scripture any less obscure. Indeed, some ancient writers occasionally expressed frustration with the 'obscurity' of texts and the 'obscurantism' of their interpretation. For example, in the *Preparation for the Gospel,* Eusebius of Caesarea (c. AD 263–339) records the words of the second century Platonist philosopher, Atticus, who comments on a difficulty with Aristotle's understanding of the immortality of the soul: 'Aristotle would know this if he . . . did not cloak the difficulty of the question in obscure language, thus avoiding any controversy like cuttlefish making themselves hard to catch by their darkness'.[29] The analogy of a 'cuttlefish' is an instructive one, for as Aristotle himself observed, a 'cuttlefish' obscures itself in its own ink the moment it senses that it might be grasped.[30] One might make a similar observation about a number of ancient and more recent commentaries on scripture. The irreducible strangeness of scripture should never be a licence to shroud the language and imagery of the Bible in even greater obscurity. But to acknowledge its strangeness is to recognize that our language about God should not be easily domesticated or manipulated – or at least, to recognize that the moment it is domesticated and manipulated, it either loses all power and force or, worse, becomes something which is quite monstrous and wicked.

One writer who was particularly sensitive to the way in which people domesticate and manipulate language about God was the Danish philosopher, Søren Kierkegaard (1813–55). This sensitivity turned to outright contempt when the people concerned happened to be the clergy of the established Church. In a brief observation published in a journal, Kierkegaard attacks the triviality and mediocrity of Biblical interpretation in his own day:

> The Biblical interpretation of mediocrity goes on interpreting and interpreting Christ's words until it gets out of them its own spiritless (trivial) meaning – and then, after having removed all difficulties, it is tranquillized, and appeals confidently to Christ's words!
>
> It quite escapes the attention of mediocrity that hereby it generates a new difficulty, surely the most comical difficulty it is possible to imagine, that God should let himself be *born*, that the Truth should have come into the world . . . in order to make trivial remarks. And likewise the new difficulty as to how one is to explain that Christ could be crucified. For it is not usual in this world of triviality to apply the penalty of death for making trivial remarks, so that the crucifixion of Christ becomes both inexplicable and comical, since it is comical to be crucified because one has made trivial remarks.[31]

For Kierkegaard, embracing the irreducible strangeness of scripture involves acknowledging what might be described as the 'offensiveness' of scripture. The danger is that when readers are confronted by words which are 'offensive', they invest all their exegetical energies and powers in minimizing the offence. Hugh Pyper has argued that this perspective offers a key insight to Kierkegaard's reading of the biblical text. Kierkegaard is 'the great poet of offence in Scripture' and he refuses to minimize the offence. This is an act of faith. To refuse to entertain the sheer difficulty of scripture requires not faith, but spiritlessness.[32] To deny the difficulty of scripture is to embrace a world of triviality and half-truths which only serve to deaden the human spirit and destroy humanity's relationship with God.

In *Sickness unto Death*, Kierkegaard, adopting the pseudonym of Anti-Climacus, writes that:

> The Jews had a perfect right to be offended by Christ because he claimed to forgive sins. It takes a singularly high degree of spiritlessness (that is, as ordinarily found in Christendom), if one is not a believer (and if one is a believer, one does believe that Christ was God), not to be offended at someone's claim to forgive sins. And in the next place, it takes an equally singular spiritlessness not to be offended at the very idea that sin can be forgiven. For the human understanding, this is almost impossible – but I do not therefore laud as genius the inability to believe it, for it *shall* be believed.[33]

For the human understanding this is impossible, and yet as Kierkegaard has already asserted: 'What is decisive is that with God everything is possible'.[34] For Kierkegaard, the words 'Your sins are forgiven' are the most offensive words in scripture. However sophisticated our hermeneutics or skilled our exegesis may be, these words offend our notions of justice and injustice, of reward and punishment, of integrity and responsibility. For Kierkegaard, these words are not trivial. They are scandalous. They serve to underline and emphasize the irreducible strangeness of scripture.

A Guide for the Perplexed

One of the striking things about this description of the strangeness of scripture and the way in which theologians have responded to this through the centuries is that it mirrors – almost exactly – many of the concerns of scripture's more recent secular detractors. The point is that scripture is difficult. It is obscure. It is offensive. Above all, it is perplexing. And in following in the footsteps of Maimonides and writing *A Guide for the Perplexed*, it is important to emphasize that the very act of making these texts more accessible reveals – paradoxically – that they are also challenging and difficult. They invite us into what, Karl Barth, the great Reformed theologian of the Twentieth Century, described as 'the strange new world within the Bible'.

This is not to suggest that the purpose of the *theological* interpretation of scripture is to shroud the text in further obscurities. Rather it is to challenge and subvert the dominant ideology which has characterized the emergence of biblical criticism since the eighteenth and nineteenth centuries. The argument goes something like this: for centuries, the interpretation of scripture was constrained by the shackles of ecclesiastical dogma. Then a moment of liberation came in the eighteenth century with the Age of Enlightenment. This marked humanity's coming of age and the emancipation of human consciousness. Its leading thinkers insisted on the objective and universal claims of reason in establishing questions of truth and meaning. And this had significant implications for the interpretation of scripture. An idle appeal to the authority of revelation was no longer sufficient. Its truth was no longer self-evident, and so, modern biblical criticism emerged. Advocates of modern biblical criticism viewed with scepticism anything that hinted at a more dogmatic or theological frame of reference: for example, biblical scholars would no longer be content to interpret Johannine Christology through 'Chalcedonian-tinted' spectacles. Such a perspective would only serve to obscure the writings of the New Testament. Biblical scholars, schooled in the rigours of historical criticism, would bring an element of dispassionate objectivity to the exercise.

In response, a good number of contemporary theologians have come to reject the claim that Christian doctrine is 'a moldering scrim of antique prejudice obscuring the meaning of the Bible'.[35] Eschewing the claims of historical criticism and literary theory, they have sought to promote the *theological* interpretation of scripture and have often drawn on the insights and exegesis of pre-modern writers like Augustine and Gregory. Theologians have argued for a 'return to allegory'. They have advocated 'figural readings' of the Old Testament. They have made a variety of claims about the superiority of pre-modern exegesis.

Tracing the development of biblical interpretation from Augustine of Hippo onwards, it would be easy to assume that in this *Guide to the Perplexed,* I will proceed in similar vein. Disappointing as this may be to some readers, I should disclose right at the outset that I will not do so. Instead, I will argue that the relationship

between historical criticism, literary theory and the development
of Christian doctrine is much more complex than at first it appears.
The problem with the dominant ideology surrounding the emergence
of biblical criticism is that historical criticism and literary theory
are not simply the product of modern habits of thought. As George
Steiner argues, these modern disciplines may in fact draw on far
more ancient antecedents:

> The discipline of reading, the very idea of close commentary
> and interpretation, textual criticism as we know it, derive
> from the study of Holy Scripture or, more accurately, from the
> incorporation and development in that study of older practices
> of Hellenistic grammar, recension and rhetoric. Our grammars,
> our explications, our criticisms of texts, our endeavours to pass
> from letter to spirit, are the immediate heirs to the textualities
> of western Judaeo-Christian theology and biblical-patristic
> exegetics. What we have done since the masked scepticism of
> Spinoza, since the critiques of rationalist Enlightenment and
> since the positivism of the nineteenth century, is to borrow
> vital currency, vital investments and contracts of trust from
> the bank or treasure-house of theology. It is from there that we
> have borrowed our theories of the symbol, our use of the iconic,
> our idiom of poetic creation and aura . . . We have borrowed,
> traded upon, made small change of the reserves of transcendent
> authority. Very few of us have made any return deposit. At its key
> points of discourse and inference, hermeneutics and aesthetics
> in our secular, agnostic civilization are a more or less conscious,
> a more or less embarrassed act of larceny.[36]

In other words, biblical scholars who assert that their enterprise
is essentially part of a 'secular' project are insufficiently alert to
the fact that the tools they use have been formed and shaped in
the crucible of Christian doctrinal development. But it is also true
to say that Christian theologians have always engaged with and
drawn upon the insights of contemporary forms of historiography
and literary theory, whether they are those associated with the
'older practices of Hellenistic grammar and rhetoric' or more
recent developments in the fields of historical criticism and literary
theory. In spite of the posturing of 'secular' biblical critics on
the one hand, and advocates of the 'theological' interpretation

of scripture on the other, the emergence of biblical criticism should not simply be described with reference to a moment of radical discontinuity at some point in the eighteenth century. The Age of Enlightenment marked a number of significant shifts in the history of biblical interpretation – particularly with regard to the relationship between revelation and reason, and the development of modern historiography – but there were also a number of striking points of continuity.

So there are two tasks at the heart of this particular guide: first, I will seek to describe those elements of continuity and discontinuity in the history of biblical interpretation in relation to developments in historiography and literary theory; and secondly, I will also describe the way in which a number of theologians in the twentieth and twenty-first centuries have sought to negotiate those elements of continuity and discontinuity as they continue to wrestle with the irreducible strangeness of scripture. *Chapter 2* will describe some of the significant developments in historiography and how they have come to shape modern biblical criticism. *Chapter 3* will describe some of the corresponding developments in the field of literary criticism. *Chapter 4* will offer a survey and analysis of a number of different ways in which theologians have responded to these developments. *Chapter 5* will explore and assess the debate and conflict that has been generated by different interpretations of scripture, particularly with regard to questions of authority in the life of the Church. Finally, I will offer some observations about how these perspectives might be drawn together in order that the art of reading scripture might become both a critical and a spiritual exercise.

So the purpose is not to demonstrate to those who are perplexed by the scriptures that the Bible is just a compendium of common sense if only you apply a few simple rules of interpretation. Whether it is the jealousy and rivalry of Jacob and Esau, the violence of Judges, the flaws in David's character, the sensuousness of the Song of Songs, the injustice of Job or the emotional range of joy and lament in the Psalter, when we actually bother to read the Bible, we learn something of its capacity to resist the description of human experience in one-dimensional or trivial terms. The truth is that the Bible is uncomfortable, difficult, challenging and perplexing. It is all these things because – as Augustine and Gregory recognized – the words of scripture capture something of our response to the extraordinary passion, the incalculable risk and the sheer mystery of divine love:

> So anyone who thinks that he has understood the Holy Scriptures or any part of them, but cannot by his understanding build up this twofold love of God and neighbour, has not yet succeeded in understanding them.[37]

CHAPTER TWO

Making History

St Augustine's account of his own conversion after reading a passage from St Paul's Epistle to the Romans seems at first sight to be entirely clear. He describes the reading of scripture in terms of complete and utter perspicuity. And yet, this same passage from Augustine's *Confessions* became the subject of some controversy in the course of the twentieth century. In the *Recherches sur les 'Confessions' de saint Augustin,* Pierre Courcelle proposed that Augustine's account of his conversion was not as straightforward as it first appeared. He argued that Augustine's description of 'sitting under a fig tree', selecting a passage at random as if drawing a lot, and hearing the voice 'of a child' needed to be understood in the light of more ancient conventions of reading and interpretation. Courcelle thought that the fig tree could have had a purely symbolic value in Augustine's imagination. It may have represented nothing other than 'the mortal shadow of sin'. Moreover, Augustine's reference to the child's voice might be a literary device, a way of representing the divine response to Augustine's questioning. Courcelle argued that the *Confessions* were essentially a theological work. His argument unleashed an avalanche of criticism and debate. As Pierre Hadot points out, most of Courcelle's critics 'were victims of the modern, anachronistic prejudice that consists in believing that Augustine's *Confessions* is primarily an autobiography'.[1] Courcelle took the view that when reading theological works of this kind, it was often difficult to tell the difference between a symbolic enactment and an account of a historical event. Nevertheless, it was important to recognize that one of the characteristics of this particular kind of literary work was that the language of symbolic enactment and historical event was often combined.

Clearly, the conventions of ancient historiography were rather different from the conventions that we follow today. Did Augustine actually sit under a fig tree? Did he hear the voice of a child singing from an open window? It is intriguing to note that when reading scripture, we are often confronted by exactly the same kinds of questions: Did Joshua conquer the city of Jericho? Did King David actually send Uriah the Hittite into battle in order that he might steal Bathsheba, his wife? Did a census take place while Quirinius was the governor of Syria? Did the Magi visit Bethlehem? When exactly was Jesus put to death? We may respond to these questions by asserting that as theological works, the books of the Bible often combine the language of symbol, metaphor, myth with real historical events. We must judge them according to the conventions of ancient historiography and ancient literary criticism. We would be doing them a great disservice if we were to read them by the conventions of modern historiography.

And yet, distinguishing between the conventions of ancient and modern historiography is not as simple as it might at first appear. Early Christians were still interested in historical events. Thus, alongside the writings of the Old Testament, the first Christians also came to treasure the teaching of the first apostles and their immediate successors, particularly their memories of the life and teaching of Jesus. They held on to a number of their writings, including their letters, and they came to place enormous value on the authority of their testimony. Justin Martyr (c. AD 100–165) refers to 'the memoirs of the apostles' in his *First Apology* and the *Dialogue with Trypho the Jew*.[2] He notes that these memoirs or gospels were read along with the writings of the prophets every Sunday in the church at Rome. Intriguingly, it seems that these texts were recorded not in the form of a papyrus scroll, but in a papyrus codex or a leaf book, rather like a modern book. A codex was essentially a notebook, which was easily portable and which was often associated with a text in a draft form. Most of the first-century codices retrieved in recent archaeological discoveries show that codices contain documents such as business accounts, receipts, inventories, school exercises and personal notes. This suggests that the material was to be regarded as provisional in some way. Given that they bear evidence of editorial activity and emendation, the fact that the gospels were written in codices may go some way to describe the fluidity of their textual development. It also explains some of the theories about the written and oral sources used by the writers of the synoptic gospels.

Given the fluidity of these traditions, it may come as no surprise that there were also other writings, which emerged in the course of the second and third centuries. These works, later regarded as 'apocryphal', presented something of a challenge to the church fathers, who regarded both their teaching as heterodox and their testimony as unreliable. St Irenaeus of Lyons, who lived in the second century, proved to be a formidable adversary of those who sought to promote the authenticity of these apocryphal works, particularly the Valentinians and proponents of other Gnostic heresies, 'knowledge falsely so-called'. In *Against the Heresies*, Irenaeus says that 'these people compile old wives' tales and then, transferring sayings and words and parables, want to accommodate the words of God to their fables'.[3] He goes on to enumerate their false teachings and their curious exegesis of more familiar narratives. To describe the inadequacies of their interpretations, he uses the analogy of a large mosaic of a king, which had been carefully created by a skilful artist out of precious stones. The Gnostic comes along and rearranges the stones to make the image of a dog or fox, while pretending that it was in fact the image of a king. It was in this context that Irenaeus and others attempted to establish some clear constraints on the *canon* of the New Testament. The arguments advanced by Irenaeus to achieve this are significant. The most important feature of Irenaeus' argument is that he appeals to the tradition to legitimate his claims about the canon, and in doing so he makes a clear distinction between the faith that is handed on by the apostles and the contents of the canon: 'And then, if the apostles had not left us the scriptures, would it not be best to follow the sequence of the tradition which they transmitted to those to whom they entrusted the churches?'[4]

This sets up a curiously circular argument about the relationship between scripture and tradition. On the one hand, the scriptures are normative for the development of subsequent tradition. On the other hand, the establishment of the canon of scripture itself is dependent upon the tradition handed down within the churches. Irenaeus draws on the testimony of Papias and Polycarp in particular to demonstrate that the four evangelists were reliable witnesses to the tradition of the apostles. Polycarp was particularly important. Irenaeus regarded him as the strongest witness to the tradition because Polycarp had met a number of the apostles. More importantly, Irenaeus had met Polycarp and provided a direct personal link between Christ and himself. But this direct connection ensured the authenticity of his teaching:

> [Polycarp] always taught the doctrine he had learned from the apostles, which he delivered to the church, and it alone is true. All the churches in Asia bear witness to this, as well as the successors of Polycarp to this day, and he was a witness to the truth of much greater authority and more reliable than Valentinus and Marcion and the others with false opinions.[5]

The premise that the authority of apostolic teaching is derived from and dependent upon these authentic traditions provided the basis of Irenaeus' critique of Gnostics such as Valentinus and Marcion. As his argument unfolds, Irenaeus seeks to demonstrate that there should only be four gospels, that Luke wrote Acts, that the church required a comprehensive list of Pauline and Catholic Epistles and that the writing of the Book of Revelation came at the end of the reign of Domitian. Although scholars have debated the origins of the canon, it seems clear that the determining factor for Irenaeus was whether the writings of the New Testament reflected the real and authentic testimony of the apostles. This determined whether a book should be included in the canon or not.

Although modern biblical scholarship might sit uneasily with Irenaeus' bullish claim that the canonical gospels reflected the verbatim records of the first apostles, the emphasis given by Irenaeus to the value of apostolic testimony invites further reflection on the role of testimony in shaping the Christian vision. Irenaeus was not being particularly innovative in emphasizing the value of testimony. We see a similar emphasis in the Johannine writings: 'This is the disciple who is testifying to these things and has written them, and we know that his testimony is true' (Jn 21.24). Presenting this 'testimony' was not simply about providing the raw data in order to enable the modern commentator to say exactly what happened. The writings of the New Testament describe a series of events, which are presented in such a way as to render their 'testimony' intelligible in terms of the language and discourse of the Old Testament. This 'testimony' draws on these earlier writings for its inspiration and guide. At the same time, the writings of the Old Testament are used in a way, which is bold, creative and innovative. The 'testimony' of the New Testament is presented in such a way as to demonstrate the fulfilment of God's promises in the death and resurrection of Jesus Christ. This 'testimony' seeks to demonstrate God's faithfulness to the covenant with Israel in the Old Testament. The consequence is that this 'testimony' is contested almost from the very beginning, not because the occurrence of the event reported is disputed but because aspects of the interpretive framework used to explain its significance and meaning are not shared. In other words, the ways in which the writings of the Old Testament were read by the earliest Christian communities were disputed by other Jews. Their interpretation was contested.

The fashioning of this apostolic testimony served a clear theological purpose. The writers of the New Testament sought to demonstrate the coherence and faithfulness of God's action in the world. Any reading of the first few chapters of a canonical gospel or a Pauline letter will demonstrate that these writings resonate with an abundance of quotations and phrases from the Old Testament. The 'testimony' of the New Testament sought to bear witness to God's faithfulness to his promises. By contrast, many of the 'apocryphal' New Testament writings negotiated these issues in a very different way, either by drawing a contrast between the God of the Old Testament and the God of the New Testament, or by ignoring the Old Testament completely. And this observation points to the paradox that lies at the heart of the 'testimony' of the New Testament. While the writers of the New Testament sought to render their 'testimony' intelligible with reference to the Old Testament, they were seeking at the same time to find the words to describe the profound *novelty* of what had been revealed in the death and resurrection of Jesus Christ. Indeed, when Paul went into the synagogue in Thessalonica and 'argued with them from the scriptures, explaining and proving that it was necessary for the Messiah to suffer and to rise from the dead, and saying, "This is the Messiah, Jesus whom I am proclaiming to you"' (Acts 17.2b–3), it is significant that in the riot that ensued Paul and other Christian believers are described as 'these people who have been turning the world upside down' (Acts 17.6). These words give expression to the disruptive character of the testimony presented within the New Testament. They are trying to explain a range of experiences and insights that have caused them to reinterpret, to rework and to rewrite Israel's story in order to amplify its meaning and significance.

When we consider the development of the canon in this way, I want to suggest that it is perhaps more helpful to think of the Bible as a project rather than as an object. The development of the canon is dependent upon a tradition of apostolic testimony handed down within the churches. The memoirs and letters of the apostles and their immediate followers seek to bear witness to what God has revealed in Jesus Christ. At the same time, the writings of the Old Testament serve to render that witness intelligible. Indeed, when we consider the theological debates generated over centuries between the Churches and their disagreements about the precise list of books contained within the canon, it becomes increasingly difficult to describe the Bible as a single object. When we also reflect on the advances made by textual critics since the time of Erasmus and the revisions made to the biblical text in the light of the discovery of more ancient manuscripts, we begin to recognize that there are further elements of fluidity about the canon. Moreover, when we consider the way in which these texts have been translated and retranslated into more and more languages, and the extraordinary array of different versions that are available today, it becomes increasingly difficult to identify the Bible with a single object. But to acknowledge the fluidity of the Christian canon does not mean that we have to relativize everything that it has to say. Understanding the Bible as a project means recovering the emphasis placed by Irenaeus on apostolic testimony. The purpose of identifying a canon, the purpose of reviewing textual variants in order to establish the reliability of the text, the purpose of translating the text into every single language on the planet, is to enable the Church to hand on apostolic testimony about Jesus Christ from one generation to the next.

And yet, this testimony has been contested from the very beginning. When the New Testament writers wrote about the mystery of the incarnation, they were describing events, which took place in space and time. They were writing about events, which took place at the beginning of the first century on the eastern edge of the Roman Empire. For the writers of the New Testament, a series of events in the life of a Palestinian peasant during the reign of the Emperor Tiberius (AD 14–37) had universal significance. By contrast, the Roman historian, Tacitus (AD 56–117) could write, 'Under Tiberius nothing happened'.[6] These words are a provocative reminder about the disruptive character of apostolic testimony. They are also a reminder that the meaning and significance of a number of historical events is contested. One of the consequences of this is that Christian theologians and biblical interpreters have been challenged by the questions of historiography at almost every turn. This chapter describes the way theologians and biblical scholars have responded to the challenge.

The Development of Early Christian Historiography

While one might assume that debates over the contents of the Christian canon were essentially an internal matter for the Christian church, a more accurate picture emerges when one recognizes that debates about the reliability of their scriptures were also shaped and influenced by the need for early Christian apologists to provide a clear and robust account of the intellectual foundations of their faith. In the course of the first three centuries of the Christian era, a number of pagan thinkers had challenged the central tenets of the Christian faith. One of their principal lines of attack was to call into question the *origins* and *provenance* of the Christian church and the authenticity of their foundational documents. These pagan critics were quick to exploit perceived inconsistencies in the writings of the New Testament. For example, around AD 175, the Platonist philosopher, Celsus, wrote a comprehensive attack on the Christian faith in his treatise *On True Doctrine*. Fragments of this work are recorded in the counterblast produced by Origen of Alexandria some decades later. One of the remarkable things about Celsus is that his writings suggest that he has taken some trouble to engage with

the writings of the New Testament, particularly the gospels. The
passages quoted by Origen contain allusions to Matthew, Luke
and John. Celsus had noticed that there appeared to be some
inconsistencies between the genealogies of Matthew and Luke.
In a rather prescient discussion of the 'Messianic Secret', he notes
that at some points in the gospel narrative, Jesus wishes to remain
hidden and concealed, and yet at other points, his identity is fully
disclosed by 'a voice from heaven'. Origen objects that Celsus is
seeking to convict the writings 'of discrepancy'.[7] He refutes Celsus
by observing that there is a proper distinction to make between
revealing something to a multitude and revealing it to a select
gathering. It is apparent from *Against Celsus* that Celsus himself
has engaged with a range of writings associated with Christians
but he is not too bothered about the detail. This enables Origen
to counter his arguments relatively successfully.

By contrast, the Neoplatonist philosopher, Porphyry (AD
234–c.305) was a much more challenging adversary. Again only
extracts of his writings against Christians survive and much of
the material has to be gleaned from the writings of Eusebius of
Caesarea. It is clear from these extracts that Porphyry was not
only skilled in the forensic analysis of texts but he also had a
deep knowledge and understanding of the Christian scriptures.
He knew that there were discrepancies between the genealogies
in Mt. 1.1–16 and Lk. 3.23–38. He criticized Mark's conflation
of Mal. 3.1 and Isa. 40.3 and its attribution to the prophet Isaiah
at Mk 1.2–3. He took issue with Matthew's attribution of a
passage from the Psalms to Isaiah. In the account of the Gadarene
demoniac, he noted that Mark included details which were not
found in Matthew's account. And he discovered numerous
inconsistencies between the gospels in their respective passion
narratives.[8]

As far as Porphyry was concerned, the evangelists were
writers of fiction. They were not observers or eyewitnesses of
the life of Jesus. These criticisms presented a serious challenge
to Christian theologians and biblical scholars. They needed
to develop arguments to refute those of their detractors. This
was a task to which Eusebius of Caesarea (c. AD 263–339) was
absolutely committed. Eusebius sought to address the issues
presented by Porphyry, to explain the discrepancies in the
gospels and to refute his contention that the gospels contained

little of historical value. He also produced a detailed comparison of the four canonical gospels by means of a numbering system which was incorporated in what became known as the Eusebian Canons. These tables which adorn many ancient and medieval manuscripts of the gospels provide a kind of synopsis, which enables the reader to compare the similarities and differences of the accounts provided by the evangelists. Early Christian commentators put considerable energy and ingenuity into explaining or minimizing these differences. There is an evident concern to demonstrate the 'accuracy' of the gospel accounts. Indeed, Eusebius' wider contribution to the development of historiography is worthy of further comment. Arnaldo Momigliano has suggested that by drawing on the contents of the library established by Origen in Caesarea Maritima, Eusebius presented a rich anthology of documentary evidence in his writings which served to transform the practice of historiography as it developed in the fourth century AD. Momigliano recognizes the great debt of modern historiography to ancient Greek historians like Herodotus and Thucydides, but he also acknowledges the influence of Eusebius in amassing appropriate evidence to defend his arguments:

> Having started to collect his materials during Diocletian's persecutions, Eusebius never forgot his original purpose which was to produce factual evidence about the past and about the character of the persecuted Church. He piled up his evidence of quotations from reputable authorities and records in the form that was natural to any ancient controversialist.[9]

His *Ecclesiastical History* and his more polemical writings consist of dozens of extended quotations from a whole variety of different sources. The selection and quotation of these sources demonstrates the same kind of commitment to the identification and presentation of authentic testimony that we have seen in the writings of Irenaeus. The critique of pagan philosophers such as Celsus and Porphyry served to sharpen the terms of debate and to focus the minds of Christian theologians on the historical events which lay behind the biblical narrative.

Moreover, just as arguments emerged between Christians and pagans about the writings of scripture, so also arguments continued between Christians and Jews about the interpretation of the Old Testament. Origen had lived in the cities of Alexandria and Caesarea Maritima. In both cities, there were large Jewish populations, and it is clear that Origen was familiar with the members of the Jewish community. In *Against Celsus*, he refers to discussions with Jews.[10] He was also familiar with the writings of Philo of Alexandria and the Jewish historian, Josephus. In recent years, scholarship about the history of biblical interpretation has tended to emphasize the areas of continuity between Jewish and Christian exegesis with specific reference to Jewish patterns of exegesis. So Richard Hanson argued that 'the exegesis of the primitive Christian Church was a direct and unselfconscious continuation of the type of exegesis practised by ancient Judaism in its later period'.[11] The idea that Jewish and Christian forms of interpretation constituted a distinctive tradition of reading and reasoning has had a telling influence on recent debate. For example, in *Biblical Interpretation in Ancient Israel,* Michael Fishbane argues that the resources for rabbinic exegesis of scripture evolved from native cultural forms. Thus rabbinic exegesis was not dependent upon interaction with the world of pagan scholarship. While this judgment about rabbinic exegesis may be correct, there is a danger in ignoring the fact that the Judaism of the first three centuries of the common era may need to be drawn more broadly. Maren Niehoff's study of the exegetical work of Philo of Alexandria and his predecessors suggests that Jewish interpreters in Alexandria were familiar with the conventions of ancient historiography and employed similar kinds of argument. For example, some interpreters were uncomfortable with the description of the Binding of Isaac (Genesis 22) because it appeared to legitimate child sacrifice. In a detailed survey of Philo's writing and an analysis of the kind of arguments in which he engages, Niehoff concludes that there were Jews in Alexandria who offered an historical interpretation of the Binding of Isaac. They noted the similarity of the planned sacrifice with pagan practices, and then noted the contrast with Moses' emphatic rejection of these earlier forms of child sacrifice. They suggested that this pointed to the rejection and abolition of more primitive practices. Drawing parallels with the way in which Aristotle and others interpreted some of the more challenging passages in Homer, Niehoff suggests that these Jewish interpreters were able to contextualize the passage in Genesis 22 and identify a significant development within Judaism:

> Philo's colleagues shared their historical perspectives with Greek scholars, such as Aristotle and Aristarchus, while differing considerably from a more traditional exegete such as Philo. Their surprisingly modern position is based on the understanding that Moses revised the more primitive stages of the Jewish religion and introduced important reforms.[12]

While one should not overstate the case presented by Niehoff, one should not underestimate the ways in which Christian interpreters were informed by the conventions of ancient historiography either directly by virtue of their education or indirectly as a consequence of their interaction with Jewish scholars and exegetes. Indeed, we can see evidence of this in the way in which early interpreters made sense of confusing or perplexing passages in scripture. One example might be the coded reference to the 'abomination of desolation' in Mk 13.14. In the *Catena in Marcum*, the commentator notes that there are a number of possible interpretative options. The 'abomination' might refer to 'soldiers coming into the temple' or to 'the statue of the man who captured the city at that time', while the 'desolation' might refer to the destruction of the temple and its subsequent abandonment in AD 70. Intriguingly, the commentator quotes Josephus and suggests that the phrase might refer to a particular incident when Pontius Pilate brought his soldiers into Jerusalem in the middle of the night bearing the standards of Caesar. These standards carried effigies of Roman gods, and Pilate's action provoked an aggressive response from the Jewish residents of Jerusalem. Josephus presents this incident as the catalyst for the first Jewish Revolt, a view with which the commentator in the *Catena in Marcum* appears to concur: 'the revolt took its starting-point from that moment, and there was no respite until the time when the temple was burnt down, and the city was left desolate'.[13] Note the style and character of this argument. The writer is appealing to a particular historical event to illuminate the meaning of a biblical passage. In doing this, the writer is following the conventions of ancient historiography.

Descriptions of patristic exegesis have tended to take as their starting point a distinction between Antioch and Alexandria. In

broad brush terms, biblical critics associated with the Catechetical
School in Alexandria tended to emphasize a more allegorical
reading of scripture. Given the allegorical interpretation of
scripture outlined in Book 4 of *On First Principles,* Origen would
be the principal exemplar of this approach. By contrast, those
associated with the city of Antioch tended to adopt a more literal
reading of the Bible. Theodore of Mopsuestia is presented as one
of the great exemplars of the Antiochene tradition and a feisty
critic of Alexandrian exegesis. Commenting on the Alexandrians'
use of allegory and their attempt to extract a spiritual meaning
from the text, while ignoring its real historical meaning, Theodore
of Mopsuestia warned those who 'say that paradise did not exist
as paradise nor the serpent as the serpent. I should like to say to
them that by breaking up history, they will have no history left'.[14]
The Antiochene approach sought to place greater emphasis on the
literal sense of the text.

More recent scholarship has suggested that this simple
distinction between Alexandrian and Antiochene approaches
requires a more nuanced analysis. Frances Young has argued
that the differences in theological temperament between some
of the principal protagonists in Christological controversies
during the fourth and fifth centuries, particularly with regard
to their handling of scriptural texts, owe more to the patterns of
education associated with Alexandria and Antioch.[15] Alexandrian
exegesis was influenced by the philosophical schools, where a
more speculative approach was encouraged. On the other hand,
Antiochene exegesis was influenced by the predominance of
rhetorical schools within Antioch. Indeed, we know that a number
of prominent Christian theologians, including one of the great
preachers of the early Church, John Chrysostom (the 'golden-
mouthed') had sat at the feet of Libanius, one of the greatest
teachers of rhetoric in the ancient world. One of the reasons why
people learned the art of rhetoric in the ancient world was in
order to become proficient in arguing a case in a court of law. This
means that those schooled in the art of rhetoric were accustomed
to a more forensic approach to the analysis and interpretation of
texts. This meant they were alert not only to questions about
the context of a particular passage in a text, but also the questions
of historical context that enabled the reader to understand its
meaning. Augustine had also been a teacher of rhetoric in Milan.

In *Hermeneutics and the Rhetorical Tradition*, Kathy Eden points out the parallels between the arguments presented in Augustine's treatise *On Christian Teaching* and Cicero's *On Invention*, a handbook for orators:

> Like Cicero in the *De inventione*, . . . Augustine considers not only the immediate textual context . . . but also the work as a whole, what Cicero had called *omnis scriptura* (*De inventione* 2.40.117) and what Augustine . . . understands as the *summa* of Scripture, or *caritas*. And like Cicero, Augustine also recommends considering the whole set of circumstances that inform the composition – times, places, persons, and so on.[16]

Augustine recognized that when confronted with the ambiguity of the biblical text, one needed to be attentive to the textual context, to be alert to some of the vagaries of translation and also to understand its historical context.

This interest in history arose not simply out of some kind of principled commitment to the idea that Christianity was 'a historical religion'. It also emerged as a reaction to the critique presented by pagan commentators such as Celsus and Porphyry. Christian biblical scholars were forced to defend the testimony of the apostles, recorded in their scriptures, on historical grounds. Writers such as Origen and Eusebius amassed a huge amount of documentary evidence in order to do this. The forensic approach associated with the practice of rhetoric was also helpful in presenting robust and coherent arguments to explain some of the vagaries of the text. The arguments about the historicity of the gospels may have become more marked since the rise of modern biblical criticism, but a commitment to discover whether the gospels presented accurate and credible testimony about Jesus was also an important characteristic of early patristic commentary and exegesis. The first four centuries of the Christian church saw the flowering of a comprehensive range of commentaries on books of both the Old and New Testaments. Some of these commentaries have now been lost, but extracts from them can still be found in the anthologies or *catenae* that were produced from the fifth century onwards. These texts which reproduced the comments of the fathers in the margins around the text of scripture itself were the principle means by which biblical scholarship was made accessible until the time of the Reformation. In Western Europe, the *Glossa ordinaria* and the *Catena aurea* (the latter compiled at the behest of St Thomas Aquinas) provided a compendium of ancient Christian commentary. The biblical text was embedded in and surrounded by an interpretative tradition: 'an island of scripture floating in a vast sea of commentary'.[17] And yet as these anthologies were copied, edited, translated and recopied, some of the spark and insight of the original commentaries was lost. By the end of the fifteenth century and the beginning of the sixteenth century, scholars such as Erasmus became increasingly dissatisfied with the inaccuracies and infelicities of this manuscript tradition. Inspired by the humanist spirit and the revival in classical scholarship, they argued for a return to the sources. Most importantly, they argued that scholars should return to the Biblical texts in their original languages. This led to a remarkable resurgence and interest in biblical scholarship.

The Return to the Sources

In the winter of 1513, Martin Luther (1483–1546) was preparing a series of lectures on the psalms. He had recently been appointed as a lecturer in biblical studies at the University of Wittenberg. Luther decided to commission a new textbook for his class. He instructed the University printer to produce an edition of the psalms with wide margins and lots of space between the lines. Rather than being embedded in the glosses, comments and interpretations of others, the text of the scriptures would stand alone. The students would write the glosses and scholia (short extracts from established sources) provided by their lecturer between the lines and in the margins of the text. Luther extended this practice to subsequent courses of lectures on Romans, Galatians and Hebrews. We should not for a moment ignore the significance of Luther's instruction in the context of the Reformation. When the Reformers spoke about 'sola scriptura' or 'scripture alone', they were not simply making a claim about the authority of scripture. They were also describing the geography of the page in the books that they were using.

The Protestant Reformation of the sixteenth century emerged when theologians and biblical scholars, educated according to humanist principles, returned to the Biblical texts in their original languages. They contrasted what they found with the ecclesiastical and spiritual practices of their own day. The critical attitude towards the life of the Church of the high middle ages and the zeal for reform which emerged from all this dramatically changed the Reformers' understanding of the relationship between the Bible and the Church. Key to the Reformers' insights was a deep distrust of the use of allegory in reading scripture. A privileged status was given to the *sensus literalis* or the 'literal sense' in reading scripture. The Reformers wanted to know the plain sense of the text. That was all that mattered. Most importantly, the Reformers sought to place the Bible in the hands of the Christian believer by translating it into the vernacular. This presented a number of challenges, not least attempting to identify the most reliable form of the original Hebrew and Greek.

The contribution of Erasmus of Rotterdam (c. AD 1466–1536) in addressing some of these challenges should not be underestimated. A Roman Catholic priest, Erasmus was one of the great classical scholars of his era. He was particularly interested in establishing the original Greek text of the New Testament. To do this, he needed to establish the reliability of the manuscript tradition. No literature is ever transmitted without variation of its text creeping in, and the Bible was no exception. Even with the advent of printing, there was still room for variation and error, but variation was inevitably greater in earlier literature copied out by hand. Variations arose which were purely accidental – spellings, omissions, mistranslations, repetitions, the accidental writing of a similar word (misheard or misread). Variations also arose in the context of doctrinal dispute and debate. Erasmus was familiar with some of these inconsistencies in the text and he sought to resolve the differences and to reconstruct an original version of the text unsullied by the mistakes and omissions of generations of copyists. This involved the extensive and patient study of a whole range of different manuscripts, drawing on the philological insight and textual analysis of the most up-to-date critical scholarship. His edition of the New Testament in Greek was published in 1516. A second edition was published in 1519. This text was used by Martin Luther as the basis for his translation of the New Testament into German.

Translation was often the source of some controversy during this period, particularly as the Reformers championed the translation of the scriptures into the vernacular. In *The Literary Culture of the Reformation,* Brian Cummings notes that the translation of the Bible into English by William Tyndale provoked a strong response from Thomas More. More objected that in the absence of an English version of the Bible which everyone regarded as 'canonical', a vernacular Bible would lead to a range of diverse and contradictory interpretations. The creation of a variety of different translations would only serve to undermine the integrity of the Christian faith. According to More (and in spite of the irony that the Latin Vulgate was itself a translation), the translation of scripture would only lead to 'equyuocacion' – words could be used to mean whatever you wanted them to mean. He objected in particular to the way in which Tyndale avoided words such as 'church', 'priest' and 'charity', and replaced them with 'congregation', 'senior' and 'love'. For More, some of the key terms of catholic ecclesiology were lost in this process, and the reader was left with the impression that the use of words like 'church' and 'priest' was a later innovation of the tradition. Such words had no place in the world of the New Testament.

Note again the style and character of this argument. It is informed by a clear historical perspective. There is an implied distance between the world of the New Testament and subsequent developments. In other words, the distinction between scripture and tradition requires and demands a commitment to a historical reading. This became an important device in the rhetoric of the Reformation. Indeed, this emphasis on understanding passages in their historical and textual context was a central characteristic of the interpretative approach associated with Erasmus. Drawing on the insights of Cicero, Erasmus 'recommends investigating those very circumstances of production covered under the rhetorical principle of *decorum*: speaker, audience, time, place and so on.'[18] We have seen exactly the same kind of emphasis in the writings of Augustine. These insights informed in turn the work of translators, including William Tyndale.

What is clear from this discussion is that the whole process of translating the scriptures into the vernacular drew on the best insights of contemporary scholarship. The translators of the scriptures were schooled in the principles of the humanist tradition, and they drew consciously on this tradition in assessing questions of historical and textual context in rendering their translations of the original biblical languages. This was essential to the whole enterprise of returning to the sources and stripping away the accumulation of later tradition. And yet, the process of translating the scriptures left an ambiguous legacy. The translation of the biblical text into the vernacular certainly achieved Tyndale's aim to open up the scriptures to the population at large – or at least the literate classes – but (paradoxically) reading the text in the vernacular required less investment in the intricacies and techniques of biblical scholarship.

Jonathan Sheehan argues that the proliferation of vernacular Bibles in the sixteenth and seventeenth centuries constituted a 'big bang' in the development of biblical scholarship. But he also suggests that the 'big bang' was followed by a 'big crunch'. The crunch came 'when the project of biblical translation ground to a halt and a canon of vernacular Bibles was set into stone in the seventeenth century'.[19] In Sheehan's view, the establishment of influential and authoritative translations like the King James Bible of 1611 accentuated a separation between reading scripture and biblical scholarship. This was partly a consequence of the fact that translators often resolved and reconciled ambiguities and gaps in the text. Once concealed, readers were less alert to some of the challenges of reading scripture critically. This was reinforced by the development of a range of theological views which emphasized the authority of scripture in theological debate. As time continued, this emphasis became more marked as a number of Protestant theologians developed the doctrine of the inerrancy of scripture. In stark contrast to the days when there was no Bible, scripture had become a closed canon of inspired documents containing timeless truths. The Bible came to provide a compendium of dogmatic statements. Thus attention to questions of historical context became less pronounced in biblical interpretation. Although this was one of the unforeseen and unintended consequences of biblical translation, the dissociation which emerged between reading the Bible in the vernacular and sustained engagement with critical scholarship provides the necessary backdrop for the recovery of biblical criticism in the eighteenth century. It is one of the factors that enables us to see why the 'epistemic break' associated with the Enlightenment was so pronounced.

An Ugly, Broad Ditch

It has become fashionable among a number of contemporary theologians to knock 'the Enlightenment'. In the imagination of some commentators, the Enlightenment is the source of all the ills suffered by the contemporary church, the perceived 'lack of belief' and scepticism prevalent in contemporary culture. My own view is that such negative judgements should not distract us too long in assessing the impact of the eighteenth century on the emergence of modern biblical criticism and, more particularly, historical criticism. There is a danger of over-generalization. To employ a phrase like 'the Enlightenment' without distinguishing between the vast array of thinkers, movements and cultures, embraced by that phrase hardly does justice to a critical evaluation of its impact and significance. Two observations are helpful in assessing its impact: first, the thinkers of the eighteenth century did not simply reject the Bible, although some did. The majority wrestled with it, they questioned it and they sought to make sense of it. Secondly, it is important to emphasize that this thinking and reflection did not occur in isolation from the social and political currents of their day.

The age of Enlightenment marked a number of significant shifts in the development of biblical interpretation. The eighteenth century was a self-consciously enlightened and emancipated age. Emancipation was sought in both political and religious terms. The Bible had played an ambiguous role in these developments in the course of the sixteenth and seventeenth centuries. On the one hand, the Bible was employed to defend the *status quo*. On the other, it inspired calls for reform. Its writings spawned a whole host of revolutionary movements. For example, when King James I sponsored a translation of the scriptures in the seventeenth century, he did so not because he thought that the quality of its prose would be more edifying but because he knew that the Authorized Version would replace a popular vernacular version, the Geneva Bible. This version adopted a more radical Protestant agenda. It also contained a number of marginalia challenging the authority of monarchs. These marginal notes were political dynamite. The King and his courtiers knew that these little subversive comments presented a challenge to his authority. A new translation without such marginalia was a political priority.

The story of the seventeenth century is one of profound religious conflict. Many of these conflicts stemmed from different interpretations of the Bible. But as arguments over political issues developed in the course of the seventeenth century, the authority of the Bible itself was diminished. So the historian Christopher Hill points out that when a Member of Parliament made a speech in the House of Commons and sought to support his arguments by quoting passages of scripture, his words were met with derision by fellow MPs. This was not because the House of Commons was particularly ungodly or that his fellow MPs lacked piety. It was because the previous decades had taught them that a quotation from scripture was not sufficient to settle an argument. As Hill puts it, 'Twenty years of frenzied discussion had shown that text-swapping and text-distortion solved nothing: agreement was not to be reached even among the godly on what exactly the Bible said and meant'.[20] Such appeals to scripture were no longer persuasive in political debate.

This development is significant because it provides tangible evidence of a growing dissociation between revelation and reason in public discourse. An uneasy dualism between human reason and divine revelation had begun to emerge. The reasons for this are complex, and, as the quotation of Christopher Hill suggests, it is illuminating to consider the broader developments in Western thought and theology in the context of the political and social issues of the day. Nevertheless, it is fair to say that by the time of the Reformation, the idea of 'revelation' had become increasingly reified. Rather than a direct encounter with the divine mystery which embraced human thought and experience and which engaged the human subject as a participant, 'revelation' had become a little list of 'things to be believed'. In other words, 'revelation' had become an object, a thing (among other things) or a fact (to be placed alongside other facts), rather than a way of relating to the divine mystery. At the same time, rather than reason being a means of participating in the life of God (as Augustine, Gregory and Thomas Aquinas believed) and an integral part of a theology of revelation, it had become something quite distinct. It became an expression of human autonomy. Increasingly, people began to assert their intellectual freedom in opposition to the claims of ecclesiastical dogma. These developments were particularly pronounced in Britain and in Germany. Although space does not allow me to rehearse all of the arguments, a couple of vignettes about three leading thinkers – Gotthold Ephraim Lessing (1729–81), Johann Philipp Gabler (1753–1826) and William Wrede (1859–1906) – will provide some insight into the issues at play in the course of the eighteenth and nineteenth centuries.

Gotthold Ephraim Lessing was a writer, philosopher, dramatist and art critic. He revelled in controversy and did not fight shy of antagonizing Lutheran pastors and theologians. In the course of his career, Lessing had made the acquaintance of a Professor of Oriental Languages called Hermann Samuel Reimarus. On his death, members of Reimarus's family sent Lessing the script of an unpublished work, entitled *Apology for Rational Worshippers of God*. Its contents were controversial. Lessing judged that the script was unprintable, but he decided to publish extracts from it, which appeared as anonymous fragments in instalments. The first fragment provided a defence of Deism and Rationalism. Rejecting orthodox Christian belief about the doctrine of the Trinity, Reimarus affirmed that since Jesus was a teacher of rational, practical religion, anyone who was rational and followed his practical ethical teaching was basically a Christian. In Reimarus' view, the problem was that the simplicity of Christ's teaching had been corrupted by later ecclesiastical dogma. The second fragment contained an argument on the nature of revelation. He argued that God could not make special revelations to everybody, since the continuous succession of miracles would disrupt the natural order, and God would be contradicting himself. Therefore, God could only make these revelations occasionally and to particular individuals, in whose testimony others must put their trust. In other words, for the contemporary believer, there could be no direct revelation, only human testimony concerning revelation. According to Reimarus, this was an inadequate basis for theological reflection. In response, he asserted the primacy of nature over revelation as the starting point for thinking about God. The third fragment provided a detailed analysis of the Israelites crossing the Red Sea (Exod. 12.37f.) which stated that 600,000 fighting men, with families, retainers, equipment, livestock and supplies, crossed the Red Sea in a single night. Reimarus calculated that if the Israelites moved in a column 10 deep, the length of the column would have been 180 miles, and would have taken 9 days to cross the Red Sea. He therefore concluded that the account in Exodus could not be reliable. The fourth fragment asserted that the books of the Old Testament were not written to reveal a religion. The fifth fragment 'On the Resurrection Narrative' analysed the inconsistencies among the evangelists, concluding that since they disagreed about the details of Jesus' resurrection from the dead, they must be mistaken about the fact.

Lessing himself did not agree with all these arguments. For instance, on the resurrection narratives, he suggested that because experience shows how eyewitnesses of any given event will give surprisingly different accounts of it, such contradictions and inconsistencies are only to be expected. However, Lessing's own celebrated tract, 'On the Proof of the Spirit and of Power', was to take up the issues surrounding the reliability of historical testimony about miracles with considerable passion and force. The title comes from Origen's *Against Celsus* 1.2, where Origen cites 1 Cor. 2.5 as if Paul's words referred to the two main props of traditional apologetic: prophecy and miracle. Lessing challenges the confidence placed by traditional apologists in prophecy and miracle. For Lessing, it is axiomatic that 'accidental truths of history can never become the proof of necessary truths of reason'. For instance, if the resurrection of Christ is a past event, it cannot prove the truth that Christ is the Son of God 'of one substance with the Father', which is quite simply contrary to reason: 'That, then, is the ugly, broad ditch which I cannot get across, however often and however earnestly I have tried to make the leap'. Lessing is clear that although he accepts that in Christ prophecies were fulfilled and he does not deny that Christ performed miracles, testimony about them is not sufficient to provoke faith in the teachings of Christ. 'What then does bind me? Nothing but these teachings themselves. Eighteen hundred years ago they were so new, so alien, so foreign to the entire mass of truths recognized in that age, that nothing less than miracles and fulfilled prophecies were required if the multitude were to attend to them at all. But to make the multitude attentive to something means to put common sense onto the right track'.

There is a radical empiricism about Lessing's approach that eschews any confidence in the testimony of others. He is not confident that he can trust the testimony of others, about the miracles of Christ, because he has no analogous experience. As Lessing commented with a hint of irony, 'I live in the eighteenth century, in which miracles no longer happen'.[21] The clear inference of this statement is that the only thing that counts is his immediate experience of observable events. Any event that occurs in the past presents insurmountable epistemological difficulties. It depends on the testimony of others and there is no guarantee that such testimony can be reliable. It cannot provide any assurance of religious truth. In Lessing's view, historical testimony about the life of Jesus is not a sufficient basis for determining the validity of religious belief. Consequently, the only thing that will bind him to the Christian faith is the teachings of Christ. An emphasis on historical testimony is displaced by a corresponding emphasis on the inner personal quality of religious truth conceived in moral terms. For Lessing, the power and authority of historical testimony is significantly diminished.

A rather different approach is adopted by Johann Philipp Gabler. In 1787, following his appointment as a professor at the University of Altdorf, Gabler gave an inaugural address entitled *An address concerning the proper distinction between biblical and dogmatic theology and the proper determination of the goals of each*. Gabler argued that a sharp distinction needs to be made between biblical theology and dogmatic theology. In his analysis, the basic difference was that biblical theology was 'historical' in origin. By this he meant that biblical theology takes as its starting point the perspective of the authors in determining the meaning of the text. By contrast, the claims of dogmatic theology were determined by more contemporary agendas and confessional interests. While these agendas and interests might be perfectly legitimate in dogmatic terms, the historical orientation of biblical theology was supposed to provide greater rigour and a more solid starting point for theological reflection. His aim was to seek 'a solid understanding of divine matters' and to discourage 'that depraved custom of reading one's own opinions and judgments into the Bible'.[22]

Gabler's analysis has sometimes been misinterpreted. Some commentators assume that Gabler attempted to distinguish between 'biblical theology' as an historical description of the particular theological outlook of an author in his original context, and 'biblical theology' as a constructive enterprise that drew on the insights of the Bible. In other words, any historian could describe a 'biblical' theology in the first sense, but only a theologian could construct a 'biblical theology' in the second sense. Gabler's analysis was rather more nuanced than that. In making a distinction between 'biblical theology' and 'dogmatic theology', his purpose was to lay bare the bedrock of history in order to penetrate beyond later dogmatic formulations and thus overcome the potential for disagreement about theological meaning. Gabler was looking for a way in which historical criticism could be used in reading the Bible in order to create a more robust and rigorous form of dogmatic theology. In his confidence that the Bible could only have one meaning (which was the meaning intended by the original author), Gabler believed that the application of an historical method would serve to promote genuine theological agreement. It would avoid the 'multiplicity of change' associated with dogmatic theology, where 'each theologian philosophises rationally about divine things, according to the measure of his ability or of the times, age, place, sect, school, and other similar factors'. Surely, he argued 'the sacred writers are not so changeable that they should in this fashion be able to assume these different types and forms of theological doctrine'.

Intriguingly, the factors which influence dogmatic theologians are presented as human constructs which serve to occlude and shroud the divine meaning of the Bible:

> But let those things that have been said up to now be worth this much: that we distinguish carefully the divine from the human, that we establish some distinction between biblical and dogmatic theology, and after we have separated those things which in the sacred books refer most immediately to their own times and to the men of those times from those pure notions which divine providence wished to be characteristic of all times and places, let us then construct the foundation of our philosophy upon religion and let us designate with some care the objectives of divine and human wisdom. Exactly thus will our theology be made more certain and more firm, and there will be nothing

further to be feared for it from the most savage attack from its enemies.[23]

The idea of 'biblical theology' was intended to introduce greater rigour into theological discourse, and to provide a means of evaluating the truth of a range of dogmatic proposals by determining what the original authors of the biblical texts believed about God. It served to enable the reader to distinguish between the circumstances and particularities of the writer's context and the eternal truths about God contained in his writings. He wanted to provide a thorough historical foundation for dogmatic theology. But in doing this, the distinction between history and theology became rather blurred. His understanding of 'biblical theology' served a clear apologetic purpose.

The tension between these two positions is instructive when one considers the role of historical criticism in relation to the construction of theological proposals in subsequent decades. On the one hand, Lessing's approach leads to the marginalization of history in constructing dogmatic formulations. There is no point in attempting to draw on historical testimony in exploring theological truth. It is not that such testimony is simply unreliable. Reference to an historical event does not provide sufficient proof to demonstrate the truth of a dogmatic statement. It does not necessarily follow from the observation that the tomb was empty that Jesus Christ is the Son of God. On the other hand, Gabler suggests that historical criticism plays a vital part in identifying and distilling timeless truths about the reality of God. It serves to provide some kind of objective point of reference in order to test the truth of dogmatic statements. Is this doctrine consistent with the biblical witness? Indeed, the development of historical criticism in the modern period is a telling commentary on the emerging tension between these two different positions.

Lessing's caution about suggesting that historical testimony might be a vehicle for divine truth became more marked when adopted by others in the course of the nineteenth century. In the 1880s, a group of young scholars at the University of Göttingen began to meet regularly to study Christian origins. The group consisted of William Wrede (1859–1906), Albert Eichhorn (1856–1926), William Bousset (1865–1920) and Hermann Gunkel (1862–1932). This little group became known as the

History of Religions School. They were disenchanted with the way in which previous generations of scholars had employed historical insights in much the way that Gabler had advocated. What they noticed was a tendency to desert the rigours of historical criticism when the historical foundations appeared to conflict with doctrinal formulations. This point was made forcefully by Ernst Troeltsch (1865–1923), who challenged the 'supernaturalism' advocated by some of his contemporaries. Troelstch recognized that nothing could escape the ravages of the historical-critical method: 'Once it is applied to biblical scholarship and church history, (the historical method) is a leaven which transforms everything and which finally causes the form of all previous theological methods to disintegrate'.[24] This meant that Christianity needed to be studied in a broader context of the history of religion and culture. Thus, the focus of the *History of Religious School* was the practice of *religion* in the ancient world rather than the study of *revelation.* They saw little evidence of the timeless verities about the reality of God that Gabler sought to identify in the biblical text. They were more interested in the history, origin and sources of traditions, which lay behind and shaped the life of the early Church.

In an important and significant essay on 'The Task and Method of New Testament Theology So-called', William Wrede insisted on the strictly historical character of New Testament theology. There could be no confusion between historical criticism and the claims of dogmatic theology:

> Biblical theology has to investigate something from given documents – if not an eternal thing, still something intellectual. It tries to grasp it as objectively, correctly and sharply as possible. That is all. How the systematic theologian gets on with its results and deals with them – that is his own affair.[25]

The purpose of historical criticism was simply to ascertain the facts. Those interested in the study of scripture might succeed in surrendering its theological character, but as far as Wrede is concerned, it should no longer be treated any differently from any branch of intellectual history, let alone the history of religion. He is nervous of any suggestion that the historical description of the writings of the New Testament should in any way fulfil the demand that biblical scholarship must serve the church. The historian must be independent of such demands and independent of the constraints of the canon. Wrede observes that 'the church rests on history, but historical reality cannot escape investigation, and this investigation of historical reality has its own laws'.[26] The clear inference is that these laws prevent historians from speaking in terms of supernatural causality. Thus the proper task of New Testament theology is to discover what early Christians believed, thought, taught and hoped. This was not the same kind of exercise as reading the New Testament as a compendium of doctrinal concepts. Moreover, the preaching of Jesus and the theology of Paul the Apostle needed to be understood in the context of contemporary Judaism. Wrede insisted that a purely historical account of early Christianity could be described by any reliable historian. At the same time, he resisted the suggestion that the New Testament revealed a series of doctrinal concepts. Such a view presupposed a theological position. Moreover, the designation 'New Testament theology' was itself problematic – hence Wrede's use of the term 'So-called' to qualify it. Whether the term referred to a theology which the New Testament contained, or a theology with a biblical character, neither definition did justice to the fact that the proper academic interest of those engaged in the study of the New Testament was the history of early Christian religion and theology. The question of how one might read these texts as Christian scripture in order to hear God's address or to demonstrate God's faithfulness was not a matter for those engaged in historical criticism. Such theological concerns had no place in historical inquiry. Indeed, attempting to address such questions would only serve to distort the work of the critic. Nevertheless, Wrede holds on to the conviction that 'the church rests on history', but it is not immediately clear what this means. This tantalizing comment is never fully explained in the course of his essay.

The Challenge of Historical Criticism

For early Christian commentators, historical inquiry was motivated by a profound theological interest. Irenaeus of Lyons may not have had all the critical tools, socio-scientific models and archaeological finds that we have at our disposal, but when he read the Hebrew Scriptures and the books which eventually came to form the canon of the New Testament, he was seeking to demonstrate that he could find in them authentic testimony about Jesus. The writings of the Old Testament, particularly the prophets, pointed to the expectation of the Messiah, and the task of the interpreter was to demonstrate how those expectations had been fulfilled in Jesus. Moreover, Irenaeus sought to demonstrate that the New Testament contained reliable and authentic testimony, because it contained *apostolic* testimony. Pagan commentators were often scornful of these claims. As a consequence, writers such as Origen of Alexandria and Eusebius of Caesarea borrowed and traded upon the conventions of ancient historiography in order to provide a rigorous apology for the Christian faith. And yet, this survey of the development of historical criticism has demonstrated that a profound tension has emerged between history and theology. No doubt, Irenaeus saw in the Gospels the verbatim records of the first apostles, but modern scholars would view those claims with suspicion. When Albert Schweitzer, in his survey of the quest for this historical Jesus, noted that the study of the Life of Jesus in the course of the nineteenth century 'had loosed the bands by which He had been riveted for centuries to the stony rocks of ecclesiastical doctrine',[27] his comment betrays the fact that the relationship between the claims of Christian doctrine and the task of historical criticism had altered dramatically in the course of the previous 200 years. Indeed, his comment not only serves to underline the ambiguity of the relationship between historical criticism and the claims of Christian theology. It also invites us to confront some challenging questions: how do modern theologians negotiate Lessing's ditch? How do they do justice to the conventions of modern historiography?

In the course of the last century, theologians and biblical scholars have responded to these questions in a number of different ways. One of the more subtle and interesting responses is associated with the name of Rudolf Bultmann (1884–1976). Bultmann was himself a disciple of the *History of Religions School*, but he did not make a facile distinction between the work of the biblical critic and that of the theologian. He was an able advocate of the principles of form criticism, which he employed in the exegesis of the Synoptic gospels, but he was not easily satisfied with attempts to describe a division of labour between the biblical critic and the theologian in terms of exegesis and interpretation. He recognized that the assumption that the biblical critic might speak with dispassionate neutrality while the theologian could only dissemble in the face of the prejudices and presuppositions of a confessional position was far too simplistic. It rendered the biblical critic blind to his or her own presuppositions and prejudices. In his essay *Is exegesis without presuppositions possible?*, Bultmann argued that the historian cannot be considered a blank slate on which the text writes its pure message. The interpreter has his own questions and way of asking questions. If biblical texts are to be understood historically – and Bultmann asserts that they have to be 'because they speak in a strange language, in concepts of a faraway time, of a world picture that is alien to us' – then the historian must concede that his or her understanding is affected by the life context in which he or she stands. It follows that a particular understanding of the subject-matter of the text is always presupposed in its exegesis. Bultmann concludes that no exegesis is without presuppositions. The interpreter will always have a pre-understanding of the text. This pre-understanding is then confirmed or challenged by the exegesis of the text, in the light of which the interpreter may go on to develop a theological perspective. Although some biblical critics might question whether one needs to go on to develop a theological perspective, Bultmann's perspective is influential in that it has alerted a whole generation of biblical scholars to the ideological biases and prejudices at work in biblical criticism.

Bultmann's own theological biases and prejudices reflect his Lutheran inheritance of faith and the influence of an existentialist philosophy that had emerged in the face of the perceived collapse of classical metaphysics. For someone whose name is associated with the pioneering methods of historical criticism (particularly form criticism), these influences created in Bultmann a curious antipathy towards those who sought to reconstruct historical events, particularly when it was simply motivated by what he perceived to be an antiquarian interest. James Barr has suggested that Bultmann's project was a consequence of his Lutheran inheritance of faith:

> Surely his entire theological position can be plausibly read as deriving from a profound and extreme application of the

Lutheran understanding of justification by faith. If he thought that faith should not be built upon the reliability of historical reports about the life of Christ, this was not (as Anglo-Saxon critics have often supposed) a result of 'historical scepticism', but because faith itself would be in danger of destruction if it relied upon such a support.[28]

My own view is that Barr is correct up to a point. This radical application of Lutheran teaching does explain the orientation of his basic convictions, but we should not neglect the fact that Bultmann's existentialism provided the intellectual framework that enabled him to express those same convictions in a more contemporary idiom.

Bultmann's thinking was heavily influenced by two philosophers, Wilhelm Hermann (1846–1922) and Martin Heidegger (1889–1976). Like them, Bultmann made an important distinction between *historie* and *geschichte*. The former describes incidental historical events, while the latter is concerned with the events of personal existential significance. The importance of this distinction becomes abundantly obvious in Bultmann's *New Testament Theology*. This work focuses almost exclusively on Johannine and Pauline literature within the New Testament. For Bultmann, the central question which both Paul and John were addressing was the question of human existence. Heidegger had made a distinction between authentic and inauthentic existence. Basically, human existence is inauthentic when a human being seeks a false security. In seeking this false security, a human being is enslaved to the world. Authentic existence lies in terms of 'freedom' and a true self-understanding. So, when it comes to commenting on John's Prologue, for example Jn 1.10–11, Bultmann notes that the world failed to believe in Jesus as the Revealer and recognize him, for: 'It could only occur in the act of abandoning one's own chosen, false self-understanding and in receiving the gift of a proper understanding of oneself in relation to the Creator'. The purpose of the incarnation was to present human beings with this ultimate existential question: we are challenged to choose between inauthentic existence and authentic existence, between death and life. For Bultmann, the incarnation is not simply something that happened in the past. It is a present eschatological event. It is 'eschatological' in the sense that it is an *ultimate* question. So the purpose of the New Testament witness is not to provide material that will serve some kind of weird antiquarian interest with the past. The testimony of the New Testament poses an ultimate question about our existence, about matters of life and death. Because of this emphasis in his theology, Bultmann is curiously sceptical of questions about the historical Jesus and attempts to reconstruct his life. He is more interested in the way people responded to the proclamation (or *kerygma*) of the gospel. Thus in developing a form critical analysis of the synoptic Gospels, and asking questions about the situation in life (or *Sitz im Leben*) in which a particular pericope emerged, the presumption is that the focus of inquiry should not be on the historical Jesus but on the way in which the first Christian disciples responded to the gospel. This means that there is a subtle shift in the precise subject-matter of historical inquiry. Bultmann appears to negotiate Lessing's ditch by suggesting that one may not need to cross it after all.

And yet, Bultmann's approach is problematic for a number of reasons, not least because it neglects some of the basic questions about the historicity of the gospels. For all the rhetoric, the figure of Jesus Christ can so easily become a kind of 'cipher', divorced from the realities and contingencies of real human existence. When one considers the particular context in which Bultmann was writing (in Nazi Germany) and the way in which his sophisticated reading of the New Testament plays down the significance of the historical Jesus, it is worth pondering how it also became much easier for others to ignore challenging questions about the Jewishness of Jesus. It is no accident that more recent attempts to explore the quest for the historical Jesus have tended to focus precisely on the relationship between Jesus and Judaism. But it is also fair to say that many theologians continue to hold that questions of historicity are absolutely fundamental to the theological enterprise.

This emphasis on the importance of historicity is explicit in the writings of Tom Wright, the former Bishop of Durham. Wright has written extensively on the historical Jesus. He has proved himself adept at employing historical-critical methods in order to demonstrate weaknesses in the arguments of more sceptical scholars who would naturally prefer to interpret the writings of the New Testament without the disconcerting encumbrance of theological considerations. And yet, sceptics have in turn taken him to task for his own confusion of the claims of Christian theology and historical scholarship. Conscious of these criticisms, Wright writes about a number of methodological issues that are presented by the use of historical criticism in reading and interpreting ancient texts in *The New Testament and the People of God*. He advocates a form of biblical criticism that charts a middle course between the kind of positivist view of history that sees it as little more than a collection of 'facts' and more postmodern approaches that emphasize the ideological commitments and subjective judgements of the interpreter.

> I propose a form of *critical realism*. This is a way of describing the process of 'knowing' that acknowledges the *reality of the thing known, as something other than the knower* (hence 'realism'), while fully acknowledging that the only access we have to this reality lies along the spiralling path of *appropriate dialogue or conversation between the knower and the thing known* (hence 'critical').[29]

Wright recognizes that the historian will always have an active rather than a passive role in the writing of history. In this regard, his earlier writings were probably more alert to some of the developments within contemporary historiography than a good number of other biblical scholars writing at the time. He is dismissive of what he regards as the impossibility of 'mere history' and suspicious of those who claim to be more objective and dispassionate in their reading of the New Testament texts. That said, it is fair to say that he looks for a much greater affinity between historical scholarship and the claims of Christian theology. Nowhere is this more evident than in his analysis of the resurrection narratives in *The Resurrection of the Son of God*. The book provides an exhaustive compendium of Jewish and pagan attitudes towards death and the afterlife in the ancient world in order to address the question: What happened on Easter morning? He argues that the resurrection narratives in the gospels should be regarded as reliable and authentic accounts of the bodily resurrection of Jesus Christ. He argues that the historicity of the story of the empty tomb in the gospels and the accounts of Jesus' appearances to his disciples together provide both the necessary and sufficient reasons for the rise of early Christian belief about the resurrection. No Christian belief that Christ had been raised from the dead would have arisen if Jesus' body was still in the tomb. There is a clear apologetic strand in his writing, and one cannot help but be struck by the force of his rhetoric and its similarity to those who argued against pagan critics like Celsus and Porphyry in the ancient world. And yet, he directly and deliberately disavows the idea that the simple repetition of this kind of rhetoric will address the legacy of the Enlightenment:

> The tools of thought, which we need . . . cannot be those of pre-modernism any more than those of modernism. To what extent the ones I am offering belong to 'postmodernism' is a matter that does not much concern me . . . To proclaim the death of the Enlightenment worldview is not yet to announce what will rise to take its place. It may be that the study of Jesus, which cannot but focus on questions of death and resurrection, will have something to say on the matter.[30]

Wright sought to respond to this challenge by presenting his epistemological foundations in terms of 'critical realism'. And yet, there is a serious question as to whether he has succeeded in this enterprise. Wright's attempt to bridge the gulf between historical criticism and the claims of Christian doctrine has perhaps done more to convince Christian believers that they can believe in the resurrection of Jesus Christ with conviction and integrity, than it has to convince secular biblical critics that one can appeal to historical arguments to demonstrate the historicity of the bodily resurrection. Wright provides not so much a *proof* for the resurrection, as a reasoned explanation for his view. Indeed, one sympathetic reviewer, referring to the 'remarkable epistemological optimism of Wright's historical stance', asked whether one could in fact sustain the claim that by honing the historian's tools with greater care, the evidence would demonstrate that the Resurrection of the Son of God is 'the *only* possible conclusion, the *only* one that is both "necessary" and "sufficient" (as the Conclusion suggests)'.[31] The problem is that while we may accept the historicity of the empty tomb and the accounts of visions, signs and wonders, the resurrection of Jesus Christ is still only one possible way of explaining these phenomena. It is not the only way. Moreover, while the early Christians may have believed that they were talking about something that had taken place in *history*, the resurrection was not a matter of public record in quite the same way as the crucifixion. When the New Testament speaks of the resurrection, it does so in the context of presenting apostolic *testimony*. As Markus Bockmuehl notes, '. . . for all their insistence on the facticity of the resurrection, the early Christians never claimed that accessible empirical "events" were intrinsically "necessary" and "sufficient" to establish that truth'.[32] As the final words of St Thomas in John's gospel demonstrate, their acceptance of this apostolic testimony was an act of faith (Jn 20.28). While Wright's mastery of the art of historical criticism is impressive, it is not always clear that his epistemology does justice to the faith which animated the response of the first disciples and which continues to animate the life and witness of Christians today.

A similar commitment to the importance of historical criticism can be found in the recent writings of Pope Benedict XVI. In the *Foreword* to the first of his three volumes on *Jesus of Nazareth,* Benedict sketches the broad outlines of the methodological approach that he has adopted and reflects on the significance of historical questions for both the exegetical enterprise and also the exploration of theological questions:

> The first point is that the historical-critical method – specifically because of the intrinsic nature of theology and faith – is and remains an indispensable dimension of exegetical work. For it is of the very essence of biblical faith to be about real historical events. It does not tell stories symbolizing supra-historical truths, but is based on history, history that took place here on this earth. The *factum historicum* (historical fact) is not an interchangeable symbolic cipher for biblical faith, but the foundation on which it stands: *Et incarnatus est* – when we say these words, we acknowledge God's actual entry into real history. If we push this history aside, Christian faith as such disappears and is recast as some other religion. So if history, if facticity in this sense, is an essential dimension of Christian faith, then faith must expose itself to the historical method – indeed, faith itself demands this.[33]

Benedict emphasizes the importance of the historical-critical method in appropriating the biblical text, but he goes on to add a number of important qualifications. First, the historian can explore questions and offer a range of hypotheses about the original text, its use of sources, the interests and concerns of the original author, but there is a limit to the degree of certainty offered by these hypotheses. This suggests that there are limits to what the historical-critical method can deliver. Consequently, one must look to other 'complementary' methods and approaches. This perspective was thoroughly endorsed by the Pontifical Biblical Commission in its publication of *The Interpretation of the Bible in the Church* in 1993. Secondly, Benedict went on to observe that while it is possible to analyse each of the books of the Bible in their original historical context, 'the unity of these writings as one "Bible" . . . is not something it can recognize as an immediate historical datum'.[34] At this point, he introduces the project of 'canonical exegesis' developed by a number of 'American scholars' over the last 30 years, and their insistence that individual texts need to be read in the context of the entire witness of scripture. The unity of Scripture is 'a theological datum' which drives forward the task of theological exegesis:

> Modern exegesis has brought to light the process of constant rereading that forged the words transmitted in the Bible into Scripture: Older texts are reappropriated, reinterpreted, and read with new eyes in new contexts. They become Scripture by being read anew, evolving in continuity with their original sense, tacitly corrected and given added depth and breadth of meaning. This is a process in which the word gradually unfolds its inner potentialities, already somehow present like seeds, but needing the challenge of new situations, new experiences and new sufferings, in order to open up.[35]

Benedict attempts to bridge Lessing's ditch by supplementing *historical fact* with the *theological datum* of the canon. On the one hand, he emphasizes the *historical fact* of the incarnation, which demands to be addressed with all the precision and rigour of the historical-critical method. On the other hand, he finds support in the *theological datum* of the canon of Scripture. This enables the theologian to assert that the real meaning of the Old and New

Testaments can only be discerned when one reads them in the light of a Christological hermeneutic, 'which sees Jesus Christ as the key to the whole'.[36] The problem is that when one begins to look at the way in which Benedict employs the historical-critical method in some detail, his prospectus looks less convincing. Geza Vermes, one of the great pioneers of the 'third quest' of the historical Jesus, has noted that Benedict has a tendency only to follow the rules of the historical-critical method when it suits him. Benedict seeks to provide a single coherent narrative that often shies away from comparing contradictory statements in the gospels. In his second volume on the Passion narratives, Benedict does begin to think about the radically different chronologies for the trial and crucifixion offered by the Synoptic tradition on the one hand, and the Fourth Gospel on the other. These chronologies are basically irreconcilable, but Benedict seeks to find as many resonances between them as possible by opting for the Johannine chronology and enriching it with elements of the Synoptic timetable. Similarly, in his account of the resurrection narratives, Benedict wants to affirm that the resurrection is an historical event 'that bursts open the dimensions of history', but concedes that the resurrection narratives within the gospels are 'not binding in every detail'. In other words, there are some inconsistencies between the gospel narratives that cannot be easily reconciled. At a number of points, Benedict appears to be balancing rather precariously, at one moment placing greater weight on the historical, at another moment on the theological, then again on the historical. It perhaps demonstrates that in straddling the two sides of Lessing's ditch, he has taken on a difficult and rather unenviable task.

Some rather more nuanced approaches to the relationship between historical criticism and the theological interpretation of scripture are indicated in the writings of two modern Roman Catholic New Testament scholars, Raymond Brown and Joseph Fitzmyer. Both Roman Catholic priests, they recognized that there was a profound tension between the task of the historical critic in assessing the testimony of the New Testament and the role of the theologian in articulating the faith of the Church. For example, in the first edition of *The Birth of the Messiah*, Raymond Brown addressed the *factum historicum* of the Incarnation head on. He noted in particular the debate about the historicity of the virginal conception and came to two important conclusions: first, while the *scientifically controllable* biblical evidence left the question of the historicity of the virginal conception unresolved, on balance he thought that there was better evidence for historicity than against; and secondly, because the virginal conception was a doctrine infallibly taught by the ordinary magisterium, obedience demanded that he should believe it. Brown was criticized for this position from a number of different quarters: there were those who argued that you could prove the virginal conception exegetically; there were some who asserted that Church teaching did not require belief in the virginal conception; there were others who argued that theological arguments should not subvert the exegetical task and there were still others who presented an argument that was diametrically opposed to that of the first group. They insisted that there was exegetical evidence to disprove the virginal conception! Brown was vilified by secular biblical critics for writing 'servile letters' which would attract the *imprimatur* of his Bishop, while at the same time he noted that 'ultraconservative Catholics also resent the imprimatur when it is given to a book such as mine that embodies modern biblical criticism because that affirmation interferes with their desire to impose their narrow views as church doctrine and to condemn as heretical what, in fact, is perfectly tolerable within the range of Catholic thought'.[37]

Responding to these points in a subsequent edition of *The Birth of the Messiah*, Brown argued that the relationship between scripture and doctrine was more complex than many of his critics were willing to concede. Those who saw doctrine as something which had come to obscure the meaning of scripture or was irrelevant to the exegesis of scripture were in danger of forgetting that 'doctrine was not simply derived from the Scriptures; for when the Scriptures were written, they gave expression to what was already believed and taught. And surely that is true in the case of the infancy narratives: Belief that Mary conceived as a virgin did not first come from reading what Matthew and Luke wrote; rather Matthew and Luke wrote their accounts to express a faith that they already had in the virginal conception'.[38] In other words, while the emergence of historical criticism could be regarded as an attempt to loosen the ties between scripture and 'the stony rocks of ecclesiastical doctrine', an awareness of the role of Christian doctrine in shaping the New Testament writings and the canon of scripture was absolutely essential in the exegetical task. But note that Brown is making a rather different point to the former Pope. Rather than using the canon of scripture as a *theological datum*, he is pointing to a particular set of beliefs that predate the formation of the canon and even the writings of the New Testament themselves. Joseph Fitzmyer presents a rather different argument. In Rom. 5.12–21, St Paul draws a contrast between Adam and Christ: sin entered the world through Adam (verse 12), while 'the abundance of God's grace and his gift of righteousness' (verse 17) came through Christ. Fitzmyer notes that in this passage Paul appears to acknowledge the existence of hereditary or 'original' sin:

> Indeed, the Roman Catholic exegetical tradition has almost unanimously . . . interpreted it, especially 5:12, in terms of the universal causality of Adam's sin on the sinfulness of human individuals.[39]

He goes on to note the way in which the Council of Trent decreed that Rom. 5.12 'is not to be understood in any other way than as the Catholic church . . . has always understood it'. The clear inference is that Rom. 5.12 gives expression to the doctrine of 'original sin'. Fitzmyer suggests that one might need to be a little more circumspect in drawing this conclusion: 'Care must be taken, however, to understand what Paul is saying and not to transform his mode of expression too facilely into the precision of later dogmatic development'. He points out that at no point does Paul use the phrase 'original sin', a term which appears to have originated in the Western tradition at the time of St Augustine of Hippo. At the same time, he also takes advantage of the rather studied ambiguity of the Tridentine decree by noting that the tradition also embraces a number of different interpretations of Paul's words. This means that he can go on to affirm that the doctrine of original sin builds on what Paul teaches in Rom. 5.12: 'Paul's teaching is regarded as seminal and open to later dogmatic development, but it does not say all that the Tridentine decree says'.[40] Fitzmyer is making the point that there is no reference in Paul to the way in which sin was transmitted from one generation to the next. It was Augustine who introduced ideas of propagation or heredity. While he is content to admit that Paul's words about

Adam and sin might be open to Augustine's later interpretation, he is careful to distinguish between his close historical-critical reading of Paul's words and later doctrinal development. He is alert to the danger of reading too much into Paul's words, but willing to accept that the Church might be guided by the Spirit in its subsequent development of doctrine.

These examples from Brown and Fitzmyer share a common theme. Both assert that alongside scripture lies another important resource for Christian doctrinal reflection. This is *tradition*. Raymond Brown suggests that there was a tradition of Christian believing that predates the writing of the scriptures, and that this same tradition informed and animated the production of the scriptures. Thus the virginal conception was already believed by those who wrote the infancy narratives in Matthew and Luke. By contrast, Fitzmyer asserts that the scriptures informed and animated the development of a subsequent tradition. Paul may not have believed in a fully developed doctrine of original sin, but this later doctrinal development was entirely consistent with his statements in his *Epistle to the Romans*.

The tension between scripture and tradition presupposed in the arguments presented by Brown and Fitzmyer brings us back to the points made about tradition in the writings of Irenaeus of Lyons. Brown presents a very similar argument to that of Irenaeus in holding that there was an apostolic tradition that animated the proclamation of the Christian gospel and informed the writers of the New Testament before the New Testament came to be written. Fitzmyer, on the other hand, is suggesting that there was a process of doctrinal development which lay alongside the formation of the canon and continued after its formation. Both are willing to concede that in reading the Bible through the lens of historical criticism, a biblical scholar who is also a Christian believer is bound by the same laws of historical investigation as any other scholar. The subtlety and nuance of their contribution lies in recognizing that it is perfectly legitimate to widen the scope of historical inquiry beyond the writings of the New Testament. So for Brown, it is perfectly legitimate to say that it was not possible to prove the historicity of the virginal conception on the basis of the testimony provided within the infancy narratives of Matthew and Luke, but it was possible to argue that these accounts may have given expression to a doctrine that was already believed.

Admittedly, this may not *prove* the virginal conception, but it does serve to authenticate the reliability of apostolic testimony as it is reflected in both scripture and tradition. Similarly, Fitzmyer recognizes that a close reading of Paul demands that we resist the temptation to project later doctrinal formulations back into his writings. Rather than thinking of the tradition as something that predates the writings of the New Testament, he emphasizes the way in which the New Testament has generated a rich tradition of interpretation, which has emerged in the light of the gaps and lacunae in the text. Thus Paul may write about the reality of sin, but he does not speculate about the way in which sin is transmitted from one generation to the next. Such reflections belong to later writers like Augustine. They may well be a legitimate development of the original apostolic testimony, but no-one is pretending that by employing the historical-critical method we can demonstrate that Paul presented in Rom. 5 an Augustinian understanding of original sin. The important point is that, in borrowing and trading upon the conventions of modern historiography, these writers have learned to be more circumspect in exploring the relationship between historical criticism and doctrinal development.

Such a conclusion might be construed as representing a loss of nerve in the face of modern historical criticism. Surely to acknowledge the vulnerability and fragility of the scriptural witness in the face of historical criticism and to allow space for doctrinal development is a recipe for disaster, creating only uncertainty and doubt about the authenticity and reliability of scripture? I am not persuaded or convinced that this is the case. First, this survey has demonstrated that Christians in the ancient world employed the conventions of ancient historiography in order to provide an apology for their faith. That apology was not intended to be a sorry excuse, but a vigorous and robust defence. In their corresponding response to the demands of modern historiography, it is essential for Christian theologians to continue to engage in fruitful dialogue with other biblical scholars and historians. It is also necessary to acknowledge the limits of the historical enterprise. While we should not fight shy of subjecting the foundational documents of the Christian faith to historical scrutiny, it is not easy to describe how exactly one might *prove* the doctrine of the resurrection or the doctrine of the virginal conception by subjecting the gospel narratives to the rigours of historical criticism. Moreover, Biblical scholars have been quick to point out the biases and presuppositions in the positions adopted by theologians when they have attempted to do so. At the same time, in their race to adopt the moral high ground of being more neutral, dispassionate and objective in their account of Christian origins, those same Biblical scholars have sometimes been less adept at spotting their own ideological assumptions, and subjecting them to necessary critique. And this is precisely where being attentive to the limits of historical methods can be helpful. Those engaged in the study of modern historiography are much more aware of the ways in which questions of ideology, race, class and gender, as well as religion, inform the study of history. Debates about historical method are very much alive in the academy, and biblical scholars and theologians have something to contribute to that debate. By participating in an ongoing dialogue with its attendant and occasionally uncomfortable scrutiny and challenge, theologians will continue to demonstrate that they are profoundly committed to the search for truth.

Secondly, this chapter began with some reflections about the emergence and development of the canon of scripture. It perhaps highlighted that while we cannot be Christians in the modern world without the Bible and the history of its interpretation, somehow the first Christian communities managed it. But they did so by placing enormous value on the testimony of the apostles. This testimony consisted of memories and stories about Jesus Christ, above all about his death and resurrection. This testimony formed part of a tradition, a tradition to which the scriptures themselves bear witness. And yet, this testimony cannot and should not be dressed up in the clothes of unalloyed certainty. It is worth pondering the characteristics of the testimony in the gospels regarding the resurrection of Jesus. There is the tentative testimony at the end of St Mark's gospel, which simply records that the women 'said nothing to anyone, for they were afraid' (Mk 16.8). St Luke's account of the disciples on the way to Emmaus oscillates between elusiveness and recognition, as the disciples come to recognize Jesus in the breaking of bread (Lk. 24.13–35). Similarly, John the Evangelist entrusts the task of proclaiming the resurrection of Jesus to Mary Magdalene, whose testimony – because of her gender – would hardly be accepted in a court in the ancient world. This testimony was and is vulnerable and fragile. And that is the point. It demands and requires a response of faith and trust.

To acknowledge the vulnerability and fragility of this testimony is to recognize that it is *apostolic* testimony, testimony that is animated by faith and trust in God. Thus the theological interests that motivated early Christian theologians and biblical scholars to engage with the intellectual demands of historical inquiry are as significant today as they were in the time of Origen and Eusebius. Their commitment to history was motivated not by a desire to accumulate ancient curiosities, but by a passionate intensity that recognized that in the events recorded in scripture they were confronted with questions of life and death. The writing – indeed, the making – of history betrayed a clear apologetic interest. Describing this testimony in a manner which acknowledges and respects the conventions of historical criticism is a challenge faced squarely by many advocates of the theological interpretation of scripture. It is also a challenge occasionally avoided by others. In responding to the challenges posed by historical criticism, theologians have to negotiate two different risks: either the risk of surrendering the theological character of apostolic testimony in the reconstruction of historical events, or the risk of subverting the conventions of historical criticism to such a degree that historians begin to doubt that they are engaged in the same kind of enterprise. The way in which a number of different theologians negotiate these challenges in their reading of scripture will be the subject of Chapter 4.

CHAPTER THREE

Telling Tales

In the sixth century, a Christian writer and monk, called Hadrian, edited a grammatical textbook made up of different figures of speech gleaned from the scriptures. Its title was *An Introduction to the Sacred Scriptures*.[1] Modelled on the grammatical textbooks that were used in the ancient world, this little manual presented a grammatical analysis of the language and imagery of the Bible. After enumerating the inevitable anthropomorphisms which characterize language about God, Hadrian went on to survey a whole range of different figures of speech, giving in each case some examples from scripture. He lists examples of metaphor, simile, metonymy, allegory, hyperbole and irony, as well as rhetorical devices which may be less familiar to the modern reader. It draws mostly (although not exclusively) on images from the Old Testament, and he seeks to analyse the text with reference to its meaning and its composition.

Hadrian's purpose in compiling this text is not immediately clear. He does not give a reason. This means that Hadrian's *Introduction to the Sacred Scriptures* can be interpreted in two distinct and competing ways: first, one might suggest that by imitating the grammatical textbooks of the ancient world, Hadrian was seeking to demonstrate the literary worth and value of the biblical text. Thus one might conclude that the purpose of Hadrian's little textbook is to demonstrate that the language and imagery of the Bible imitate the language and imagery of other literature. Those engaged in the task of interpreting the scriptures needed to have a reasonable knowledge of basic grammar and they needed to understand the principles of ancient literary criticism. As Augustine writes in his treatise *On Christian Teaching*: 'The literary-minded should be aware that our Christian authors used all the figures of speech which teachers of grammar call by their Greek name of tropes, and that they did so more diversely and profusely than can be judged or imagined by those who are unfamiliar with scripture or who gained their knowledge of figures from other literature'.[2] Thus the Bible needs to be read like any other book.

Alternatively, the fact that Hadrian writes a grammatical textbook drawing exclusively on examples from scripture might reflect an anxiety about using existing grammatical textbooks which drew on pagan literature. Indeed, there were a number of Christian writers in the ancient world who had mixed feelings about the benefits of a classical education. A Syrian Church Order, dating from the third century, had said 'have nothing to do with pagan books'.[3] In the fourth century, John Chrysostom, in the third book of a treatise written *Against the Opponents of Monastic Life*, proposed that Christian parents should entrust their children to monastic schools in order to escape the corrupting effect of the prevailing educational system and the pernicious influence of pagan literature. These misgivings about pagan influence encouraged some writers to demonstrate the superiority of the Christian scriptures over the writings of pagan philosophers and poets. So the Venerable Bede (c. 673–735), repeating Hadrian's exercise and providing a similar summary of the figures of speech found in scripture, provides a much more explicit justification for his purpose in writing:

> And indeed the Greeks boast that they were the discoverers of such figures and tropes. But so that you might know . . . that Holy Scripture holds pride of place over other writings, not only in authority, because it is divine, and in utility, because it leads to eternal life, but in antiquity and in its very circumstance of speaking, it has pleased me to show with examples collected from Scripture that the masters of secular eloquence can offer nothing in the way of schemes or tropes that did not appear first in it.[4]

For Bede, the purpose of the exercise was to demonstrate that pagan literature was no match for the Bible. The Bible was not like any other book.

Hadrian has left a rather curious and ambiguous legacy. His manual alerts us to the fact that the biblical interpretation of early Christian commentators drew on the practices and conventions of ancient literary criticism. But it also serves to illustrate a profound tension between reading the Bible like any other book and demonstrating that the scriptures are quite unlike any other book. This tension is mirrored in modern debate about the place of literary criticism in the reading and interpretation of scripture. In the middle of the nineteenth century, Benjamin Jowett, the Regius Professor of Greek in the University of Oxford, caused considerable controversy in the Church of England when he published an essay in a volume called *Essays and Reviews*. In his essay 'On the Interpretation of Scripture', he argued that one should 'interpret Scripture like any other book'. Jowett was more of a classicist than a theologian. His mind had been trained to read texts carefully and forensically, and he was convinced that such 'a critical spirit in history and literature' should affect the interpretation of scripture. He was convinced that the skills that he had learned as a classicist could be employed fruitfully in the interpretation of scripture. Jowett was struck by the way in which successive interpreters of scripture – the Protestant and Catholic, the Unitarian and Trinitarian – had invoked the 'inspiration of scripture' to authorize a variety of different theological proposals:

> Where there is no critical interpretation of scripture, there will be a mystical or rhetorical one. If words have more than one meaning, they may have any meaning. Instead of being a rule of life or faith, Scripture becomes the expression of the ever-changing aspect of religious opinions. The unchangeable word of God, in the name of which we repose, is changed by each age and each generation in accordance with its passing fancy. The book in which we believe all religious truth to be contained, is the most uncertain of all books, because interpreted by arbitrary and uncertain methods.[5]

Thus for Jowett, it was axiomatic 'that Scripture, like other books, has one meaning, which is to be gathered from itself without reference to the adaptations of Fathers or Divines; and without regard to *a priori* notions about its nature and origin.

It is to be interpreted like other books, with attention to the character of its authors, and the prevailing state of civilization and knowledge, with allowance for peculiarities of style and language, and modes of thought and figures of speech'.[6] But the irony is that the nuance of his argument was completely ignored in the controversy, which subsequently engulfed him. Jowett went on to argue that by attempting to interpret scripture like any other book, the interpreter would learn that scripture was 'unlike any other book', for in reading the scriptures, 'there grows upon us the witness of God in the world, anticipating in a rude and primitive age the truth that was to be, shining more and more unto the perfect day in the life of Christ, which again is reflected from different points of view in the teaching of His Apostles'. It appears that Samuel Wilberforce, the Bishop of Oxford, did not read on. He took exception to *Essays and Reviews*. He warned his clergy of the dangers of the book's rationalism. In particular, he took issue with Jowett's essay. Wilberforce took the view that the natural inference of Jowett's essay was that he was repudiating the doctrine of biblical inspiration. Meanwhile, Dr Pusey, one of the leaders of the Oxford Movement, brought charges against Jowett in the Chancellor's Court. The case against Jowett was quickly thrown out, but the damage to his reputation was done.

Brooke Foss Westcott (1825–1901), no slouch when it came to the demands of biblical criticism, was troubled by the controversy that followed the publication of *Essays and Reviews*. His letters reveal that he did not feel that Jowett's arguments could be easily defended. In one letter, he described them quite simply as 'erroneous', but he was more troubled by the 'violent and reckless language' they provoked in Jowett's opponents. He felt that the vague charges of 'infidelity' and 'atheism' brought against the writers were unfounded. In his view, the essays should never have been published, but the reaction they received suggested 'that the mass of intelligent readers are at present wholly unfit to form a calm judgment in questions involving many of the forms of criticism'. In Westcott's opinion, a calmer and more dispassionate debate would reveal that 'Holy Scripture has nothing to fear from the most searching criticism'. He would willingly meet the essayists on their own ground.[7]

And yet, the ecclesiastical politics characteristic of the nineteenth century meant that this was not exactly the time for calm and

dispassionate debate. Jowett's claim that the Bible should be read
'like any other book', and his insistence that one should apply
exactly the same conventions of literary criticism, whether one
was interpreting the writings of Plato or reading the writings of the
Christian Bible, provoked rather vigorous reactions. Intriguingly,
reactions to the publication of *Essays and Reviews* were in some
respects more vociferous and forceful than reactions to *The
Origin of Species* by Charles Darwin. Westcott saw that reactions
to *Essays and Reviews* were often motivated by fear, but what lay
behind this fear is less easy to describe. Some may have feared that
the 'revealed truth' of the Bible was under threat and with it the
whole Protestant religion. Others may have been concerned about
the unforeseen consequences of suggesting that the Bible should
be 'read like any other book'. This was not necessarily to object
to the use of literary criticism in reading scripture. After all, as
Hadrian's little manual suggests, commentators had employed
literary forms of analysis in reading scripture for centuries. For
example, Origen had noticed the differences in style between the
Pauline letters and the Epistle to the Hebrews, and some of his
pupils had questioned the authorship of the Book of Revelation
by John the Apostle on similar grounds. The real problem was
that to suggest that the Bible should be 'read like any other book'
suggested that something needed to change in the way in which
the Bible was construed. There was an anxiety that bringing the
tools of literary criticism to bear on the interpretation of scripture
might serve to detract from the religious orientation of the text.
The fear was that something important might be lost. The Bible
might come to be regarded as little more than one book alongside
a host of other books. It might become little more than a cultural
artefact set adrift from its religious moorings.

  When one begins to engage with the ways in which literary
criticism have been employed in the course of biblical scholarship
since the time of Jowett, some of these fears and anxieties may
have been well-founded. There is some evidence to suggest that the
transition of the Bible from religious text to cultural artefact was
already beginning to happen during this period. In recent years,
advocates of literary approaches to the reading of scripture have
often tied their explorations of literary criticism to an avowedly
secular vantage point. For example, in the General Introduction to
The Literary Guide to the Bible, Robert Alter and Frank Kermode

present the Bible principally in terms of a literary artefact. Addressed to the 'educated modern reader', their essay reflects on the puzzle presented by this miscellany of documents made up 'of ancient stories, poems, laws and prophecies'. The description of these writings in terms of their genre underlines the fact that 'the power of the Genesis narratives or of the story of David, the complexities and refinements of the Passion narratives, could be studied by methods developed in the criticism of secular literature'. But they go on to assert that the reader should not suppose that they did not care about the religious character of the Bible. They argue that both religious believers and more secular readers would both have something to learn from the application of literary methods to the interpretation of scripture: first, they point out that the Bible, as a book, achieved its effects through the form of a written language. Any written text requires and demands interpretation, regardless of whether we regard it 'as the report of God's action in history, as the founding text of a religion or religions, as a guide to ethics, as evidence about people and societies in the remote past, and so on'. Secondly, a closer knowledge and awareness of the biblical text would inform and invigorate the practice of literary criticism: 'an increasing neglect of the Bible in our secularized times has opened a gulf between it and our general literature, a gap of ignorance which must in some measure falsify the latter'. So the modern secular commentator reading John Milton would not be able to match the way in which an agnostic Victorian reader like Matthew Arnold would have picked up Milton's biblical allusions and references. The kind of intimacy with biblical narratives which previous generations enjoyed by virtue of either shared belief or the shape of the school curriculum could no longer be assumed. Secular criticism would only be impoverished by this lack of knowledge and awareness. Thirdly, they comment on what they saw as 'a more striking development: the Bible, once thought of as a source of secular literature yet somehow apart from it, now bids fair to become part of the literary canon'. One of the ironies about this particular guide is that it deliberately excluded a whole range of different literary methods from its critical apparatus. There is little reference to feminist, psychoanalytic, deconstructive, ideological and postcolonial approaches within the guide. Alter and Kermode acknowledge the impact of these different methods of literary criticism, but largely choose to ignore them: 'it is unnecessary to specify these methods here. . . . Modern criticism is a fine breeding ground of neologisms; we avoid them for the most part . . .'[8]

As their argument unfolds, it becomes clear that the concerns of the secular critic are perhaps uppermost in their minds. Their observation about the Bible as part of a 'literary canon' perhaps confirms that they regarded the Bible more as a cultural artefact than as a religious text. Part of the reason for this lay in their need to negotiate the secularism of the educational system in North America. The US constitution demanded the separation of Church and State. This meant that State-sponsored Universities and Colleges could not teach theology as part of their curriculum. If the Bible were to be included in the curriculum, its inclusion might be justified on the grounds that the Bible belonged to a wider canon of 'world literature'. So, the development of Biblical studies as a discipline took a rather different form in the United States in comparison with Northern Europe, where theology was often taught in Universities from a confessional standpoint. This led to a proliferation of 'Bible as literature' courses in North American Universities, and this stimulated further interaction and conversation between Biblical scholars and literary critics. Alter and Kermode's guide was principally designed to serve the needs of students in 'Bible as literature' courses, rather than the needs of seminarians and theology students.

And yet, whatever we might suppose about the intention of the authors, the development of these literary insights has also served to stimulate further theological reflection about the interpretation of scripture. This chapter tells the story of the way in which literary approaches to reading scripture, far from confirming the worst fears of Jowett's critics in marginalizing the Bible, have opened up the riches of Biblical narrative and poetry for further theological reflection. At the same time, a more literary approach to reading scripture has also offered the opportunity to demonstrate the ways in which the Christian scriptures continue to animate Western culture in the twenty-first century.

A Literary Artefact

The Literary Guide to the Bible reflected a major sea change in both Old and New Testament studies. It also reflected wider changes in the world of literary criticism. Until the 1920s, literary criticism had been taught in Universities with a strong historical and philological interest. It is no accident that the practices of source criticism, form criticism and redaction criticism, which are often associated with traditional approaches to biblical criticism, were formed in this environment. During this period, the divide between historical and literary approaches was less pronounced. But, in the 1920s and 1930s, with the advent of New Criticism (sometimes associated with T. S. Eliot) in Britain and North America, this emphasis began to change. Rather than regarding a text as a window through which one could look at the interests of the original author and the context which he or she inhabited, a text was to be regarded as a picture or a portrait with its own aesthetic value. New critics advocated a close and intensive reading of the text itself, without speculating about the intention of the author or the response of the reader. They were dismissive of the 'intentional' fallacy, which privileged the role of the author, and the 'affective' fallacy, which privileged the role of the reader. They promoted instead the idea that a text enjoyed a certain autonomy. This emphasis on the autonomy of the text was important for subsequent developments in literary criticism.

It is fair to say that this emphasis was rejected initially by biblical scholars. They remained stubbornly committed to the strong historical and philological interests of a previous generation of literary critics. But, in the 1960s and 1970s, this began to change. Biblical scholars began to engage with recent developments in the field of literary criticism, and to recognize that, in the words of Robert Alter, there was an art in biblical narrative. Stimulated by renewed interest in questions of literary theory, following the publication of Northrop Frye's *Anatomy of Criticism* in North America and subsequent developments in European philosophy and French literary criticism, biblical scholars began to engage with various forms of literary theory, including structuralism and deconstructionism.

One of the key proponents of the literary approach to the study of the Hebrew Bible was Robert Alter. In *The Art of Biblical Narrative*, he described this approach in the following terms:

By literary analysis I mean the manifold varieties of minutely discriminating attention to the artful use of language, to the shifting play of ideas, conventions, tone, sound, imagery, syntax, narrative viewpoint, compositional units, and much else; the kind of disciplined attention, in other words, which through a whole spectrum of critical approaches has illuminated, for example, the poetry of Dante, the plays of Shakespeare, the novels of Tolstoy.[9]

Alter took issue with the way in which source critics of a previous generation had assumed that the writings of the Old Testament were little more than a chain of disparate documents held together like pearls on a string. Thus Chapters 37–38 of the Book of Genesis may well be a mixture of J and E sources, but such an analysis does not do justice to the complex interrelationship between the story of Joseph being sold into slavery and the story of Judah's complex relationship with Tamar. For the source critic, the latter story is simply a curious interpolation. For the literary critic, this same story is full of similar motifs to the previous narrative. Alter points out that both stories contain an element of separation. Joseph is separated from his brothers, just as Judah is separated from his brothers by going to marry a Canaanite woman. Jacob mourns for the death of his son, Joseph, just as Judah mourns for the death of his sons, Er and Onan. Judah is dishonest in his dealings with Jacob, and unscrupulous in his dealings with Tamar. Judah uses the blood of a goat to stain Joseph's garment, while the promise of a kid plays a part in his own deception by Tamar. The point of these literary connections and repeated motifs is to demonstrate that both stories have been woven together into a single complex narrative.

Similarly, David Clines has pointed out the value of attending to the Book of Jonah as a story 'for it is not necessary to disbelieve, or to believe, in the story's historicity in order to understand it'. Attending to the narrative of the Book of Jonah, rather than wrestling with questions of historicity or attempting to isolate a single point or message from it, enables the interpreter to enter more imaginatively into the 'serious concerns of the author are lightly and teasingly sketched'.[10] Clines suggests that similar insights can be applied to the 'historical' books. Indeed, as he explores the way in which the character of King David is presented, Clines notes that 'the quest for a single theological message' can inhibit our appreciation of the biblical narrative. It can fail to capture the complex levels of characterization in 2 Sam. 9–24 and 1 Kgs 1–2 where we discover the tension between David as king and David as a human being (husband and father). David is a complicated figure: at one moment he is generous to a fault, the next moment he is portrayed as little more than a grasping tyrant (2 Sam. 11). David Gunn makes the point that the narrative portrayal of David offers no opportunity for strait-laced 'moralizing but rather a picture of the rich variety of life that is comic or ironic in its contrasting perspectives and conflicting norms. Not that the author is amoral or immoral; but his judgement is tempered by his sense of the intricacy and ambivalence of the situations that confront his characters. . . .'[11] While the biblical narrative may appear to emphasize David's rectitude and Solomon's wisdom, the temptation to see in these monarchs the pattern of true kingship is often thwarted by the inclusion of the word 'except'. David 'did what was right in the Lord's eyes and did not turn aside from anything that he commanded him all the days of his life, *except* in the matter of Uriah the Hittite' (1 Kgs 15.5). The 'matter of Uriah the Hittite' is a reference to David's callousness in sending Uriah, the husband of Bathsheba, into a battle that he was bound to lose with the intention of ensuring that David could marry his widow. Gunn points out that the little word 'except' can have a powerful and subversive effect on the way we read this sentence. One might read it as something of an afterthought so that 'the matter of Uriah the Hittite' is the exception that proves the rule. Alternatively, if one reads the narrative carefully and recognizes that the matter of Uriah the Hittite was 'the pivotal episode in David's life, representing a peak of grasping for whatever was good in his own eyes', the reader is offered a much more complex and ironic judgment of David's character. Attending to these more literary questions has the capacity to enrich our reading and interpretation of these narratives. It offers a rather more exciting strategy of interpretation than source criticism. But, more importantly, it becomes rather more challenging when we begin to consider the way in which God is portrayed in these narratives.

One of the noticeable weaknesses of Robert Alter's approach is that he perhaps placed too much emphasis on narrative (excluding consideration of other genres within the Biblical corpus). Unsurprisingly, *The Art of Biblical Narrative* has a great deal to say about narrative but it does not have much to say about poetry.

It is significant that there is so much poetry in the Old Testament. One of the most obvious examples of this is the Song of Songs. This is a love poem and, largely because of the 'obliqueness' of its language, it has been interpreted in a variety of different ways. In rabbinic thought, it was often interpreted in terms of the relationship between God and Israel. Maimonides thought that the Song described the yearning of the soul for union with God. Among patristic writers, it was interpreted as an allegory about the relationship between Christ and his Church. In her recent commentary, Cheryl Exum takes issue with these interpretations: 'The Song is not an allegory; there is no indication that the poet ever intended it to be given an esoteric interpretation'. She argues that the Song is a love poem about erotic love and sexual desire: 'The poem's genius lies in the way it shows us as well as tells us that "love is strong as death" (8.4), and in the way it explores the nature of love'. By attending to the 'controlling poetic strategies' of the Song, she seeks to explore the way in which the poetry of desire functions and the techniques it employs: 'We cannot understand the Song, much less appreciate how it succeeds as a love poem, without paying attention to the *way* it presents its vision of love, to its emotional sequences in time and the accompanying shifts in technical management'. If Gunn is struck by the use of *irony* in his reading of narrative, Exum emphasizes the importance of *metaphor* in making sense of poetry: 'Striking and unusual metaphorical descriptions of the body are not at all uncommon in love poetry, though for some reason they seem to be a stumbling block for literal-minded commentators on the Bible's only love poem'. This presents a significant interpretative challenge for the commentator. Our expectation of a commentator like Exum is that she will provide authoritative guidance about how we might interpret these metaphors, and yet, as Exum acknowledges, the point of the metaphors employed in the imagery of the Song of Songs is that they resist a single definition. Thus Exum suggests that her observations should not be understood 'in any definitive sense, for it is not the case that there is only one correct way to approach them'.[12] For Exum, this appears to be an intrinsic characteristic of metaphor and poetry. And yet, she is also aware of the way in which the contemporary reader sets the interpretative agenda. This is reflected in contemporary interest within the humanities in questions about the construction of gender, sexuality and the body, and the recognition that the Song of Songs provides an obvious text for exploring these issues. But it is also consistent with the way in which the ideas of Stanley Fish and others in alerting us to the active role of the reader have become more commonplace:

> A focus on the reader leads one to ask different questions, not only of the text but also of the interpretation it has elicited, and sometimes of the interpreters themselves – their motivations, stated and unstated, conscious and unconscious.[13]

This shifting emphasis from text to reader has opened up the text to a whole variety of different reading strategies, including feminist interpretation and queer theory. It has also opened up the study of the reception history of the Song of Songs, particularly in the arts and music. As biblical scholars have begun to explore the many 'afterlives' of the Song, scholars have come to appreciate the many and varied ways in which this ancient Hebrew love poem continues to animate aspects of Western culture.

By contrast, the development of literary criticism in relation to the New Testament took a little longer to get going. Indeed, it has perhaps always been rather less advanced than it has in the study of the Old Testament. In the course of the 1970s, the Markan Seminar of the Society of Biblical Literature became a key forum for debate and discussion about literary approaches to the Gospel of Mark in particular and to the interpretation of the New Testament in general. It is fascinating that the interpretation of the Gospel of Mark has often provided the crucible in which new strategies for reading have been tested, established and then overthrown. The fruits of this research can be seen in the publication of *Mark as Story: An Introduction to the Narrative of a Gospel* by David Rhoads and Donald Michie in 1982. There had been a number of monographs published in the course of the 1970s that looked at particular aspects of Markan narrative, but this was the first time that a thorough description of the gospel narrative had been attempted. Rhoads and Michie employed 'narrative criticism' in their reading of the gospel. Stephen Moore has noted that their use of literary approaches was somewhat eclectic. They emphasized the intrinsic unity of Mark's text and they contended that the Gospel told a story that generates a world of people, places and events. In speaking of this 'story-world', they argued that narrative criticism recognizes that knowledge of the history and culture of the first-century provide crucial insights in reading Mark's narrative. However, it is not interested in reading Mark in order to reconstruct historical events about Jesus or about Mark and his community: 'it brackets historical questions and looks at the closed universe of the story world'.[14] A distinction is made between the 'real author' and the 'implied author', between the 'real reader' and the 'implied reader'. The 'real author' is the person who actually composed the story. The 'implied author' refers to the image of the author, which the text progressively creates in the course of the reading. The 'real reader' is any person who has access to the text – from those who first read or heard it read, right down to those who read or hear it read today. The 'implied reader' is the reader, which the text presupposes and in effect creates. To negotiate the gap between the 'real reader' and the 'implied reader', one must be capable of performing the mental and affective operations necessary for entering into the narrative world of the text and responding to it in the way envisaged by the real author through the implied author. A text will continue to exercise its influence in the degree to which 'real readers' (that is, us) can identify with the 'implied reader'. The major task of exegesis lies not in identifying the original intentions of the author, but in facilitating the identification of the 'real reader' with the 'implied reader'.

Nevertheless, Rhoads and Michie still emphasized the intentions of the author in developing plot and character, and in creating suspense and irony. In emphasizing the intention of the author, they were doing a bit more than simply extending the insights of redaction criticism. Stephen Moore suggests that the key influence on their reading of Mark was Seymour Chatman's work on narrative and narratology. In *Story and Discourse* (published in 1978), Chatman had combined two traditions of literary theory: a French structuralist tradition, with an emphasis on plot, character and narrative time, and an Anglo-American tradition centred on the narrator's manipulation of point of view, commenting overtly and covertly on the action and plot of the story. But while Chatman exercised some influence over Rhoads and Michie, the precise genealogy of 'narrative criticism' in the writings of other advocates is not always so clear: sometimes authorial intention is accepted as an integral part of the reading strategy; sometimes it is not. Such confusion is a potential source of difficulty, particularly if one is alert to more recent developments in the field of literary theory. Indeed, literary critics know no such movement as 'narrative criticism'. It is an approach developed by a number of biblical critics that draws on a rather eclectic selection of secular insights and questions which it brings to the text. David Rhoads was a biblical scholar and Donald Michie was a literary critic. Their collaboration resulted in a ground breaking, significant and interesting reading of Mark, but their joint working also resulted in a kind of hybrid method of reading whose genealogy and provenance are not always immediately clear. Indeed, Stephen Moore and Yvonne Sherwood regard 'narrative criticism' as a rather half-baked affair: 'Narrative criticism, for all it undeniable novelty in the 1980s, seems now in restrospect to have been a singularly painless extension of redaction criticism'.[15] More recent developments in biblical scholarship have seen a more sustained engagement with poststructuralism and more recent developments in critical theory. Moore laments the way in which biblical scholars have adapted various methods in literary studies. Partly as a consequence of his criticisms, literary approaches to the Bible have tended in more recent years to focus much more intentionally on questions of method and to be much more explicit about their conversation partners in the field of literary theory.

One important and significant conversation partner in this enterprise has been Frank Kermode. In *The Genesis of Secrecy*, Kermode provides a commentary on the work of commentators – a book 'about interpretation, an interpretation of interpretation'. He addressed directly the distinction made by biblical scholars between history and literature: he argued that it was essential that the contemporary interpreter of a text should not simply be satisfied with discussing the historical questions surrounding 'what it is written about'. The interpreter must acknowledge the narrative quality of the text and attend to 'what is written'. He was critical of those scholars who succumbed to the temptation to dissolve the text into its elements rather than to observe the depth and range of its interrelations. Kermode presented himself self-consciously as a 'secular critic', one more at home in the world of secular literary criticism than biblical studies. His primary interest was the study of hermeneutics. However, because the history of the rules and theory of interpretation were so closely linked with that of biblical exegesis, his fascination with questions of hermeneutics and his conviction that 'the gospels need to be talked about by critics of a quite unecclesiastical formation' led him to produce a series of lectures on the interpretation of Mark's narrative. Kermode was drawn by what he perceived as the 'enigmatic quality' of Mark's gospel, a quality which he accounted for in a number of different ways. For instance, in the chapter on 'Why Are Narratives Obscure?' he alerted the contemporary reader to the fact that what one might consider to be the 'natural' reading of the text would not necessarily have been recognized as such by earlier interpreters. To describe one's own reading as *natural* is 'only (a) way of authenticating, or claiming as universal, a habit of thought which is cultural and arbitrary'. Kermode promoted the view that such narrative lends itself to multiple interpretations. For the Church fathers, the parables were loaded with hidden meanings: 'The Holy Ghost does not give details merely to please or reassure; in all his works every word and every figure is charged with sense'.[16]

In his discussion of St Luke's parable of the Good Samaritan (Lk. 10.25–37), Kermode reflected in turn on C. H. Dodd's reflections on St Augustine's interpretation of the parable in his introduction to *The Parables of the Kingdom.* Following Dodd, Kermode noted that patristic writers, from Irenaeus to Augustine, interpreted a number of parables on several occasions with some variation. The fact that these writers of the early church did not attribute a 'fixed' meaning to the text should in itself alert the reader to the enigmatic quality of the text. These many and varied interpretations formed 'structures of explanation' which stood between the text and interpreter 'like some wall of wavy glass'.[17] Confronted with such a distorted perspective on the text, Kermode suggested that the attempt by an interpreter to recover the original meaning of a text could only prove to be an 'illusory quest'.

Kermode's essay has generated considerable debate and has attracted a number of critics, particularly from those who place greater emphasis on the role of the reader in interpretation. According to Stephen Moore, Kermode's argument proves ultimately unsatisfactory in that however much 'the urbane Cambridge don has absorbed a heady dose of French poststructuralism somewhere', he continues to locate the 'interminability of interpretation' within the text itself. As Moore notes, 'perusing the *Genesis of Secrecy* one does get the impression that there is something hard and essential for him behind the wall of glass'.[18] Indeed, there is a tendency among literary critics of Mark's Gospel simply to duplicate the claims of redaction and composition critics in emphasizing, not so much the sophistication of Mark's theological programme, as his accomplishment as a story-teller. Moore contrasts this with the approach of Stanley Fish, the great advocate of reader-response theory, who describes the enigmatic quality of the hermeneutical exercise in terms of the sheer variety of interpretations rendered by a series of interpretive communities. Nevertheless, Kermode's argument is perhaps more nuanced than Moore allows. While Kermode contends that there is a class of narratives which have to mean more, or other, than what they manifestly say, the 'interminability of interpretation' rests not simply on an intrinsic property of the text but is also determined by a decision of the interpretative community to ascribe 'canonical status' to a particular text. Kermode does not attribute the obscurity of Mark's narrative to any single factor, but seeks to describe the enigmatic quality of this one text in the light of a range of factors and influences: 'Whatever is preserved grows enigmatic; time, and the pressures of interpretation, which are the agents of preservation, will see to that'.[19]

However, it is Kermode's description of 'carnal and spiritual senses' in the interpretation of Mark's narrative, which has perhaps generated the greater controversy. Kermode was intrigued by the unsettling way in which the parables, recorded by Mark, have the capacity to 'proclaim a truth as a herald does, and at the same time conceal a truth like an oracle'.[20] This was not simply a consequence of the 'riddle-like' quality of the genre, subverting obvious expectations and manifest senses. By his own admission, Mark appeared to suggest that parables have the express purpose of concealing a mystery that was to be understood only by insiders. Kermode notes the curious words attributed to Jesus: 'To you has been given the secret of the kingdom of God, but for those outside everything is in parables; so that they may indeed see but not perceive, and may indeed hear but not understand; lest they should turn again, and be forgiven' (Mk 4.11–12). For Kermode, the sense of Jesus' saying is plain. Only the insiders can have access to the mysteries and can understand the true meaning of these stories.

Kermode comments on the teacher's irritation with the disciples, an irritation born from the fact that the disciples did not know that even plain stories mean more than they seem to say and that they may contain mysteries inaccessible to all but the most privileged interpreters. There are the naïve interpreters who *see* and *hear*, while an elect band are invited to *perceive* and *understand*. As one elect band succeeds another, there is a 'perpetual *aggiornamento* of the latent senses' contained in the text. Such an invitation to move beyond the constraints of the simple primary sense encourages the reader to seize on the spiritual meaning. The challenge presented by a biblical text to an avowedly secular literary critic like Kermode lies in the fact that among initiates, a preference for spiritual over carnal readings – or for interpretations that are hidden from outsiders – has been firmly established almost from the moment that the Christian canon came into existence. Kermode has in mind the extraordinary transformation of the Hebrew Bible when it was joined to the New Testament:

> This joining, which occurred late in the second century, was of a kind that permitted Christian interpreters to assume that the more obvious senses of the Old Testament, including the historical meaning, were of small or no importance, were dangerous illusions, even. The Old Testament made sense only insofar as it prefigured Christianity. The rest of it – a great deal – was deafness, blindness, forgetfulness.[21]

The paradox of Christian exegesis of the Old Testament is that the insiders turn out to be outsiders, and the outsiders become the insiders. Kermode marvels at the way in which a whole literature produced over many centuries and which sustained and continues to sustain Jewish religion and culture 'is now said to have value only insofar as it complies with the fore-understanding of later interpreters'.[22] Kermode notes that there were Christian interpreters, like Theodore of Mopsuestia, who objected to the contention that the true sense of the Old Testament could only be fulfilled and made plain in a series of 'absurd spiritual allegories'. For them, the diminishing of the historical record of the Old Testament amounted to 'the dangerous destruction of history'.[23]

Kermode suggests that their opinion was not heeded, and that they did not prevail. Consequently, multiple meanings proliferated to such a degree that it became increasingly difficult to say what the text actually meant.

This is the anxiety at the heart of Kermode's essay: can a text simply be made to mean whatever you want it to mean? Are the multiple meanings that interpreters see in the text a consequence of some intrinsic characteristic of the text? Or are they the consequence of the varied interests and concerns of the readers? Can there be any limit to the extent of their ingenuity and creativity in interpreting these texts? Like Exum, in her recognition of the inability of the commentator to give a single definitive description of the poetry of the Hebrew Bible, Kermode wants to make the point that he sees no way beyond the 'interminability of interpretation' in the reading of the gospels. As 'multiple meanings' proliferate, his essay tails off into a rather despondent elegy on the unenviable task of interpreters, thwarted by the enigmatic and 'endlessly disappointing'[24] quality of the text, reduced to squinting expectantly through walls of wavy glass, while recoiling fearfully from their own distorted shadows reflected on the surface.

The Literal Sense

Kermode's view was challenged by the theologian, Hans Frei. No stranger to dialogue with contemporary literary criticism, Frei's understanding of the priority of narrative in theological discourse emerged out of a sustained engagement with the writings of Erich Auerbach. Auerbach's book *Mimesis*, published in 1946, was hailed as 'a landmark' in understanding the literary importance of the Bible. In the *Eclipse of Biblical Narrative,* Frei argued that modernity marked a profound change in the way in which scripture came to be construed and used. Prior to the development of historical criticism in the eighteenth century, the biblical text had been read realistically, that is, as a literal account of reality: 'The words and sentences meant what they said, and because they did so they accurately described real events and real truths that were rightly put only in those terms and no others'.[25] And yet following the Enlightenment, this emphasis was lost. As people discovered other ways of mapping out reality, their attempts to use the Bible for the purpose of reconstructing Christian origins or as a guide to interpreting archaeological evidence only served to distort and lose sight of the biblical narrative. In Frei's view, this eclipse of the biblical narrative would have catastrophic consequences for the theological interpretation of scripture.

For Frei, the problem with Kermode's approach is that he neglected the priority given to the literal sense within Christian exegesis of both the Old and New Testaments. The prevalence of allegorical and figural readings of scripture did not mean that the literal sense was superseded in the way that Kermode suggests. For Frei, it was axiomatic that 'description of the Christian religion, especially in the West, has included a description of its sacred text in which at the very least certain portions regarded as central were to be read not allegorically or spiritually but literally. Another reading may be allowed, but it must not offend the basic literal sense of those crucial sections'.[26]

Frei's argument rests on an extended redefinition of the phrase, 'the literal sense'. He noted that the phrase might be used in three different ways: first, as an appeal to the author's intention. This might refer either to the intention of the human author, but it might also refer to a 'divine author' or the coincidence of divine and human intention. Accompanied by a theory of divine inspiration, the literal sense might even include and overlap with figurative or typological senses, which may have been part of the literal sense for God but not for the human author. Frei notes that such an appeal to 'authorial intention' has had some curious unforeseen effects in the theological interpretation of scripture. While restricting the interpreter's interest to the intention of the human author has provided encouragement to those engaged in historical criticism, the merging of appeals to 'authorial intention' with theories of divine inspiration has been fairly catastrophic. While an emphasis on divine inspiration may provide an ingenious way of insisting on the primacy of the literal sense, Frei concedes that the difficulty with such mental gymnastics is that they can lead ultimately to biblical literalism and inerrancy. Secondly, Frei suggests that the literal sense refers to a positive and realistic regard for the New Testament narrative, pointing the reader to the Bible's narrative world as God's story, that when combined with other narratives within the canon of scripture not only renders the identity of God or

his self-identification as an agent in this storied context but
also invites the reader to accept this world as the proper setting
for understanding his or her life and the lives of others: 'the
narrated world is as such the real world and not a linguistic
launching pad to language transcending reality, whether ideal
essence or self-contained empirical occurrence'. In this context,
it is worth remarking that the parables of the Kingdom are more
like metaphors than allegories. Thus the figural reading of the
parables associated with Augustine and other patristic writers
place the parables firmly in the context of the wider narrative
of the Gospel. Whatever their original intent, these parables
came to be used as figurations of Jesus that substantiated his
messianic identity. In this way, the parables served to identify
Jesus of Nazareth rather than provide a series of enigmatic clues
about the meaning of the overall narrative: 'In the context of
the *full* narrative – pericopes together with the passion and
resurrection – Jesus identifies the Kingdom of God and is only
secondarily identified by his relation to it: He is himself the
parable of the Kingdom'.[27] Thirdly, Frei notes that the literal sense
is the way the text has generally been used in the community,
by which presumably he means his own ecclesial community.
He sees the origins of this Western Christian emphasis on the
importance of the literal sense in the *peshat* of early Jewish
interpretation. This latter way of conceiving the literal sense
marks a decisive shift from some of his earlier writing. Instead
of simply presenting the literal sense as an attribute of a certain
genre of narrative, he places much more emphasis on a practice
of reading, which follows a recognizable pattern established by
a community of Christian readers. Consequently, the principle
reason why Kermode's distinction between 'carnal and spiritual
senses' is an inadequate account of the Christian interpretive
tradition lies in his contention that the relation between 'letter'
and 'spirit', characteristic of the Western Christian tradition, is
not equivalent to the relation between manifest and latent sense:
'The primacy of the *sensus literalis* is in effect an assertion of the
fitness and congruence of the "letter" to be the channel of the
spirit. It is the assertion that the text is more nearly perspicuous
than not and that, therefore, the dialectic insider/outsider as well
as disclosure/concealment must end in asymptotic subordination
of the latter to the former in each pair'.[28]

Frei's commitment to the priority of the literal sense rests on nothing more than his observation that this has always been characteristic of the Christian interpretive tradition in the West. This commitment enables Frei to affirm that when Christians engage with the narrative of scripture they can continue to speak about *truth*. It is at this point that the contrast with Kermode becomes clear and apparent. For Kermode, *truth* is irretrievable, because he perceives *truth* as an underlying essence, buried below the surface of the text, obscured by 'absurd spiritual allegories', which are nothing more than the accumulated deposits of human ingenuity in constructing different layers of *meaning*. For Frei, the purpose of engaging with scripture is to enable the reader to reflect on the reality of God and the *truth* of the Christian Gospel.

But Frei also recognized that for centuries Christians had not always read passages in scripture absolutely *literally*. This was particularly true of Christian readings of the Old Testament. In response to this, Frei proposed the recovery of the literal and figural sense in the reading of scripture. He was particularly intrigued by John Calvin's use of the Old Testament. While Luther tended to accentuate the contrast between the Old and the New, between the Law and the Gospel, Calvin emphasized the unity of the biblical canon and the assertion that 'the meaning of all of it is salvation in Jesus Christ'.[29] Frei explored the importance of 'figural' or 'typological' reading in Calvin's use of the Bible. He noted the way in which Calvin used the juxtaposition of types and anti-types to enrich his reading of scripture. Calvin emphasized the way in which the biblical canon constituted a unitary whole which bore witness to divine action.

To explore the significance of 'figural' reading in more detail, he drew directly on the literary theory of Erich Auerbach. In his essay *Figura*, Auerbach makes an important distinction between allegorical and figural readings of the Old Testament. Although figural readings were a form of allegorical reading, they were distinct in that they were consonant with the preservation of historical reality. He justifies this argument with reference to Tertullian's reading of Numbers 13.16, where, according to Tertullian, the naming of Hoshea son of Nun as Joshua is a 'figure of things to come' heralding a second, future event: the coming of Jesus Christ. Auerbach asserts that 'the naming of Joshua-Jesus is a phenomenal prophecy of prefiguration of the future Saviour; *figura* is something real and historical which announces something else that is also real and historical'.[30]

Frei embraces this analysis, but he goes on to relate the figural reading of scripture to a theology of divine providence. Figural interpretation was quite different from 'allegory' because it involved a historical reference. It demanded 'the effective rendering of reality with the pattern of meaning that is dependent upon it'. It was not enough to read a series of Old Testament passages as allegories of the Christian drama of salvation. If the story of Exodus was a *type* or *figure* of the drama of Easter, the Christian Passover, then the pattern and shape of the story pointed to the unfolding of God's revelation and providence in history. Thus "figural interpretation" was to be clearly distinguished from 'an arbitrary allegorizing of texts in the service of preconceived dogma'.[31] Two distinct historical events, in their concrete reality and particularity, are related to one another, and this relationship reflects a single divine intention. Of course, this represents something of a departure from Auerbach's own argument. In developing the idea of 'figural reading', Auerbach is more interested in questions of human interpretation than the issue of divine intention. But Auerbach does not simply bracket or ignore the theological import of this kind of figural reading. He suggests that the problem inherent in the way that Christians understand reality is that they fall prey to the temptation to engage in ever more speculative and figurative readings of scripture. In some ways, he prefigures precisely the problem identified by Frank Kermode. Auerbach was critical of allegorical readings because they vitiated the historical emphasis of the narrative. Frei shares these misgivings. Nevertheless, it is important to recognize that while Frei's thinking has been heavily influenced by the work of a leading literary critic, he also accentuates and extends Auerbach's insights about the distinction between the 'figural' and the 'figurative'. As a literary critic, Frei can suggest with Auerbach that Christian figural reading extends rather than effaces the Bible's realistic, literal sense. But as a theologian, Frei departs from Auerbach in presenting a renewed and vigorous emphasis on Christian figural reading as evidence of divine providence. It is not simply a question of human interpretation.

Frei's contribution to the debate is very significant indeed. Frei acknowledges that Christian interpreters have engaged in figurative and allegorical readings of the text. In this respect, he recognizes that Frank Kermode has a point. But he goes on to suggest that such hermeneutical adventures serve to subvert the Western Christian tradition's dominant and over-riding concern with the *literal sense*. He supports his argument by drawing on the insights of another literary critic, Erich Auerbach. But in doing so, he extends and expands the range of Auerbach's argument. A point about human interpretation is re-presented in terms of divine intention. There is a curious parallel here with the way in which theologians and biblical scholars have employed the historical-critical method. They acknowledge it is indispensable in the exegetical task, while at the same time seeking to refine or redefine it so that it can accommodate 'a worldview in which events are not adequately explained through reference to intra-mundane causalities'.[32] Frei also elaborates Auerbach's argument beyond intra-mundane causalities. Although the ditch described by Lessing (in the previous chapter) may not be as pronounced in the field of literary theory, there is an intriguing distinction to make between the *theological* and the *literary*, just as there is between the *theological* and the *historical*.

That said, in engaging as a theologian with the currents of thought in contemporary literary theory, Frei's achievement is considerable. He has reasserted the importance of *narrative* in the theological enterprise, and this has stimulated and provoked all sorts of developments in the field of 'narrative theology'. Learning to read the Bible 'like any other book' and attending to the depth of its literary potential have served to enrich and expand the theological imagination. As David Clines points out, simply searching the text for a religious truth or a moral lesson in order to make a series of dogmatic statements will only sap the life out of the story. Employing literary methods to attend to the biblical narrative offers the potential to engage in a deeper and more satisfying interpretation of scripture.

Frei's emphasis on the distinction between the *literal* and the *figural* has also been significant. But one of the difficulties – and the dangers – is that an emphasis on the pre-eminence of narrative in the biblical corpus can sometimes cause us to ignore a whole range of other genres in scripture. The Bible is not all about narrative and story. There is also genealogy, law, history, epistle, prophecy, proverb, lamentation, confession, apocalypse, exhortation, praise, parable and poetry. However useful the distinction between the *literal* and the *figural* may be in interpreting biblical narrative, it is rather more limited in providing a satisfying description of the language and imagery of the Bible. With its different genres of writing and its many different figures of speech, the Bible presents language and imagery, which is often analogical and metaphorical, particularly when talking about God. While the emphasis on the *literal sense* is helpful in providing a foil for the more eccentric figurative interpretations of biblical narrative, it is unhelpful if the reader concludes from this that theological language can be *literally* literal. Indeed, it is precisely the obliqueness and allusiveness of biblical language and imagery, which grants it a capacity to speak afresh in every situation, in a way which the defined and the precise simply cannot do.

The point about the allusiveness of language is reinforced by Harold Bloom in *Where Shall Wisdom be Found?* For Bloom, a sense of connotation is essential in the effective reading and interpretation of a text: 'Without a sense of connotation, the reader would be tone-deaf, and all figurative language would become a form of irony'.[33] This distinction between 'denotation' and 'connotation' perhaps clarifies some of the issues at the heart of the debate over the use of the 'literal sense' in the theological interpretation of scripture. For Frei and others, the 'literal sense' enables the reader to affirm the capacity of a text to 'denote' meaning and truth. And yet, in marginalizing more figurative interpretations of a text, I suspect that there is a danger in imposing arbitrary limits on the 'connotation' of a text, arbitrary in the sense that such limits do not always provide an adequate description of the allusiveness of the language and imagery of the Bible. If we become deaf to the allusiveness of its language and imagery, then the danger is that we will also fail to hear its echo and to observe its influence in the art, music and literature of Western culture.

The Bible, Literature and Western Culture

Stephen Moore points out that over the last two decades interest in the literary criticism of the Bible has increased exponentially. He notes the irony that whereas 'deconstruction and other forms of poststructuralism, extending to New Historicism, were not taken up in New Testament studies until long after their first flowering, and even their eventual decline, in literary studies, . . . most of the major developments of the 1990s in literary studies, in contrast – cultural studies, postcolonial studies, queer theory, masculinity studies, and autobiographical criticism – had all been taken up in New Testament studies even before that decade had come to an end'.[34] In the last decade, scholars have become more interested in the complex relationship between the Bible and its reception in Western culture. Scholars have explored the 'afterlife' of particular texts within the Bible. This has involved thinking about the way in which Biblical narratives are refashioned and retold in a variety of different media. Such resource has served to enhance our understanding of the Biblical text and of later works that have been influenced by the Bible. So there has been an explosion in literary studies of the Bible in recent years. It appears that biblical scholars have taken Jowett's exhortation to read the Bible 'like any other book' to heart.

At times, these developments have been viewed with some suspicion. In its earliest phases, the literary criticism of the Bible appeared to be associated with a secularizing agenda. In some respects, this was an inevitable consequence of the need to negotiate the secularity of the educational system in the United States of America. It also reflected the desire to assert a greater degree of freedom within the academy. Embracing the latest form of critical theory was a way of demonstrating that biblical studies belonged fully in the University and was at liberty to celebrate its freedom from the shackles of ecclesiastical dogma. As Stephen Moore and Yvonne Sherwood point out, it marked 'our emphatic distance from the kind of thing that colleagues in other disciplines tended to imagine we were up to, when they did not imagine outright that we were testifying, praying in tongues, and issuing altar calls in the classroom'.[35] But there is some irony in the fact that at precisely the point that biblical scholars arrived in the promised land of cultural theory, the leading lights of that strange land were simultaneously turning their attention to religion. Jacques Derrida explored a range of religious themes in his writing. Similarly and intriguingly, a number of prominent European philosophers have written extensively in recent years on the writings of St Paul. When Derrida died in 2004, Stanley Fish, the author of *Is There a Text in this Class?*, was called by a reporter, who asked 'what would succeed high theory and the triumvirate of race, gender, and class as the centre of intellectual energy in the academy'.[36] Fish responded with one word, 'Religion'. Indeed, the work of Hans Frei serves as an example of the way in which the theological interpretation of scripture can be enhanced by a sustained engagement with the literary criticism of the Bible.

But Fish's comment and the fruits of Frei's exploration of narrative have, ironically and perhaps providentially, brought us full circle. Jowett's critics were anxious that reading scripture through the lens of literary criticism would lead to a diminishing interest in the Bible as a resource for theological reflection. The anxiety was that scripture would be reduced to a literary artefact. This would only serve as yet another capitulation to the forces of secularism. And yet, the tensions that we have identified in the unfolding story of reading the Bible 'like any other book' have opened up a range of insights that would have been unimaginable to Jowett and the other writers of *Essays and Reviews*. As Frei's work suggests, the insights of literary criticism may in fact serve to restore aspects of our appreciation of holy scripture which have been lost or obscured. These insights might also serve to mediate between the faultlines of the sacred and the secular.

The idea that reading the Bible like any other book might offer the prospect of *mediating* between human culture and divine truth, between the secular and the sacred, was proposed in 1969 by the French Dominican scholar, Marie-Dominique Chenu, in a brief article entitled, 'La littérature comme "lieu" de la théologie' or 'Literature as the locus of theology'. Chenu, like Henri de Lubac, Jean Daniélou and Yves Congar, was associated with the *ressourcement* movement which came to exercise a powerful influence over the agenda of the Second Vatican Council. *Ressourcement* is a French word that has no simple English equivalent: it embraces a range of ideas, including 'a return to the sources' and 'renewal'. Chenu argued that Roman Catholic theology needed to recover its roots in the scriptures, which had animated the writings of the fathers and represented the soul of theology. In addition, Chenu noted the profound irony that nineteenth century neoscholastic manuals, which were used to train Roman Catholic clergy, were filled with abstract propositions and ideas, while French literature of the nineteenth century was filled with literary allusions to the Bible. In Chenu's analysis the reason for this paradox was that French novelists regarded the Bible as 'part of the common property of humanity', while theologians did not. Chenu suggested that, by emphasizing the literary value of scripture, theologians might find a way of mediating between human culture and divine truth:

> The Bible, the ultimate measure of all Christian theology and, one may say, itself theology in superabundance, is a picture book, a book of images. The self-revelation God made in it to the world has entered into association with a literary not with a theological type of comprehensibility. The Bible is a literature. God is revealed in it not through a system of ideas . . . but through a history, and through many stories, through people with individual faces and various destinies . . . since God did not think it robbery to become a writer, it is only just if people recognize him in this capacity and take the Bible as, formally, literature, . . .'[37]

In Chenu's understanding, recognizing that the Bible was part of the common property of humanity reflected something of the mystery of the incarnation. The fact that divine revelation was entrusted to a set of literary texts spoke of an act of *kenosis*, of self-emptying. The Bible embraced the common features of human literature, while at the same time raising those common features to a dignity for which 'nature left to its own resources could never have hoped'. In this respect, the Bible served to mediate between the sacred and the secular, between theology and culture.

The idea that a literary approach to reading scripture enables us to see traces and intimations of the language and imagery of the Bible in poetry and narrative, in art and music, and that this phenomenon should provoke theological reflection, speaks of a profoundly *catholic* sensibility. It is 'catholic' in the sense that it recognizes that human culture, like creation itself, can be a vehicle of divine grace. The world is a revelatory kind of place. We can appreciate the artfulness of those direct and self-conscious representations of biblical narrative in the Isenheim altarpiece or one of Handel's oratorios. We can also see intimations of the Book of Jonah in Herman Melville's *Moby Dick*, and allusions to Noah's Flood in Jeanette Winterson's *Boating for Beginners* or Julian Barnes *History of the World in 10½ Chapters*. We can see subversions of the biblical narrative in Margaret Attwood's *The*

Handmaid's Tale and Nikos Kazantzakis' *The Last Temptation of Christ*. We can see all sorts of biblical images in fiction and even in film. Noticing or remarking on such interpretations and reworkings of the biblical text is not simply an occasion for yet another virtuoso demonstration of the most recent form of poststructuralist literary theory. These 'rewritings' also challenge us to recognize the way in which the scriptures continue to animate a whole range of different aspects of Western culture. And this provides rich and challenging material for further theological reflection as we listen to the echoes of divine speech in contemporary culture. In the words of Karl-Josef Kuschel, we see in this literature a form of provocation: whereas theologians are sometimes content to retreat into ready made formulae – about the two natures of the pre-existence of Christ – literature often brings the reality into view: 'the child in the manger and the man on the gallows, the man of suffering, whose life began under the shadow of a massacre'.[38] We might add that what is true of literature is also true of a literary reading of scripture. It opens our eyes to the intimations of God's presence in our own lives. It enables us to make connections between the stories of scripture and our own experience. In Chapter 4, we will explore the ways in which a number of contemporary theologians respond to the challenge of reading the Bible like any other book.

CHAPTER FOUR

Seeking Inspiration

In recent years, there has been a renewed interest in the *theological* interpretation of scripture. Miroslav Volf describes this as 'the most significant theological development in the last two decades'.[1] The reasons for this development are manifold: first, in spite of the extraordinary and welcome advances made in the discovery of ancient manuscripts and our knowledge and understanding of the world in which the biblical texts emerged, *a growing dissatisfaction with the methods of historical criticism* has emerged. This discontent has taken a number of forms. For some, it is simply a question of historiography. Partly because of the impact of postcolonial and liberationist perspectives, they have become alert to the ideological blindness of the academy in its claims to 'objectivity'. Others question the emphasis on the search for the original meaning of the biblical text, an emphasis which has sometimes left Christians completely at sea when they are asked to relate a journey into ancient history to the world in which they live. Increasingly frustrated with those who dissect and dismember the biblical text in the name of historical research, advocates of a variety of different approaches, including the canonical method and narrative theology, have sought to emphasize that this kind of historical criticism often ignores the final canonical form of the text and the integrity of the biblical narrative. Secondly, more *recent developments in literary theory* and our understanding of the art of interpretation have led a number of theologians to question the way in which advocates of the historical-critical method assume that the meaning of a text can be fixed with reference to the intention of the author. Drawing on the insights of the 'reader-response' theory of Stanley Fish and others, some have suggested that the study of the reading subject is just as important as the object that is read. Moreover, claims to 'objectivity' in reading and interpreting a text are immediately suspect, particularly when the claim to 'objectivity' is conjoined with the insistence on a 'secular' approach to the study of the Bible. The work of Hans-Georg Gadamer and Hans Jauss has led to a renewed interest in the reception history of the Bible and a growing awareness of the way in which the history of the Bible's interpretation mediates between the reader and the text. Given that many of those interpretations were theological (although not exclusively so), an interest in the theological interpretation of scripture has gained greater prominence. Finally, *the fragmentation of the study of theology* into a number of discrete disciplines (particularly in the United Kingdom and North America) has also contributed a renewed interest in the theological interpretation of scripture. In recent decades, there has been some tension between those who think of themselves as 'biblical scholars' and those who think of themselves as 'theologians'. Biblical scholars are criticized for their lack of theological awareness while theologians are criticized for their misuse of the biblical texts. Where a truce is drawn, a rather arbitrary distinction is sometimes made between the 'exegesis' of biblical scholars and the 'interpretation' of theologians. The problem with this uneasy agreement is that it flies in the face of recent developments in hermeneutics. There is no simple way of distinguishing between what the text *meant* and what the text *means*.

The consequence of all this is that even within the field of theology itself, there is a bewildering cacophony of different voices and movements, each clamouring to be heard and claiming to have some purchase on the interpretation of scripture. All of this contributes to make the *theological* interpretation of scripture a rich and creative field of Christian theology. Over 40 years ago, David Kelsey attempted to make sense of the different ways in which the Bible was used by a number of Protestant theologians. In *The Uses of Scripture in Recent Theology*, Kelsey noted that this diversity had been caused in part by a range of different understandings of biblical authority. Rather than presenting a single account of the doctrine of the authority and inspiration of scripture, Kelsey presented seven detailed comparisons of the ways in which a number of theologians addressed these questions. Moreover, Kelsey was interested in the way in which these theologians actually used scripture in order 'to authorise their theological proposals'.[2] While it was legitimate to explore how they *construed* scripture, it was also worth looking at the ways in which they actually *used* it. Kelsey's study is useful because, even though the case studies are no longer 'recent', his essay alerts us to some significant differences in the way in which theologians of the twentieth century made sense of scripture. But it also provides rich and extensive evidence that theologians are often guided by 'a discrimen' in construing and using scripture to authorize their theological proposals. By 'discrimen', Kelsey means 'an imaginative judgement' about the construal of scripture. This imaginative judgement tries to catch in a single metaphor the characteristics of divine disclosure in and through scripture.

Kelsey begins his study with a comparison of the traditional Calvinist, Benjamin Warfield (1851–1921), and a contemporary Lutheran, Hans-Werner Bartsch (1915–83). The central thrust of Warfield's argument is that the Bible is entirely and fully inspired by God. This is supported from the Church's experience and from the content of scripture itself, the classic texts being the following: 2 Tim. 3.16, 2 Pet. 1.19–21 and Jn 10.34–35. Warfield tries to show, somewhat unconvincingly, that in context each passage refers to the whole of scripture (so, when 2 Tim. 3.16 says that 'All scripture is inspired by God . . .', this refers explicitly to both the Old and New Testaments. Secondly, Warfield stresses that the basic intent of each passage is to claim that all scripture issues directly from divine origin. God is the direct cause of their writing. Starting with Jesus' use of the Old Testament in Jn 10.35, Warfield moves on to other places in the New Testament to show how Jesus and Paul interchangeably refer to what 'God says' and what 'scripture says'. The central thrust of Warfield's argument is that the Bible is *a compendium of biblical doctrines*. By contrast, Bartsch presents scripture in terms of *a conceptual apparatus*. Like many members of the 'Biblical Theology Movement', which had emerged in the postwar period, Bartsch argued that theology needed to pay attention to biblical categories or concepts, particularly the etymology and origin of Hebrew words and their translation into New Testament Greek. In a paper entitled

The Concept of Reconciliation in the New Testament, Bartsch
set out to evaluate the distinctive biblical concepts of peace and
reconciliation. His central thesis was that in the New Testament,
the event of reconciliation is understood more basically in terms
of the concept 'peace' rather than 'salvation', and that 'peace'
is a highly distinctive concept. The word has its etymological
roots in the Old Testament concept of 'shalom'. He concludes
from this that the New Testament concept of 'peace' carries
with it all the implications of the concept 'covenant' with which
'shalom' is always associated in the Old Testament. So the Bible
contains distinctive concepts enshrined in characteristically
biblical terms. Biblical language is basically a system of technical
terms and concepts. And yet this claim is deeply problematic. As
James Barr pointed out to devastating effect, there are some basic
assumptions about language here, which are difficult to sustain
in the light of recent developments in linguistics and philosophy.
Bartsch assumes that words are simply containers of meaning,
which have the same meaning regardless of context. Words do
not have a particular theological force just because they happen
to be in Hebrew or Greek. Words also take their meaning from the
company they keep. One wonders whether Bartsch's conceptual
apparatus can do justice to this insight. Nevertheless, it is worth
remarking on the similarities with Warfield. Both Bartsch and
Warfield take scripture to be authoritative because of some
intrinsic property of the text. We receive information about God
stated in divinely communicated doctrines or concepts.

For George Ernest Wright (1909–74), the presence of God
is located not in specific doctrines or concepts but in the self-
manifestation of God in historical events. In his book *God who
Acts*, Wright draws on the insights of Gerhard von Rad. He
argues that scripture tells the story of these revelatory events by
presenting a coherent 'salvation history' organized around 'several
expressions of the basic Old Testament *kerygma*, of which Deut.
26.5–9 is perhaps the most striking'.[3] The authoritative aspect of
scripture is not its doctrines or its concepts, but rather its narrative.
The Bible is not primarily the Word of God, but the record of the
Acts of God. Wright argues that no system of propositions can
deal adequately with the inner dynamics of Biblical faith. Those
dynamics only became clear in the recital of the unfolding events
of history as the redemptive handiwork of God. This 'salvation

history' reveals the character of God. Revelation is understood in dynamic terms. The scriptures present *a recital of divine providence*, which discloses the character of God.

The insight that there is an important relationship between narrative and identity is the starting point for Karl Barth's reflections on the use and construal of scripture. As a student, Barth had been well-schooled in the practices and methods of the 'History of Religions' school. When, however, he was appointed to a pastorate in the steel town of Safenwil in 1915, he discovered that he was ill-equipped to address the needs of the workers in his pastoral care. In the context of the First World War, he was also horrified that his teachers were so broadly and uncritically supportive of the German war effort. Barth went back to the Bible. The publication of his commentary on the *Epistle to the Romans* in 1919 represented a decisive shift in the relationship between biblical studies and theology. It demonstrated that historical criticism was not enough. Standard biblical scholarship did not engage with the theological content of the Bible. The Bible was not to be understood as a series of religious developments but as the Word of God. For Barth, it was axiomatic that the Bible spoke of the reality of God and this was revealed through the presence of the risen Christ. Obviously, there is a clear Christological focus to his theology, but the question remains: what does this look like? Barth responds by focussing on narrative. The stories embedded in scripture provide an 'identity description' of Jesus Christ. This means that when we read stories about the things which Jesus did, we understand that his actions are enactments of his own intentions. They define his identity. So, the true subject of theology and of scripture is the incarnate and risen Lord. The authoritative aspect of scripture is the identity of Jesus Christ, rendered and communicated through narratives about him.

This is not about a simple historical reconstruction of Jesus. What Barth is attempting to express could perhaps be illustrated by the story of the way to Emmaus (Lk. 24.13–35). The disciples come to recognize Jesus not as an isolated marvel or simply in the breaking of the bread. As they travel along the road, their companion tells them how all these things were foretold in the scriptures. Then Luke records that when they stop for a meal, they recognize the Risen Lord in the breaking of bread. In other words, the moment of recognition comes in the comprehensive context

established by holy scripture. For Barth, scriptural narrative
provides an *identity description* of Jesus Christ.

This Christological emphasis is also reflected in the work of
Lionel Thornton (1884–1961). The difference is that, for Thornton,
the authoritative aspect of scripture lies not in its narrative but
in the images employed to describe saving events. Scripture is
authoritative insofar as it expresses a revelatory and saving event
of the past and occasions its occurrence for someone in the present.
Thornton sees this saving event as part of a much wider cosmic
creative and re-creative process, which is continually unfolding
in the relationship between God and human beings. Scripture
expresses revelation in symbolic images, or events symbolically
described. Kelsey explores this theme with reference to Thornton's
book, *The Dominion of Christ*. This book draws out the typological
relationship between Adam and Christ in scripture. It emphasizes
the 'restoration of Adam's dominion in Christ, a restoration which
takes the form of integration: that is to say a return of our nature
to that wholeness of being for which we were designed'.[4] As he
explores the symbolism of the story of the Transfiguration and
emphasizes the way in which Matthew's portrayal of Jesus' entry
into Jerusalem on Palm Sunday constitutes a 'recapitulation of
David's story in David's Son', it appears that Thornton takes these
biblical images and the complex inter-relationships between them
to be the authoritative aspect of scripture. It is a form of *typological
interpretation*.

For other commentators, the authoritative aspect of scripture is
rather more diffuse. Kelsey sees some similarities between Thornton's
emphasis on images and the way in which Paul Tillich (1886–1965)
approaches the biblical text. For Tillich, the authoritative aspect of
scripture is to be found in biblical images, which he calls 'symbols'.
Tillich seeks to demonstrate that Christian symbols contain the
'answers' to the existential 'questions' people are asking today.
Drawing heavily on the resources of existentialist philosophy,
Tillich argues that these religious symbols can be understood in
terms of the function they play in revelatory events: a revelatory
event is an event in which human beings receive power by which
they are made new beings. Scriptural symbols are understood as
expressing the occurrence of revelatory events in the past, although
it is not always entirely clear how they relate to the present. For
Kelsey, this is deeply problematic: 'That lack of connection is

serious because it seems to suggest that what the theologian has to say today to and about the world does not depend on what he can say about Jesus and his significance for his world. The question is left open, Why insist that saving events today depend in any way on Jesus?'[5] In other words, the appeal to scripture is too diffuse and indirect. Scripture serves to provide an *anthology of symbols* and images, which have the potential to function in a revelatory event.

Finally, Rudolf Bultmann shares with Thornton and Tillich the view that the authoritative aspect of scripture lies in those passages that express the revelatory and saving 'Christ event' and occasion contemporary saving and revealing events. For Bultmann, the existential encounter with Christ is the essence of the matter, and there is no need to worry about the difficulties presented by the primitive dress in which the biblical faith is presented. Bultmann makes an important distinction between *kerygmatic* statements, those central words of scripture, through which God addresses the believer directly, and then *theological* statements, which articulate that experience of being addressed by God. Some of the theological statements in scripture have abstractable content. Bultmann labels these as 'myth'. It is here that Bultmann's project of demythologization comes into view. His point is that, while in their original historical contexts (e.g. gnostic religious discourse), such units may well have been used differently, these passages 'have been borrowed by the New Testament writers and put to different uses'.[6] Such mythological language is secondary. It should not be allowed to distort the kerygma, God's direct call and invitation to all human beings to embrace a life of authentic existence.

Kelsey presents a very helpful survey of the different ways in which a number of leading theologians used scripture to authorize their theological proposals in the middle of the twentieth century. Kelsey's analysis presents a range of ways in which theologians have used scripture to authorize their theological proposals, some of which are reflected in a more contemporary idiom: a compendium of biblical doctrines, a conceptual apparatus, a recital of divine providence, an identity description, a collection of images, an anthology of symbols and a mixture of kerygmatic and theological statements. In this chapter, I will draw on the questions used in Kelsey's analysis to present a survey of more

recent developments in contemporary theology. I will structure
my discussion around *nine patterns of construal*, each of which
captures an imaginative judgement about divine disclosure in and
through the scriptures:

1 Proof

2 History

3 Memory

4 Narrative

5 Canon

6 Testimony

7 Tradition

8 Resistance

9 Performance

Each will illustrate a contemporary strategy for reading scripture
from a theological perspective. The purpose of this exercise will
be to enable the reader to navigate what has become an even more
varied landscape, and to develop a more self-conscious awareness
of the different strategies adopted by theologians and preachers in
the interpretation of scripture.

Nine Patterns of Construal

1 Proof

In 1974, a group of evangelical Christians held a conference in
Lausanne, Switzerland. The *First International Congress on
World Evangelization* emerged out of a proposal by the American
evangelist, the Revd Billy Graham. It brought together over
2,500 delegates from all over the world. One of the fruits of its
deliberations was the Lausanne Covenant. This document presented
a commitment to world-wide evangelism and was designed to
provide a doctrinal basis on which evangelical Christians could

unite in mission. The drafting committee was chaired by the Revd Prebendary John Stott, then the Rector of All Souls', Langham Place, in London. The covenant opens with a confession of faith in God the Trinity. The second article is a statement about the *Authority and Power of the Bible*:

> We affirm the divine inspiration, truthfulness and authority of both Old and New Testament Scriptures in their entirety as the only written word of God, without error in all that it affirms, and the only infallible rule of faith and practice. We also affirm the power of God's word to accomplish his purpose of salvation. The message of the Bible is addressed to all men and women. For God's revelation in Christ and in Scripture is unchangeable. Through it the Holy Spirit still speaks today. He illumines the minds of God's people in every culture to perceive its truth freshly through their own eyes and thus discloses to the whole Church ever more of the many-coloured wisdom of God.
>
> (2 Tim. 3:16; 2 Pet. 1:21; Jn 10:35; Isa. 55:11; 1 Cor. 1:21; Rom. 1:16; Mt. 5:17,18; Jude 3; Eph. 1:17,18; 3:10,18).[7]

This declaration presents a classic statement of an evangelical understanding of biblical authority and inspiration. In this context, it is worth considering the nuances of some of the phrases contained within it. In *Understanding the Bible*, John Stott refers to some of these nuances directly. First, in affirming the truthfulness of scripture, 'this does not mean – to quote a common claim – that "every word of the Bible is literally true". Such a statement would need to be qualified in several ways'. For example, when Job's comforters speak about suffering, they are mistaken. Their words are recorded in order to be contradicted, not in order to be believed. In Stott's view, one cannot take any verse from the Book of Job and say 'This is the word of the Lord' because it may not be. The point is that not all the contents of the Bible are affirmed by the Bible. For this reason, scripture is 'without error in all that it affirms'. The Lausanne Covenant adds that whatever is affirmed by Scripture is true and without error, because its affirmations are God's. In arguing in this way, Stott wants to distinguish the position outlined in the Lausanne

Covenant from any kind of 'biblical inerrancy'. Secondly, Stott asserts that 'the written word of God' refers to the original Hebrew or Greek text as it came from the authors' hands: 'We claim no special inspiration or authority for any particular translation *as a* translation – whether ancient Latin or modern English, nor indeed for any particular interpretation'.[8] It is the responsibility of textual critics to establish the authentic text of scripture 'beyond any reasonable doubt'. As far as Stott is concerned, where any ambiguity remains, no doctrine of any substance hangs on it.

Stott's comments about the authentic text are open to challenge by a number of textual critics. For example, Bart Ehrman has commented on some of the textual difficulties of Jn 1.18 and the repercussions for Christology that follow from the kind of decisions made by textual critics about the most authentic reading. Whichever way one might respond to Ehrman's observations, the uncertainties provoked by the textual tradition are hardly trivial. Moreover, we are left with some challenging questions about those passages in scripture that betray evidence of later emendation and editorial activity. For example, we read at the end of John's gospel, 'This is the disciple who is testifying to these things and has written them, and we know that his testimony is true. But there are also many other things that Jesus did; if every one of them were written down, I suppose that the world itself could not contain the books that would be written' (Jn 21.24–25). But at this point, who do we regard as the author? Do we regard this passage as authentic because it is 'original', or because it is canonical?

In spite of this particular difficulty, it is important to acknowledge that Stott's book is clear and concise. But it is also worth looking at the way in which Stott uses scripture to authorize his theological proposals. For example, in discussing the divine inspiration and authority of Scripture, Stott explains that this doctrine is supported by the consistent teaching of the church, the claims of the biblical writers themselves and the capacity of readers to discern in the unity and coherence of its message the activity of a single divine author behind the human authors. But above all, it is a doctrine endorsed by Jesus Christ himself:

Some may at once retort that to rely on Christ's witness to Scripture is to employ a circular argument, which might be expressed like this: 'How do I know that Scripture is inspired? Because of Christ, who says so. How do I know that Christ says so? Because of Scripture, which is inspired'. This, our critics point out, is to beg the question, for it is *to assume the very truth we are wanting to prove*. But they have misstated our argument. When we make our first approach to the Bible, we bring with us no assumptions about its divine inspiration. We accept it merely as a collection of historical documents, containing in particular the witness of first-century Christians to Christ. As we read their testimony, we come to believe in Christ, still without formulating any particular doctrine of Scripture. But then the Christ we have come to believe in sends us back to Scripture. He gives us a new understanding of it because he endorses its authority for us.[9]

Note the characteristics of this argument. Stott emphasizes the fact that these texts are 'historical documents', so he acknowledges the importance of historical criticism in reading and interpreting these texts. And yet, Stott maintains that in employing the principles of historical criticism, we encounter the testimony of the first apostles and conclude that the divine inspiration of both the Old and New Testaments is endorsed by Jesus himself. But it is not clear that the principles of historical criticism have readily established that this is the case. While there are many passages in the gospels in which Jesus refers to the writings of the Old Testament and accepts their authority ('It is written . . .'), it is not so clear that he has provided a similar endorsement for the writings of the New Testament. Stott must rely on the argument that Jesus appointed twelve apostles, who were authorized to teach in his name. But there is no passage in the gospels that suggests that Jesus taught a doctrine of biblical inspiration that embraced the Old and New Testaments.

Stott believes that Jesus endorsed the inspiration and authority of scripture, and that by appealing to scripture, he is able to *prove* that this is the case. Like Warfield, Stott holds that the authoritative aspect of scripture lies in the doctrine it contains. There is an inevitable circularity about this argument. It is partly a consequence of the fact that Stott ascribes ultimate authority to scripture, and quite consistently seeks to appeal to that same authority to prove his arguments. If he did not do so, it would not be the kind of authority that he says it is. He would have failed to demonstrate the strength of his convictions. So, for example, when commenting on the idea that his readers should not hesitate to describe the divine inspiration of scripture in terms of 'verbal inspiration', warrant and backing for this statement are demonstrated by the 'proof' of scripture itself: 'The apostle Paul . . . could declare that in communicating to others what God had revealed to him, he used "not words taught us by human wisdom but . . . taught by the Spirit" (1 Cor. 2.13)'.[10] In this passage, scripture is used as supporting evidence to prove the truth of the doctrine proclaimed. Thus the 'written word of God' is construed in almost positivist terms. It serves to furnish the reader with evidence and proof. In the 'written word of God', Stott discovers the direct disclosure of doctrines about God.

2 History

For Wolfhart Pannenberg, divine disclosure is a rather more indirect affair. In 1961, Pannenberg edited and published a collection of essays, entitled *Revelation as History*. Pannenberg himself contributed the following essay: *Dogmatic Theses on the Doctrine of Revelation* emphasized the centrality of 'history' in theological discourse. He argued that it was not enough to view revelation as the disclosure of truths about God. Revelation must be interpreted as the self-revelation of God – God does not reveal himself *directly* (e.g. in his 'Word'), but *indirectly* through his acts in history. He presents his argument in the form of a number of theses about the doctrine of revelation: first, the self-revelation of God in the biblical witnesses is not of a direct type in the sense of a theophany, but is indirect and brought about by means of the historical acts of God; secondly, revelation is not comprehended completely in the beginning, but at the end of the revealing history; thirdly, in distinction from special manifestations of the deity, the historical revelation is open to anyone who has eyes to see and it has a universal character; fourthly, the universal revelation of the deity of God is not yet realized in the history of Israel, but first in the fate of Jesus of Nazareth, insofar as the end of all events is anticipated in his fate; fifthly, the Christ event does not reveal the deity of the God of Israel as an isolated event, but rather insofar as it is a part of the history of God with Israel; sixthly, in the formulation of the non-Jewish conceptions of revelation in the Gentile Christian Church, the universality of the eschatological self-vindication of God in the fate of Jesus comes to actual expression and finally, the Word relates itself to Revelation as foretelling, forthtelling and report.

These assertions are developed in more detail in his *Systematic Theology*. In these three volumes, the scope and extent of Pannenberg's central theses become clear. The concept of history is absolutely central to his argument: 'If theology must hold fast to the historical action of God even at the level of facticity, it cannot surrender the concept of history. On this depends the reality of what is said about the revelation of God in Jesus Christ and therefore the soberness and seriousness of belief in the God of the Bible'.[11] There are three important points about this historical emphasis in Pannenberg's thought: first, it requires a thorough engagement with the rigours of the historical-critical method. Only this kind of engagement will begin to meet the challenge of the atheist critique of religion. Secondly, Pannenberg is not satisfied by describing God's self-disclosure in terms of 'salvation history'. God's self-revelation cannot be divorced from the rest of history. It cannot be reduced to the record of a few divinely appointed events. God's self-revelation is mediated by God's action in history, *real* history. Thirdly, the saving event of the cross and resurrection of Jesus Christ is not to be regarded as a curious hiatus in the course of history. The resurrection points to the future. It is the *end* of history.

There is an important eschatological dimension to Pannenberg's thought. In taking history seriously, he engages with recent scholarship in the quest for the historical Jesus, particularly advocates of the 'Third Quest', such as Ed Sanders, who have emphasized that Jesus was an eschatological prophet and that his teaching needs to be understood in the context of Jewish restoration eschatology. Pannenberg asserts the importance of recognizing that Jesus was an eschatological prophet who looked forward to the Kingdom of God. Where he departs from a number of biblical scholars involved in the quest for this historical Jesus is in going on to assert that this expectation was fulfilled in the resurrection: 'The resurrection of Jesus from the dead, which was backed by appearances to his disciples

and also to Saul their persecutor, forms the starting point of
the apostolic proclamation of Christ and also of the history
of the primitive Christian community. Without the resurrection
the apostles would have had no missionary message, nor
would there have been any Christology relating to the person
of Jesus'.[12] At this point, another aspect of the eschatological
emphasis of Pannenberg's thought becomes evident. One can
employ the lens of historical criticism to reflect on the meaning
and significance of Jesus as an eschatological prophet, but how
does Pannenberg make sense of the resurrection in the light of
his commitment to historical criticism?

In *Jesus – God and Man*, Pannenberg presents a detailed
analysis of the material contained in the New Testament.
He identifies two separate strands: the Pauline report of the
appearances of the risen Lord, and the testimony about the
discovery of the empty tomb. Pannenberg's discussion of
the Pauline report concentrates on the evidence presented by
1 Cor. 15.10–11. He notes that 'the appearances reported in the
Gospels, which are not mentioned by Paul, have such a strongly
legendary character that one can scarcely find a historical kernel
of their own in them. Even the Gospels' reports that correspond
to Paul's statements are heavily coloured by legendary
elements, particularly by the tendency toward underlining the
corporeality of the appearances'. Pannenberg argues that it was
Paul's intention to present convincing proof. The Pauline report
lies close to the events themselves. The Pauline report reflects
earlier material, a judgement supported by a number of 'History
of Religions' scholars – 'One cannot doubt that the disciples
were convinced that they had seen the resurrected Lord'.[13]
Without the appearances, it is difficult to explain the faith of the
disciples surviving the crisis of Jesus' death. He is not convinced
by a 'psychological explanation' of this faith because it does not
explain the number of these appearances and the range of people
who bore witness to them at different time and in different
places. As for the story of the empty tomb, the trustworthiness
of this report is not necessarily shaken by the fact that Paul
does not mention it. For Pannenberg, testimony about the empty
tomb points to the primitive community in Jerusalem and the
reliability of its testimony. He notes that the tradition about
the tomb is common to all the Synoptics (even though there are

a number of discrepancies in other aspects). He suggests that the stark and abrupt ending of Mark at 16.8 indicates a break between an earlier local Jerusalem tradition and the subsequent addition of other appearance traditions. Note that Pannenberg engages in a close and detailed analysis of the text.

But even if we agree with Pannenberg's exegesis, how can the assertion that the resurrection took place be consistent with the principles of historical criticism? How does Pannenberg negotiate Lessing's ditch? He responds to these questions as follows: first, he emphasizes the importance of human finitude in addressing any epistemological question – so the argument that the resurrection violates the laws of nature demands careful analysis. Pannenberg argues that, by virtue of our finitude, human beings can only know a part of the laws of nature. Even if one can speak of the general validity of the laws of nature, one cannot necessarily make definitive judgements about the possibility or impossibility of an individual event. And this emphasis on the finitude of human knowledge is linked to the eschatological dimension of his thought. Pannenberg argues that the revelation of God will only come to its full expression at the end of time. He wants to hold onto faith's insight that this future is disclosed proleptically in the resurrection of Jesus, but at the same time he admits that 'only the future consummation of God's kingdom can finally demonstrate that the deity of God is definitively revealed already in the history of Jesus and that the God of love is truly God. On the way to this ultimate future the truth claim of the Christian message concerning God remains unavoidably debatable'.[14] Thus only with the consummation of the world in the kingdom of God does God's love reach its goal and the disclosure of the doctrine of God reach its conclusion. Until that time, theologians and biblical scholars must recognize the finitude of human knowledge:

> The knowledge of Christian theology is always partial in comparison to the definitive revelation of God in the future of his kingdom (1 Cor. 13.12). Christians should not need to be taught this by modern reflection on the finitude of knowledge that goes with the historicity of experience. They can find instruction in the biblical account of our situation before God even as believers. Recognizing the finitude and inappropriateness of all human talk about God is an

essential part of theological sobriety. This does not make our statements indifferent, but it is a condition of the truth of our statements.[15]

So Pannenberg seeks to develop a theology which maintains close contact with the findings of historical criticism, but at the same time he is alert to the limits associated with 'the historicity of human experience'. Acknowledging the historicity of human experience and reflection involves recognizing the limits of human knowledge and human knowing, and this means that all human talk of God falls short of a complete apprehension of the truth of God. Pannenberg is making two important and significant moves at this point: he is saying that the finitude of human knowledge places limits on what we can say and know about history (so the demands of historical criticism are qualified) *and* this places similar limits on what we can say and know about God (so the methods of theological inquiry are also qualified). Pannenberg is not saying that we can know nothing. On the contrary, he wants to assert that God's self-revelation in history is open to anyone with eyes to see. But he also wants to say that such vision is partial because human knowledge is partial. This means that we need to cultivate an appropriate degree of humility in making imaginative judgements about the nature of divine disclosure in history. The reading and interpretation of scripture from an historical perspective requires and demands an appropriate degree of theological sobriety.

3 Memory

Pannenberg's position is rather more nuanced than the position outlined by George Ernest Wright in *God who Acts*. Pannenberg shares with Wright the conviction that history is the chief medium of revelation. But he differs from Wright in that he is rather more circumspect in responding to the challenges of historical criticism. Wright asserts that divine disclosure occurs in the objective happenings of history. Like his teacher, William Albright, Wright assumed that a little help from biblical archaeology and further study of the history of the ancient Near East would only serve to confirm the general outline of Israel's history as given in the

Old Testament. John Rogerson, an Anglican priest and Emeritus Professor of Biblical Studies at the University of Sheffield, views Wright's bullish claims about the acts of God in history with a certain amount of bemusement. When he considers Wright's claims in the light of recent developments in the study of the Hebrew Bible, the archaeological discoveries in the second half of the twentieth century which overturned the consensus established by the Biblical archaeology school, and the contest between 'minimalists' and 'maximalists' from the 1980s onwards (when the reconstruction of Old Testament history became a matter of sometimes bitter and rancorous debate), Rogerson observes that Wright's conclusions simply cannot be accepted. For Rogerson, the most significant difficulty with Wright's argument is that when Wright claims that God acts in history, he assumes 'that history is a "thing" that can be recovered by scholarly investigation and that by means of such investigation God can be seen to have intervened actively in historical events'.[16] It is difficult to reconcile such an assumption with current trends in modern historiography.

In *A Theology of the Old Testament*, Rogerson responds to a challenge presented by Rudolf Bultmann in his *Theology of the New Testament*. Bultmann had noted that in New Testament studies there was an inevitable tension between the task of reconstruction and the task of interpretation: 'Either the writings of the New Testament can be treated as "sources" which the historian uses in order to reconstruct early Christianity as a phenomenon of the historical past, or the reconstruction serves the need of the interpretation of the New Testament writings, on the assumption that these writings have something to say to the present'.[17] Rogerson finds this distinction between 'reconstruction' and 'interpretation' helpful. From the outset, he does not want simply to reconstruct the religion of ancient Israel. Instead, he wants to explore what the Old Testament has to say to today's world. To do this, Rogerson makes three methodological moves: first, he promotes a *narrative* understanding of history; secondly, he interprets the Old Testament in the light of a theory of cultural memory; finally, he seeks to illuminate aspects of human experience with reference to the writings of the Old Testament and to illustrate his conviction that the remarkable thing about the Old Testament is the persistence of its visions of a better humanity and a better world.

Each of these moves requires further elucidation: first, in promoting a *narrative* understanding of history, Rogerson argues that our knowledge of the past is inevitably selective. When people refer to the past, they are referring to memories or records of things said or done that are stored in many different ways, and access to them only becomes possible when they are embodied in a narrative. For the past to become available to the present, it has to be narrated. If the past has to be narrated, then the narrator will often be an interested party:

> The claim of the narrative view of history is that while we do not invent the past, our narrative accounts of it are affected and shaped by factors such as our very limited knowledge of what happened in the past, and our situatednesses in nation, gender, class, political and religious commitment or lack of the same, and aims and interests in wanting to construct narratives about the past, in the first place.[18]

This brings Rogerson to make the crucial observation that 'the value of the history-like traditions in the Old Testament lies not in their approximation to history as reconstructed by modern scholars (if, indeed, there is an approximation), but in their narrative witness to belief in God'.[19] At this point, there is a rather odd shift from the role of the modern historian as a narrator to the narrative quality of much of the Old Testament itself. Nevertheless, as his argument progresses, it becomes clear that the controlling image is not narrative but *memory*.

Rogerson draws on the theory of cultural memory developed by Maurice Halbwachs and Jan Assmann to promote the idea that it is often more profitable to view the witness of the Old Testament in terms of cultural memory than history. By 'cultural memory', Rogerson is referring to much more than a personal memory or an individual memory. He is describing a collective memory or a set of communal narratives that enable a community or a society to understand themselves in the present by gaining some kind of purchase on the past. These memories are often embodied in the life of a community. Thus the acts of remembrance that take place on Remembrance Sunday in Britain would be a good example of this phenomenon. Rogerson notes that there are a number of particular examples in the Book of Deuteronomy where the people are deliberately reminded to hold on to a particular memory (e.g. Deut. 4.9 and 25.17). Holding this memory shapes their identity. The celebration of Passover is a way of handing on this kind of cultural memory. But before we imagine that cultural memory is simply the device for handing on a stable communal identity and silencing dissent and protest, Rogerson draws on the insights of Jan Assmann and Claude Lévi-Strauss, to develop a typology of 'hot' and 'cold' memories. 'Cold' memories emphasize the importance of institutions, continuity and preserving the status quo, while 'hot' memories provide the impetus for societal change and transformation. They challenge the status quo and offer a vision of hope. By way of example, Rogerson suggests that Chronicles, with its emphasis on continuity, would be an example of 'cold' history, while the Deuteronomistic History (from Joshua to 2 Kings) would be an example of a 'hot' history, reflecting a period of transformation and societal change. Thus the Old Testament contains both 'hot' and 'cold' forms of cultural memory.

With this analysis, he reflects on a number of different aspects of human experience. Whether he is using the Creation narratives to critique an anthropocentric view of the world, or drawing on the Patriarchal narratives to reflect on the ambiguities of interpersonal relationships, or the way in which prophetic texts serve not as a wild protest against the breakdown of the old order but as a way of critiquing an economic system that exploited the poor and the marginalized, Rogerson seeks to use the Old Testament to reflect on what it means to be human. In presenting a theology of the Old Testament in this way, one detects an apologetic motif in Rogerson's writing. At the end of the book, he expresses the hope that his book 'might find its way into the hands of members of the general public'.[20] The purpose of this exercise is to demonstrate that the exegesis and interpretation of the Old Testament can address the questions of society at large. He demonstrates that it is possible to use the Old Testament to think profitably and critically about money, sex and power.

Rogerson's discussion of these issues is based on the assumption that these resources lie deep in the cultural memory of Western culture. But it is not immediately clear why contemporary society would look to the Old Testament for guidance about these questions, and whether there is sufficient biblical literacy in society (even at the level of regarding the Bible as a 'cultural artefact') to make such an enterprise worthwhile. A consideration of the way in which the writings of the Old Testament have been interpreted and appropriated in either the synagogue or the church is completely absent from Rogerson's thesis. But the most curious aspect of Rogerson's theology is that God is almost completely invisible. Indeed, Rogerson admits at the beginning of the book that he will not deal explicitly with the nature of God, and that he might legitimately be challenged on the grounds that his book hardly deserves the name 'theology'. Rogerson responds by alluding to Friedrich Schiller's play *Wallensteins Lager*: 'Wallenstein never appears at all. Yet he is the *absent presence* whose personality, and differing estimations of it by his followers, affects and penetrates every part of the play'.[21] And yet, Rogerson's dramatic allusion could equally bring to mind another 'absent presence' – Godot in Samuel Beckett's play, *Waiting for Godot*. In the play, the characters wait for Godot but he never comes. His absence is an elusive presence, penetrating every aspect of the conversation between Vladimir and Estragon, but by the end of the play one is left wondering whether Godot exists at all.

Of course, such a comparison would ignore the fact that Rogerson is seeking to approach divinity via humanity: 'the more humane humans become . . ., the closer they become to what the Old Testament calls the "image of God" (Gen. 1.27)'.[22] For Rogerson, this may well involve converting theology into anthropology, but that 'is a risk worth taking'. The problem is that when he explores the question of what it means to be human and finds himself contemplating concepts such as 'divine forgiveness, divine love and divine grace', any possibility of further theological reflection is suddenly curtailed: 'The introduction of concepts such as divine forgiveness, love and grace move the discussion into an area where dialogue between the Old Testament and modern thinkers wrestling with the question "What does it mean to be human?" probably cannot be continued'.[23] There is a curious hesitation in the face of any intimation of divine disclosure in his thinking. Pannenberg emphasized that divine disclosure was indirect and demanded an appropriate level of theological sobriety. For Rogerson, it appears to be far more elusive. It is perhaps a curious indictment of contemporary intellectual debate that there appear to be some cultural memories that we are too embarrassed to talk about. Nevertheless, the significance of Rogerson's project lies in the way in which he uses the theory of *cultural memory* to negotiate the challenges of reading the Old Testament without falling into the trap of simply using it to reconstruct religious thought in the ancient world or assuming that it can be read as an indisputable guide to the history of Israel.

4 Narrative

Both Pannenberg's emphasis on the centrality of *history* and Rogerson's understanding of *cultural memory* reflect a willingness to operate from the epistemological assumptions of established intellectual discourse. And yet, this kind of approach is a source of anxiety to advocates of 'postliberal' theology. This movement, often associated with the names of Richard Niebuhr, George Lindbeck, Hans Frei, Stanley Hauerwas and David Kelsey, is sometimes also described as 'the Yale School' (all had some connection with the Yale Divinity School). It is important to recognize that there are a number of different features about the writings of each of these theologians, but they do share the same kind of antipathy towards the philosophical tradition of Enlightenment liberalism. The problem with liberalism is that it seeks a foundation for its truth-claims by appealing to wider cultural norms or universal human experience (e.g. history or memory). The attendant risk is that this establishes a framework, philosophical or cultural, which sets the context in which Christian claims must be defended. This means that the theologian is almost always on the back foot. Postliberal theologians are suspicious of grand claims about universal rationality. They reject the claim 'that knowledge is grounded in a set of non-inferential, self-evident beliefs'. Experience always comes already interpreted. It is always shaped by language and story.

In *The Meaning of Revelation*, Richard Niebuhr had maintained that the church must tell its story and understand its witness in relation to 'the story of our life'. That story is an 'irreplaceable, untranslatable' story about Jesus Christ and our 'relation to God through him'.[24] Lindbeck and Frei take up Niebuhr's emphasis on story and narrative and develop it. Frei seeks to recover the narrative emphasis of the scriptural witness in *The Eclipse of Biblical Narrative*. For Lindbeck, this emphasis on narrative is an important and significant way of resisting the temptation to adopt some kind of extra-biblical hermeneutical or interpretive framework in reading scripture. In contrast to these 'extra-biblical' frameworks that run the risk of distorting the scriptural witness, Lindbeck suggests that 'narrative' constitutes the 'interpretive framework' presented by scripture itself:

> Everyone recognises that correct interpretation requires the ascertaining of the literary genre of the work to be interpreted. What then is the literary genre of the Bible as a whole in its canonical unity? What holds together the diverse materials it contains: poetic, prophetic, legal, liturgical, sapiential, mythical, legendary, and historical? These are all embraced, it would seem, in an over-arching story which has the specific literary features of realistic narrative as exemplified in diverse ways, for example, by certain kinds of parable, novels, and historical accounts. It is as if the Bible were 'a vast loosely-structured, non-fictional novel' (to use a phrase applied to Karl Barth's view of Scripture in David Kelsey's *The Uses of Scripture in Recent Theology . . .*).[25]

The reference to Barth is important. It is clear that an emphasis on narrative draws on Barth's own use and construal of scripture. Frei had learned from Barth that the integrity of the Christian faith rests not on an appeal to universal reason or some other external foundation, but is sustained through the telling of and the commitment to the story of Jesus Christ. In this respect, 'postliberal theology' is a truly postmodern endeavour. There is no neutral vantage point from which the truth of this story can be judged. Christian doctrine cannot be justified or rejected by criteria alien to its own 'grammar'.

For Lindbeck, the benefit of the interpretative framework provided by 'realistic narrative' gives much more theological weight to the Old Testament than the historical-critical method ever would. The problem with historical criticism is that it 'tends to neglect, for example, the Exodus because so little can be reliably known about this in comparison to Jesus'.[26] By placing a greater emphasis on narrative, the fundamental identity description of God is provided by the stories of Israel, Exodus and Creation, as well as the stories of Jesus' life, death and resurrection. Stimulated by the literary theory of Erich Auerbach, Hans Frei and George Lindbeck have sought to relate these stories together through a pattern of 'figural' reading and interpretation: 'narrative and typological interpretations enable the Bible to speak with its own voice'.[27] Indeed, 'figural' reading is the principal strategy by which advocates of a narrative approach relate the stories of the Old and New Testaments.

And yet, one of the dangers in viewing the whole of scripture through the single lens of 'narrative' is that often advocates of such an approach very quickly move to make the assumption that the scriptures can be read as a *single* narrative. From Creation to Revelation, there is a single coherent story about the mystery of God. Indeed, this is one way of understanding the narrative theology of Hans Frei: 'The Bible sets forth a story of the world, from its beginning to its ending. It is the only true story of the world, all other stories being at best partial renditions of the world story disclosed in the Bible. Consequently, all other stories must be inscribed into the biblical story, rather than the biblical story into any one of them'.[28] This description of the Bible in terms of *narrative* has generated considerable debate: first, some critics have disputed the idea that the Bible can be described in terms of 'narrative' by focussing on the question of genre. Alongside 'narrative' the Bible consists of a number of different genres (e.g. law, poetry, prophecy, wisdom saying, letter, apocalypse). There is a danger of flattening out the rich texture of the language and imagery of the Bible by simply describing all of it in terms of 'narrative'. Secondly, in spite of attempts by postliberal theologians to demonstrate that by establishing a clear epistemic break with modernity (the recovery of narrative allowing the witness of scripture to speak in its own terms) their work betrays a remarkable debt to postmodern philosophy and literary theory. Frei's debt to Auerbach has already been noted, but it is worth acknowledging the way in which the philosophy of Ludwig Wittgenstein, Alasdair Macintyre and Charles Peirce often provides a means whereby postliberal theologians render their approach to epistemology intelligible in the sphere of the academy. Indeed, the unrelenting textuality of narrative theology has been the subject of recent criticism: Francesca Murphy argues that the emphasis on 'telling God's story' seems to reduce the mystery of God to little more than a story. Her criticisms are perhaps over-stated, and it does not necessarily follow that an emphasis on 'telling God's story' leads to the conclusion that 'God is a story', but it is worth pondering the extent to which that story exercises the kind of purchase on the reality we inhabit and experience that is required for faithful and honest truth-telling. Finally, it is not always clear that the narratives in scripture can be reduced to a single story. Some scholars have attempted to describe this story by drawing an analogy with the acts of a play. So Tom Wright describes Act 1 as Creation (Gen. 1–2), Act 2 as the Fall (Gen. 3–11), Act 3 as Israel (Gen. 12 – Mal.), Act 4 as Jesus (Mt. – Jn), Act 5 as the Church (Acts – Epi.) and Act 6 as the End (Mark 13 and Rev.). And yet such a description is problematic for a number of reasons: first, to describe the doctrine of creation in terms of the first act of a play does not give sufficient emphasis to God's ongoing creativity and sovereignty over creation. To describe God as the Creator should express something about the past, present and future. We see intimations of this creativity not just in the first couple of chapters of Genesis but repeated again and again in Wisdom literature, as well as the gospels, the epistles and the book of Revelation. Secondly, the narratives contained in scripture offer a variety of different perspectives. In the Old Testament, there may be an epic story told from Genesis – 2 Kings, but then it is retold – from another perspective – in 1–2 Chronicles. The prophets offer a variety of different perspectives on this story, while Job and Ecclesiastes appear to dissent from it completely. In the New Testament, the story of Jesus is told from four different perspectives, while the epistles offer yet even more ways of construing the story of Jesus through the lens of the Old Testament. There may be some common threads and features among these narratives, but that does not necessarily mean that together they constitute a single story.

In response to some of these criticisms, a rather more nuanced approach has recently been advocated by David Kelsey. In *Eccentric Existence*, Kelsey identifies three stories in scripture, which correspond to the three persons of the Trinity: the first story speaks of God's creativity 'whereby the Father creates through the Son in the power of the Spirit';[29] the second story describes God's action in drawing the whole of creation – and humankind as part of creation – to a proper end, for 'the Spirit, set by the Father with the Son, draws creation to eschatological consummation';[30] the third story describes God's action in reconciling estranged creatures to himself as 'the Son, sent by the Father in the power of the Spirit, reconciles'.[31] These three stories together form a 'triple helix'. And this enables us to describe a pattern of scriptural witness which is open and never completely closed. This means that the Bible is not reduced to a single totalizing narrative, with all the attendant risks of manipulation and control that involves. One of the difficulties with thinking about scripture in terms of a *single* narrative is that it presents a way of thinking about scripture as a 'metanarrative', a closed system which does not always welcome or allow conversation, debate and dissent. Kelsey's approach seeks to correct one of the perceived weaknesses of a 'narrative' approach – namely, that it is not always alert to the disjunctions and difficulties in the scriptures. This is particularly evident when Christian communities are wrestling with biblical texts, which appear to legitimate discrimination or justify oppression. Does the construal of scripture in terms of 'God's story' enable us to address the difficult interpretative questions provoked by these particular texts? Moreover, is the idea of a 'triple helix' sufficient to address these same issues?

5 Canon

The 'canonical approach' arose in direct response to the perceived sterility of historical criticism and 'a growing sense of frustration with the traditional critical way of reading the Bible'.[32] Often associated with the name of Brevard Childs, an Old Testament scholar and a colleague of Hans Frei and George Lindbeck at the Yale Divinity School, there is often some confusion about what exactly a 'canonical approach' describes. Indeed, it is often easier to explain what the 'canonical approach' is not, than what it is. The reason for this is that from 1970, when Childs published *Biblical Theology in Crisis*, through his commentary on *Exodus* in 1974, to his major work, *Introduction to the Old Testament as Scripture* in 1979, Childs' thought went through a series of developments and refinements. Indeed, further refinements have taken place in the light of the rather hostile critique of James Barr and the more sympathetic judgements of Mark Brett, Walter Moberly and

others. Childs eschews the notion of 'canonical criticism'. The
'canonical approach' describes more of a theological sensibility
than a particular method. But the problem remains that when
people describe the 'canonical approach', they are often describing
a moving target. Childs does not present a consistent or coherent
exegetical approach. While this often presents difficulties in debates
generated by this approach, it is at least possible to identify the
direction of travel.

In *Biblical Theology in Crisis*, Childs offered a critique of
the Biblical Theology Movement. While writers associated with
this movement were to be lauded for responding to the challenge
to recover a theological dimension of the Bible, their work was
compromised by their over-reliance on the assumptions of the
'History of Religions' School. According to Childs, representatives
of this movement regarded the methods of historical criticism as
sound. The problem lay in the fact that the methods had been
misapplied and peripheral matters had taken centre stage. He
also noted a tendency to give priority to a particular strand in
the biblical corpus – for example Walther Eichrodt saw the
distinctiveness of Israel's unique expression of faith in the idea of
'covenant' – or alternatively, to give priority to an earlier tradition
within the biblical corpus – so, for example, Gerhard von Rad
employed the insights of form criticism to argue that there was
a particular recital of salvation-history which dated from the
pre-monarchical period and formed Israel's earliest theological
articulation of its faith.

Childs argued that these attempts to reconstruct a strand or
period, which was then regarded as theologically normative, were
often speculative. They had failed to convince the wider scholarly
guild, and they had failed to secure agreement with one another.
More tellingly, as Childs points out in his *Introduction to the Old
Testament as Scripture*, '(t)he usual critical method of biblical
exegesis is, first, to seek to restore an original historical setting by
stripping away those very elements which constitute the canonical
shape. Little wonder that once the biblical text has been securely
anchored in the historical past by "decanonizing" it, the interpreter
has difficulty applying it to the modern religious context'.[33] It was
not clear to Childs that a painstaking reconstruction of the history
behind the text provided the proper context for interpreting the
Old Testament theologically. Moreover, these reconstructions of

Old Testament Theology often ignored the witness of the New Testament. In the absence of any theological reflection about the New Testament, it was difficult to see how such an artificial construct might serve to animate Christian discipleship. Childs argued that a more appropriate context for reading the Old Testament theologically was the *canon*. Indeed, this is his central insight. Although Childs' arguments have developed over the years, two features of his approach have remained constant: first, it was essential that a theologian should attend to the final form of the text. This was, after all, the text that the Church read. The theology of the Old Testament should be disclosed by the final form of the canonical text, and not by some tradition that lay behind it. Secondly, in reading the final form of the text, it was also necessary to attend to its context within the canon of scripture as a whole. Inevitably, one can see hints of Anglo-American New Criticism in Childs' thought. Rather than attempting to reconstruct what the original author meant or what the traditions behind the text were, interpreters were invited to reflect on the final form of the text itself.

Nevertheless, what this actually meant in practice is not always easy to determine. In his earlier work, *Biblical Theology in Crisis,* Childs proposed that a 'canonical approach' involved attending to the Old Testament quotations in the New Testament. His description of these passages confirmed his view 'that the New Testament consistently makes a claim to be in continuity with the Old Testament's understanding of God'.[34] This continuity amounted to more than the provision of useful background information for the proclamation of the gospel of Jesus Christ: 'The Old Testament testimony to God serves the church, not as interesting background to the New Testament, nor as historical preparation for Christ's arrival, but as the living vehicle of the Spirit through which it continues to confront God'.[35] The key point for Childs is that reading and interpreting the Old Testament is an occasion of divine disclosure. Childs wanted to assert that the scriptures did not simply tell us *about* God, but in reading and praying the scriptures, 'we are confronted, not just with ancient witnesses, but with our God who is the Eternal Present. Prayer is an integral part in the study of Scripture because it anticipates the Spirit's carrying its reader through the written page to God himself'.[36]

This comment from the conclusion of *Biblical Theology in Crisis* is significant because it enables us to understand the subsequent development of his thought in the commentary on the Book of Exodus published in 1974. Acknowledging that prayer was an integral part of the study of scripture suggested that the reader played a vital role in the act of interpretation. Thus, in his commentary on the Book of Exodus, he suggested that a 'canonical approach' meant attending to the traditions of reading the text in Jewish and Christian communities. It meant exploring the ways in which Jews and Christians had read these passages faithfully over the centuries. These readings might also inform our reading of the text. But in a subsequent publication, *Introduction to the Old Testament as Scripture,* Childs adopted a different tack. In this book, he suggested that a 'canonical approach' meant attending to the final canonical form of each of the books of the Bible and recognizing the way in which this often shifted the semantic potential of the earlier traditions contained within it. Thus Childs did not deny the results of historical criticism and was content to affirm that Deutero-Isaiah emerged in a sixth century context. But he was more interested in the semantic effects of its inclusion in the Book of Isaiah as a whole. Rather than addressing a particular historical context, the words of Deutero-Isaiah take on a more metaphorical and universal meaning in the context of the Book of Isaiah. This canonical process was the proper subject of theological reflection.

In his subsequent work, *Old Testament Theology in a Canonical Context,* this perspective is pushed further to refer not simply to the final canonical form of a book but to the canon of scripture as a whole. The canon as a whole provided the proper context for interpreting discrete passages within scripture. Thus in identifying a variety of themes and topics, he sought to demonstrate that each reference to a theme or topic in scripture needed to be read and understood with reference to the whole witness of scripture. We see a more detailed working of this approach in *Biblical Theology of the Old and New Testaments.* In this volume, Childs seeks to demonstrate that the Old and New Testaments both bear witness to Jesus Christ. The first two parts are made up of standard sections of exposition on the books of both testaments. The final section presents a summary of his theological approach in relation to ten categories of systematic theology: the Identity of God; God the Creator; Covenant, Election, People of God; Christ the Lord; Reconciliation with God; Law and Gospel; Humanity: Old and New; Biblical Faith; God's Kingdom and Rule; and the Shape of the Obedient Life: Ethics.

Childs' approach has been criticized on a number of accounts. Walter Brueggemann has noted that Childs often draws conclusions 'that are predictably congruent with consensus Calvinism',[37] a view which is only reinforced by the emphasis on covenant and the absence of reference to the sacraments in the ten categories of systematic theology which he selects. Brueggemann has also argued that Childs' project is 'massively reductionist': the fact that Childs limits the interpretation of the Old Testament to a source which bears witness to Jesus Christ means that much of the text is ignored. Where there is playfulness or ambiguity, it 'must be disregarded in the interest of a flat conceptualization'. According to Brueggemann, there is no attention to the conflicts and tensions within the text. The categories which Childs adopts prepare 'the way for a programmatic misreading' of the text. (Although to be fair to Childs, he does acknowledge the 'enormous diversity', the 'variety of different voices' and the 'differences between the testaments'[38] in his later work). In Brueggemann's view, Childs' insistence that scripture should be read 'according to the Rule of Faith' emasculates the purpose of biblical criticism, which was to emancipate the text from church control. The categories imposed by Childs present nothing less than a capitulation to the interpretive authority of the church. (Of course, this latter point reflects a vulnerability in Brueggemann's own project which we will discuss below). As far as Childs is concerned, Old Testament theology is a Christian enterprise. To describe this collection of books as 'the Old Testament' reflects a number of hermeneutical assumptions and commitments: the 'Old' is to be read in relation to the 'New'. A theological interpretation of scripture will pay attention to the history of its interpretation in the life of the church. The canon of scripture is normative and authoritative for this particular community of faith.

One of the principal difficulties with Childs' approach relates to a profound confusion over what exactly the word 'canon' describes and what it means. First, there is no comprehensive agreement in the church about the contents of the canon: Childs argues that the 39 books of the Protestant Old Testament should be regarded as canonical. He maintains that the Hebrew Bible, and not the Septuagint, should be authoritative for the theological interpretation of scripture on the grounds that this provides a common scripture with Judaism. And yet his comments about the relationship between the Old and New Testament suggest that he is not entirely serious about the possibilities for shared reading between Jews and Christians. Nevertheless, the important point is that these conflicts over the contents of the canon demonstrate that there is no clear agreement about the 'final form' of the text. Asserting the hegemony of the canon does not necessarily resolve these questions. Indeed, in some respects it draws greater attention to an area of interpretative conflict.

Secondly, there is some confusion in Childs' thought about the precise meaning of the word 'canon'. Indeed, this lack of clarity means that the term often falls prey to tactical definition. As James Barr has pointed out, the term is often vague and ambiguous:

> Sometimes it is the *canon* in the sense of the boundary of scripture; sometimes it is the final form of a book, as contrasted with earlier sources. Sometimes it is the abstract, *canon* without definite article: Childs seems not to notice that the logical behaviour of the term alters when the article is removed. Sometimes *canon* is more a context than a set of books or a form of words; and this suggests that it may be something in the eye of the beholder rather than a real thing out there in the world. Sometimes it is a sort of Holy Grail, a principle of finality and authority. All these are hardly distinguished; yet it must be obvious that they are different.[39]

But Barr's most telling criticism is that the kind of 'canonical process' that Childs identifies in relation to the redactional intention of the canonizers may well demonstrate that the editors were doing something clever in including Deutero-Isaiah in the Book of Isaiah in order to render its message more universal, but such an explanation cannot do justice to some of the curious editorial decisions to be found elsewhere in the Hebrew Bible. For example, when Childs argues that the canonizers intended to free the psalms from their cultic setting by making them testify to all the joys and troubles of human life, it was not clear to Barr how Ps. 7 'was made more universal' by the addition of a title 'saying that it was sung by David "concerning Cush a Benjaminite"'. Such a comment served to accentuate the particular and concrete rather than the general and the universal. From Barr's perspective, the canonization process was a mass of 'self-contradiction'. Childs offers no convincing evidence to demonstrate that the purpose of the Old Testament is to bear witness to Jesus Christ. It is simply asserted as a self-evident truth. It is left to Walter Moberly to provide a more nuanced treatment of this question through an exploration of the typological connections between the figure of Abraham in Genesis 22 and the figure of Jesus in the gospel accounts of Matthew and Luke. But Barr is unrelenting in his criticism of Childs' canonical approach. In his estimation, this 'is not really a biblical theology . . . it is basically a personal dogmatic theology with biblical proofs'.[40]

One of the difficulties with this debate – and the reason that Childs provokes such an unsympathetic reaction – is that he has a tendency to overstate the importance of the canon and to ignore the sense in which the canon, far from demonstrating the unity of the scriptural witness, simply provides a site of interpretative conflict. I suspect that in emphasizing the importance of the canon, Childs underestimates the significance of the technological advance presented by printing in the middle ages and the publication of the books of scripture in a single volume. This served to accentuate the unity of the scriptures. By contrast, early Christians would have been used to seeing the books of scripture in the form of separate scrolls or in codices. For them, the sense that the Bible was a single book was less pronounced. They referred to the scriptures not as 'the Bible' but as *ta biblia* – 'the books'. Childs does not do justice to the fact that the scriptures are made up of different books – offering different, even contradictory, perspectives. These differences may in fact be a source of fruitful theological reflection. But Childs wants the canon to generate consistency and coherence. And yet, the problem is that the scriptural witness will not oblige. Divine disclosure is not so neat and tidy.

6 Testimony

Walter Brueggemann's *Theology of the Old Testament* was published in 1997. Brueggemann was extremely critical of Childs, particularly on account of his tendency to 'flatten' the scriptural

witness and to lose sight of the fact that the canon was often
a site of interpretative conflict. He also wanted to acknowledge
that the interpretation of scripture could only be enhanced and
enriched by engagement with interpreters beyond the ecclesial
community, Jewish and secular. In its direct appeal to the 'Rule of
Faith', these voices were not given sufficient weight in a canonical
approach. Nevertheless, Brueggemann's study begins with the
observation that 'the primal subject of a Old Testament theology
is of course God'.[41] Indeed, his work betrays a theological interest
and a commitment to working with the canonical form of the
text which suggests that he shares rather more in common with
Childs than his sometimes sharp criticism might imply. At the
same time, he insists that the Old Testament does not provide
a 'coherent and comprehensive' account of God. There are
only 'hints, traces, fragments, and vignettes'. Thus his work
seeks to address the conflicting perspectives offered within the
scriptures directly. He does this by describing the language of
scripture in terms of *testimony* about God. In emphasizing the
significance of testimony, his thought betrays a significant debt
to the hermeneutics of testimony, associated with the philosophy
of Paul Ricoeur.

In his treatment of the Old Testament, Brueggemann draws
on Ricoeur's analogy of a trial in a court of law. The advantage
of this analogy is that he succeeds in avoiding the temptation
to reduce the witness of the Old Testament to a number of
specific themes. Rather, it enables him to explore the 'processes,
procedures and interactionist potential of the community
present to the text'.[42] These are the processes and procedures
characteristic of a court of law. The purpose of a trial is to get
to the truth of a matter, and yet the matter is under dispute.
A witness will give an account of the matter, and yet another
witness will give a competing account. The problem is that the
court has no direct access to the 'actual event' so it must rely
on this testimony. For Brueggemann, this testimony becomes a
form of divine disclosure: 'the testimony that Israel bears to the
character of God is taken by the ecclesial community of the text
as a reliable disclosure about the true character of God'. The
authority of scripture is recognized in its capacity 'to disclose
the true reality of God'.[43] The books of the Old Testament
provide a number of witnesses, each offering rather different

testimony. He first describes Israel's core testimony, then Israel's countertestimony, next her unsolicited testimony and finally her embodied testimony. Brueggemann seeks to attend to the 'polyphonic character' of Israel's testimony. Israel's core testimony emerges through an analysis of Old Testament language: first, there is the testimony in verbal sentences. These verbs illustrate God's sovereign power: he creates, he saves, he liberates. Secondly, there are all sorts of adjectives used to describe God, and he finds a rich convergence of these adjectives in the confession of Exod. 34.6–7. God is described as 'merciful and gracious, slow to anger, and abounding in steadfast love and faithfulness'. And yet, while these adjectives serve to generalize Israel's core testimony, they should not be used to define a number of core attributes about God. He notes that the terms of classical theology such as *omnipotent, omniscient* and *omnipresent* are completely lacking in the testimony of the Old Testament. To acknowledge that God is 'slow to anger' is to describe a relationship between God and his people. There is a relational quality to this testimony. These adjectives serve to characterize this relationship in a specific and particular way. Finally, Brueggemann assesses the nouns which are used to describe God. He emphasizes the fact that nouns such as 'judge', 'king', 'warrior' and 'father' are metaphors, and no one metaphor offers a full, final and comprehensive depiction of God: 'metaphors are nouns that function in Israel in order to give access to the Subject of verbs, who is endlessly elusive. The metaphor will be misunderstood and misused if it is not recognized that the One named by the metaphor is not contained or comprehended by the noun'.[44] This analysis leads Brueggemann to conclude that Israel's core testimony is characterized by a profound tension. God's sovereignty is marked by holiness, glory and justice. At the same time, God has established a relationship of enduring fidelity with Israel. The scriptural witness suggests that this commitment and loyalty is often at odds with his holiness and justice. This tension does not lend itself to easy resolution: 'no ready convergence of sovereignty and solidarity is available'.[45] There is a 'jaggedness' about the relationship between God and Israel which is never properly settled.

If Israel's 'core testimony' is characterized by tension and a lack of finality, this is underscored by Israel's 'countertestimony'. Under 'cross-examination', Israel's description of God's sovereignty and fidelity begins to look more hesitant. The wisdom tradition emphasizes God's hiddenness and absence. On occasion, God is portrayed as 'devious, ambiguous, irascible, and unstable'.[46] In the Book of Job, Israel wrestles with the problem of theodicy, while the complaint psalms question God's reliability. The Book of Ecclesiastes is described as 'a hostile witness', with its 'shrill and incessant voicing of negativity about YHWH'. If Israel's 'core testimony' legitimates power and the structure of society, her 'countertestimony' embraces the reality of pain and suffering. This 'countertestimony' is placed alongside two more forms of testimony. The 'unsolicited testimony' amounts to a series of character references by virtue of God's relationships with Israel, humanity in general, the nations and the whole of creation. Brueggemann sees in these relationships the same dynamics of brokenness and restoration, which shed some light on the character of God. Finally, there is Israel's 'embodied testimony', which refers to the way in which God's presence in the world is mediated through the Torah and embodied in the lives of prophets, priests, sages and kings.

Brueggemann does not look for an easy resolution of these different perspectives. These divergent accounts of God's character are set in profound conflict and opposition. He repeatedly underlines the ambiguity and playfulness inherent within them. He encourages the reader to recognize that the text of the Old Testament 'is remarkably open and refuses a simple or firm cognitive closure, that is, the text is available for many readings of particular texts, and seems at many points to delight in a playful ambiguity that precludes certitude'.[47] Inconsistency and ambiguity are inherent characteristics of the Old Testament canon: 'Israel's text, and therefore Israel and Israel's God, are always in the middle of an exchange, unable to come to ultimate resolution. There may be momentary or provisional resolution, but because both parties are intensely engaged and are so relentlessly verbal, we are always sure that there will be another speech, another challenge, another invitation, another petition, another argument, which will reopen the matter . . . Thus Israel's religious rhetoric does not intend to reach resolution or to achieve closure'. The testimony of the Old Testament has a 'dialectical and dialogical quality'.[48] In a footnote on the same page,

Brueggemann notes that 'the work of Mikhail Bakhtin will be crucial for future work in this direction in Old Testament study'. This is the only direct reference to the work of Bakhtin, and yet Brueggemann's frequent use of the term 'dialogical' points to the significant influence he has exercised over his thought. Indeed, the extent of this influence has become more apparent since the publication of *Theology of the Old Testament*.

Bakhtin was a Russian literary theorist, who lived between 1895 and 1975. His theory of 'dialogic' truth is based on his reading of the writings of Fyodor Dostoevsky. For Bakhtin, Dostoevsky's novels are characterized by 'a plurality of independent and unmerged voices and consciousnesses, a genuine polyphony of fully valid voices'.[49] The meaning of the novel is to be discerned in the interaction of the different characters and the dialogue of different voices. Human living is characterized by *open-ended dialogue*. To participate in dialogue is to ask questions, to respond, to agree, to disagree. For Bakhtin, 'dialogue . . . is not the threshold to action, it is the action itself. It is not a means for revealing, for bringing to the surface the already ready-made character of a person; no, in dialogue a person not only shows himself outwardly, but he becomes for the first time that which he is – and we repeat, not only for others but for himself as well. To be means to communicate dialogically. When dialogue ends, everything ends. Thus dialogue, by its very essence, cannot and must not come to an end'.[50] No word or text exists in isolation. Each word or text responds to the words and texts that precede it and is not left untouched by the words and texts which come after it. One can immediately see the resonances with Brueggemann's account of the dialogical quality of Old Testament testimony. The process of canonization, in Brueggemann's account, represents not the hegemonic victory of one particular theological trajectory, but a process of accommodation and compromise as the Priestly and Deuteronomic traditions are held in tension, both agents of divine disclosure. Brueggemann's great strength is that he sees lament and complaint as just as much a resource for theological reflection as confession and praise. But this 'dialogical approach' has not gone unchallenged. For Brevard Childs, this juxtaposition of 'core testimony' and 'countertestimony' amounts to little more than a 'contrived dialectic'. For Childs, the lament and complaint characteristic of Brueggemann's 'countertestimony' are an integral part of Israel's true faith.

Brueggemann's rather laboured grammatical analysis of verbs, adjectives and nouns is adopted in order to ensure that he does not import the categories of church tradition or systematic theology to describe God in reading the Old Testament. He is convinced that by attending to the biblical text in this way, a far more interesting and challenging character will emerge: 'if we honour Israel's rhetoric . . ., we can see a complexity, oddity, and dangerousness about YHWH, qualities that could hardly be taken into account by the conventions of positivistic history or by the modes of classical theology. YHWH, it appears, is always prepared for some new, outrageous self-disclosure, depending on the courage and freedom of Israel's boldest speakers'.[51] Brueggemann's commitment to describe YHWH without recourse to the established categories of Christian tradition leads him to make a number of inferences about the language of scripture and whether it refers to anything beyond itself. For example, in the initial sections of his *Theology of the Old Testament,* Brueggemann asserts that 'I shall insist, as consistently as I can, that the God of Old Testament theology as such lives in, with and under the rhetorical enterprise of this text, and nowhere else and in no other way'.[52] This takes us into a complex area (and as Brueggemann himself concedes, it raises questions which he himself is unable to resolve) but it does mean that we are left puzzling over the tension between the sovereignty of God (which he acknowledges) and how God 'lives in, with, and under' Israel's speech about him (which he also asserts). The more unsettling question raised by Brueggemann's rejection of the established categories of Christian tradition is how exactly his theology relates to this broader tradition: what kind of purchase does a 'theology of the Old Testament' have on Christian theology and discipleship? Brueggemann wants to emphasize the 'polyphonic, elusive testimony of the Old Testament' and so he seeks to resist a 'New Testament-christological construal'[53] of the Old Testament text. And yet, is it possible for a Christian to speak truthfully and comprehensively about the reality of God without speaking about Jesus Christ? The fact that Brueggemann's description of Israel's 'countertestimony' is framed in terms of 'a theology of the cross' suggests that he himself is only partially successful in achieving his stated aim. In spite of the detailed grammatical analysis, Brueggemann's interpretation betrays signs of a more ecclesial reading. He never totally succeeds in shaking this off.

7 Tradition

'Tradition' is a word which conjures up a range of different meanings. In the context of modernity, it has often been subject to hostile definition, encompassing a range of ideas associated with 'meaningless repetition' or a 'stifling of argument' or a 'substitute for reason'. And yet, in recent years, the notion of 'tradition' has undergone something of a transformation. Partly as a consequence of the influence of Hans-Georg Gadamer and Alasdair MacIntyre, the notion of 'tradition' has been rehabilitated. MacIntyre, in particular, has challenged the contrast often drawn between 'tradition' and 'reason'. He argues that all reasoning is shaped and constituted by a tradition of thinking and understanding: 'all reasoning takes place within the context of some traditional mode of thought, transcending through criticism and invention the limitations of what had hitherto been reasoned in that tradition; this is as true of modern physics as of medieval logic'. This means that tradition is not a substitute for reason: it is the very form of rational inquiry itself. Nor is tradition the stifling of an argument: it is constituted by an ongoing argument. In an institution like a university, part of its life will always be constituted by an ongoing argument over what a university ought to be. As MacIntyre says, 'Traditions, when vital, embody continuities of conflict'.[54]

Tradition also held a particular fascination for Hans-Georg Gadamer. His major work, *Truth and Method*, is a fascinating study of hermeneutics. Exploring how we might approach the question of truth in the human sciences, Gadamer was critical of attempts to model a critical approach to the humanities on the natural sciences. Hermeneutics could not be simply reduced to a method. At the same time, he was critical of the German hermeneutical tradition, associated with Friedrich Schleiermacher and Wilhelm Dilthey, which sought to determine the meaning of a text by recovering the intention of the original author. Instead Gadamer held that meaning was not an objective property of the text but an event in the present. It involved a fusion of horizons. To demonstrate what he meant by this, he explored the concept of *Wirkungsgeschichte*, which can be loosely translated as 'the history of effects'. This is an ambiguous term, which is often misunderstood. When Gadamer used the term, he was referring not so much to the 'history of effects' associated with a particular text as the 'historically-effected consciousness' of the reader. In Gadamer's view, our reading and interpretation are informed by the horizon of our own context, our own personal history and our assumptions and prejudices: 'long before we understand ourselves through the process of self-examination, we understand ourselves in a self-evident way in the family, society and state in which we live'.[55] All these things are a consequence of human finitude. The important point is that each of them has the capacity to shape our consciousness. Moreover, established patterns of reading and interpretation also inform and shape our consciousness. We come to a text as the always-already-read. For example, if we read St Paul's letter to the Romans, we have to negotiate the fact that Luther's exegesis has profoundly altered the way in which the letter has been read since. That is not to suggest that the interpretation of Reformation divines has since proved 'normative'. It is simply to acknowledge that contemporary biblical scholars who seek to promote the 'new perspective on Paul' need to negotiate and challenge the legacy of the Reformation, which has had a powerful effect on the way in which those texts have been and continue to be interpreted for good and ill. In other words, we come to a text informed by a tradition of reading and interpretation. All of this informs and shapes our own reading and interpretation. This does not exclude the possibility of challenging or questioning the tradition. The point is that our criticisms and rebellions will often presuppose it. For Gadamer, we belong to a dialogue with the past and our basic attitude is one of respect which does not rule out criticism. We cannot pretend that this history of interpretation is completely absent. Gadamer's account of hermeneutics perhaps explains why Brueggemann finds it so difficult to avoid the categories of Christian thought in his reading of the Old Testament.

This rehabilitation of tradition has informed the way in which a number of recent thinkers have reflected on the theological interpretation of scripture. In *Discerning the Mystery*, Andrew Louth adopted Gadamer as his chief conversation partner along with the Roman Catholic theologian, Henri de Lubac. As a patristics scholar, Louth read the scriptures through the lenses provided by the early church fathers. Louth looked back to this tradition for inspiration in reading the scriptures. He saw that many of the fathers employed allegory in their interpretation, and this enabled them to attend to the density of meaning within the text. For Louth, allegory was 'a way of entering the "margin of silence" that surrounds the articulate message of the Scriptures, it is a way of glimpsing the living depths of tradition from the perspective of the letter of the Scriptures'.[56] We can see a similar exploration of the significance of allegory and typology in the writings of Henri de Lubac.

As a leading advocate of the *ressourcement* movement, de Lubac was convinced that 'the renewal of Christian vitality is linked at least partially to a renewed exploration of the periods and of the works where the Christian tradition is expressed with particular intensity'.[57] De Lubac's reflections on tradition were stimulated not by Gadamer and MacIntyre, but by the writings of John Henry Newman, Yves Congar and Maurice Blondel. For Blondel, tradition was not a retrograde or limiting force. It animated the expansion and development of the Catholic Church. Henri de Lubac was confident that a radical return to the roots of the Christian faith would nourish, invigorate and rejuvenate twentieth century Catholicism. He wanted to recover and retrieve the spiritual understanding of scripture which he saw exemplified in the writings of the fathers and in scripture itself. To that end, de Lubac emphasized the significance of the typological and allegorical interpretations in scripture itself (e.g. Mark 4 and Gal. 4.24). The tradition showed that allegory offered a pattern of reading the biblical text which illuminated its spiritual meaning. But to judge whether an allegorical interpretation was appropriate, de Lubac recognized that one needed to guard against making the text mean whatever one wanted it to mean. For de Lubac, an allegorical interpretation needed to be judged in the light of tradition: was it possible to identify a consensus among the early Church fathers to justify such an approach?

Louth took from de Lubac the insight that theologians should take seriously patterns of divine disclosure beyond the canon of scripture. They needed to embrace also the ongoing tradition of the Church. Of course, Louth's understanding of tradition is controversial because he extends and accentuates the meaning of the word beyond anything that either Gadamer or MacIntyre would have recognized. 'Tradition' is no longer simply a consequence of human finitude. It is also a site of divine disclosure: 'If we see tradition as the life of the Holy Spirit in the Church, then we must also see it as something that brings us into the freedom that the Spirit confers, the boldness that enables us to stand in the divine presence and speak with simplicity of what is there made known'.[58]

We can see a similar emphasis in the theology of David Brown. In *Tradition and Imagination,* Brown dwells on the imaginative retelling of the birth narratives in the gospels. While academics and clergy might be embarrassed by the historical inaccuracies of the average nativity play, for Brown these imaginative retellings of the Christmas story, whether in the form of drama or the visual arts, often provide a profound insight into the way in which a tradition can change and develop. Such change and development might even disclose something new about the Christian mystery. For example, medieval artistic depictions of the Magi, representing different nationalities and different ages (young, middle-aged and old), accentuate the way in which they represent not just all the nations but the whole of humanity. For Brown, many of these imaginative retellings correspond to the way in which the infancy narratives within the gospels developed: 'The additions are not, of course, historically true, but the same could also be said of much of the narratives of Matthew and Luke'.[59] He argues that the canon of truth is not determined simply by the canon of scripture. A canon of interpretation continues to develop, which sometimes involved 'creative mistranslation; sometimes a new grid being imposed on an existing story; sometimes lacunae being filled and thus indirectly an almost wholly new story generated'.[60] All of this material provides further opportunities for divine disclosure. Intriguingly, in contrast to Andrew Louth who emphasizes the continuity between scripture and tradition, Brown concedes that at times the relationship has been characterized by discontinuity and change. Indeed, Brown readily accepts the thesis of Bart Ehrman to suggest that later copyists of the New Testament were content to alter the text where it failed to do justice to later doctrinal development:

That the New Testament would be improved will seem to some readers an outrageous claim. But that in effect has been what the tradition has done, and rightly demanded, as new social triggers required fresh resolutions.[61]

Brown uses the methodology associated with *Wirkungsgeschichte* to invite and provoke further reflection about the theological interpretation of scripture. The general tenor of his approach is distinctive. In granting the canon a certain elasticity, he challenges the pervasive influence of the canonical approach and much postliberal theology. He invites us to see that the Bible is not the only source of theological reflection. It is not the only site of divine disclosure. The Holy Spirit is active in the Church and the world, inviting the people of God to embrace transformation and change.

It is intriguing that Brown invokes 'tradition' to underscore an argument about transformation and change in the life of the Church. Tradition is dynamic. It describes not a *deposit* of faith which is static and unchanging, but a hermeneutical *process* of refraction and development. It is not a 'what' but a 'how'. It is not a body of material that provides a supplement to scripture, but a pattern of transmission that is engaged in a continual and imaginative unfolding of scripture. And yet, Louth and Brown's reflections on tradition and revelation also present some difficulties. It is not always clear to what extent the scriptures are foundational or authoritative for the development of this tradition. How does the Church determine what is a legitimate development? Moreover, both Louth and Brown have embraced the 'hermeneutics of retrieval' associated with the thought of Hans-Georg Gadamer, and yet Gadamer is criticized by Paul Ricoeur and others for adopting a certain naiveté in his attitude towards tradition. After all, a tradition can be dominating and oppressive. A tradition can constitute a dominant ideology that rationalizes the interests of the powerful in order to support them. We may need not to retrieve that kind of tradition but to be liberated from it. The posture of doubt and scepticism associated with the 'hermeneutics of suspicion' may be an essential part of the interpretative task.

8 Resistance

The 'hermeneutics of suspicion' is a characteristic of liberationist and feminist readings of scripture. Both approaches draw on a range of different methods, including different forms of historical criticism and literary theory. Both offer a disposition of 'resistance' in the interpretation of scripture. The word 'resistance' is deliberately ambiguous. It encompasses 'resistance' in the sense of taking seriously the ideological interests and concerns of the interpreter in reading scripture. Liberationist and feminist readers are suspicious of the way in which scripture can be used to legitimate the interests of the powerful. They adopt an attitude of resistance to unmask the ideological presuppositions and pretensions of these dominant readings. At the same time, they seek to lay bare within the biblical text the hidden testimony which will inform and give voice to a counter-cultural attitude of resistance in the lives of Christian discipleship. Thus there is often a tension between *retrieval* and *suspicion* in their interpretative strategies. For example, liberationist and feminist writers would see in Mary's *Magnificat* (Lk. 1.46–55) the subversive testimony of a peasant woman who gives voice to the voiceless and declares that God will not legitimate traditional systems of power: 'He hath put down the mighty from their seat: and hath exalted the humble and meek. He hath filled the hungry with good things: and the rich he hath sent empty away'. Adopting a stance of dissent and resistance, they do not simply appeal to neglected passages of scripture as proof-texts to justify their theological perspective. Sometimes, they may take a very familiar text like the *Magnificat* and challenge prevailing assumptions by identifying those elements which have been marginalized and ignored. At other times, when wrestling with passages which reinforce the *status quo* – 'slaves, obey your masters' (Col. 3.22) – or endorse the values of patriarchy – 'wives, submit to your husbands' (Eph. 5.22) – liberationist and feminist interpreters must read 'against the grain'. Such interpretation involves 'consciously *resisting* prevailing understandings of texts or dominant ideologies discerned in texts, and exploiting aporia, difficulties, and inconsistencies in textual interpretation'.[62]

The beginnings of Liberation Theology are often associated with a conference of Latin American bishops of the Roman Catholic Church, who had gathered at Medellin in Colombia in 1968. They issued a celebrated statement, which contained the following observation: 'Latin America is obviously under the sign of transformation and development; a transformation that, besides taking place with extraordinary speed, has come to touch and influence every level of human activity, from the economic to the religious . . . This indicates that we are on the threshold of a new epoch in the history of Latin America. It appears to be a time of zeal for full emancipation, of liberation from every form of servitude, of personal maturity and of collective integration'. The bishops were responding to the profound issues of poverty and deprivation in the Third World. In the light of the Medellin Conference, theologians began to speak of a 'preferential option for the poor', and they began to explore a range of economic and social questions, occasionally through the lens of Marxist analysis.

In the initial stages of this movement, the vitality of its theological expression lay in the fact that its perspective was formed in the crucible of Christian base communities. For example, Ernesto Cardenal's *The Gospel in Solentiname* is a record of a series of Bible studies in which a group of largely uneducated Nicaraguan peasants living in the town of Solentiname study stories of scripture, and, whether self-consciously or not, present an understanding of the Christian faith, from the perspective of the 'underside of history'. Christopher Rowland has called this 'Grassroots Exegesis'. Cardenal, a Roman Catholic priest and a political activist, drew this material together in order to renew the Church's commitment to alleviate suffering and oppression. It is a pattern of Bible study and theological reflection which has informed and animated a whole range of different forms of liberation theology which have emerged in a variety of different contexts across the globe: in South Africa, in the Pacific, in South East Asia, in North America and in Europe. People were encouraged to interpret their own lives and praxis in the light of the Word of God.

These contextual readings of scripture were sometimes dismissed by academics as 'naïve', or 'lacking rigour'. In *Theology and Praxis*, Clodovis Boff responded to these concerns. He identified two strategies of interpretation among Liberation Theologians: first, a *correspondence of terms*. This approach can be illustrated with reference to Cardenal's collection from Solentiname. One of the characteristics of this approach is that it equated Jesus and his political context with the contemporary Christian community and its political context. This sometimes involved a direct and naïve reading of the text that was insufficiently alert to questions of historicity in relation to the testimony about the historical Jesus. This led Boff to identify a second strategy, a *correspondence of relationships*. Boff drew on the insights of form and redaction criticism to draw parallels between scripture and its context on the one hand, and ourselves and our context on the other hand. The significance of this is that it creates a much more nuanced and sophisticated account of the hermeneutics involved in relating the words of scripture to a contemporary context. Boff recognizes that our access to the historical Jesus is mediated through the Bible. It cannot be assumed that the words attributed to Jesus were actually spoken by him. He is conscious that critical engagement with the quest for the historical Jesus will guard liberation theologians from the accusation that they read scripture uncritically or naively. At the same time, Boff was alert to the fact that academics can be blind to class conflict and the economic, structural injustice faced by the poor. Indeed, just as one can see the influence of historical criticism in the writings of Clodovis Boff, one can also see the influence of different forms of biblical theology in the earlier writings of Gustavo Gutierrez. In *A Theology of Liberation*, Gutierrez writes of 'the God who acts in history to save a people by liberating it from every kind of servitude'. One can see the clear influence of von Rad's understanding of 'salvation-history' in his work. Recognizing the traces of historical criticism and biblical theology in the writings of liberation theologians is significant because it enables us to see that liberation theologians often adopt exactly the same methods of interpretation as other theologians and biblical scholars. The difference is that they adopt a particular disposition, standing in solidarity with the poor and the dispossessed, which serves to disrupt the ideological presuppositions and assumptions of First World academics.

Similarly, we see in the writings of feminist theologians and biblical scholars the adoption of more familiar methods of historical criticism and literary theory. Although there are many diverse voices among feminist interpreters, a common perspective is the idea that Christianity has been formed and marred by a dominant patriarchal ideology. Examples of this would include patriarchal translations (for example, the Greek title *diakonis* is translated 'deaconess' or 'servant' when it is applied to Phoebe in Rom. 16.1 and 'minister' or 'deacon' when it is applied to a man); patriarchal interpretations (for example, the identification of Eve with sin) and patriarchal oversights (when characters like the Samaritan woman in Jn 4 or the rape of a woman in Judg. 19 are ignored). Such patriarchy has caused some women theologians to part company with Christianity. Others continue to engage with the Christian tradition, an engagement which reflects the full range of different approaches to biblical interpretation. So, for example, Rosemary Radford Ruether's classic work, *Sexism and God Talk: Toward a Feminist Theology* was self-consciously informed by the interpretative approach advocated by liberation theologians. It also bears some resonance with developments in the biblical theology movement in the course of the twentieth century. She seeks to work out a correlation of the prophetic-liberating tradition of Biblical faith and the critical principles of feminism. In terms of method, Ruether identifies four themes in presenting the prophetic principle of feminist theology (and one can see clear overlaps with the approach of liberation theologians). She refers to: 1) God's defence and vindication of the oppressed; 2) the critique of the dominant systems of power and their power holders; 3) the vision of a new age to come in which the present system of injustice is overcome and God's intended reign of peace and justice is installed in history and 4) the critique of ideology, or of religion: 'Prophetic faith denounces religious ideologies and systems that function to justify and sanctify the dominant, unjust social order. These traditions are central to the Prophets and the mission of Jesus'. She asserts that feminist thought seeks to radicalize this prophetic tradition within scripture, which is how she understands the phrase 'The Word of God'. The Word is the critical principle that Biblical faith applies to itself. 'It is the hermeneutical principle for discerning prophetic faith within Scripture as well as for the ongoing interpretation of Scripture as critique of tradition'. Thus feminist theology does not assert 'unprecedented ideas' – it is a rediscovery of the prophetic context and content of Biblical faith itself. Ruether saw this approach at work in the biblical studies taking place in the base communities in Latin America. The distinctiveness of her own approach lay in insisting that this prophetic-liberating principle apply to women.

Other feminist theologians and biblical scholars adopt a variety of different methods and approaches. For example, in *Texts of Terror*, Phyllis Trible adopts a rhetorical/literary approach in exploring the tragic stories of four women in ancient Israel. By contrast, Elizabeth Schüssler Fiorenza adopts an explicit historical approach in her interpretation of the New Testament. This is particularly evident in her book *In Memory of Her*: *a feminist theological reconstruction of Christian origins*. The basic contrast with Ruether's approach lies in the fact that Fiorenza does not appeal to some notion of 'women's experience(s)' or an appeal to some essential notion of what it means to be Christian or human. In her view, such approaches tend to present scripture as a 'mythic archetype'. Fiorenza seeks to use scripture as an 'historical prototype', which provides the Christian community with a sense of its ongoing history as well as of its theological identity. Fiorenza's basic thesis is as follows: the earliest Christian community was made up of a 'discipleship of equals'. Fiorenza starts with the historical Jesus and the renewal movement within Judaism which gathered around him. She draws material out of the blanks and persistent blindspots within the biblical text to argue that the historical Jesus would have exercised much more freedom in his attitude towards women, a freedom which is only partially reflected in the gospels. She appeals to an historical reconstruction of Jesus to criticize the canonical record of him. To sustain the view that Jesus drew together a community, in which men and women shared positions of leadership and ministry on an equal basis, she argues that the tradition was subject to a process of 'patriarchalisation'. Betraying a considerable debt to the 'history of religions' school and socio-scientific insights, she asserts that it was only as the earliest Jewish community interacted with the Graeco-Roman world, that the patriarchal structures of Graeco-Roman households began to undermine the original discipleship of equals. For evidence of this patriarchalization, she quotes the story told in Mark's Gospel at the beginning of the passion narrative:

> . . . three disciples figure prominently: on the one hand, two of the twelve – Judas who betrays Jesus and Peter who denies him – and on the other, the unnamed women who anoints Jesus. But while the stories of Judas and Peter are engraved in the memory of Christians, the story of the woman is virtually forgotten. Although Jesus pronounces in Mark: 'And truly I say to you, wherever the gospel is preached in the whole world, what she has done will be told in memory of her' (14.9), the woman's

prophetic sign-action did not become a part of the gospel knowledge of Christians. Even her name is lost to us. Wherever the gospel is proclaimed and the eucharist celebrated another story is told: the story of the apostle who betrayed Jesus. The name of the betrayer is remembered, but the name of the faithful disciple is forgotten because she was a woman.[63]

For Schüssler Fiorenza, the principal differences between a standard historical reading and a 'feminist-historical' reading are not so much about method as about the perspective brought to such a reading. And yet, to do this effectively, Schüssler Fiorenza must look for the hidden meanings in the text, she must exploit the aporia and argue from silence. As J'annine Jobling points out, one detects 'a close affinity with deconstructive approaches' in her interpretative strategy.

Schüssler Fiorenza has been criticized for her reconstruction of Christian origins from a number of quarters. From those steeped in the established patterns of historical criticism, there is an uneasiness about the ideological bias betrayed by her approach. Robert Morgan suggests that the purpose of unmasking history as ideology is to argue for less ideology rather than an alternative one. Nevertheless, such a view perpetuates the questionable assumption that we can somehow jump out of the complex web of social, personal and power relationships that we all find ourselves in to present a neutral, objective standpoint. The value of Schüssler Fiorenza's approach is that she is completely clear about her interests and values in writing. She does not dissemble. But while such a criticism might be predictable from a male academic, Schüssler Fiorenza's ideas about a 'discipleship of equals' have come under criticism from fellow feminist critics. For instance, Luce Irigaray's review of In Memory of Her conveys her initial enthusiasm for Fiorenza's work, particularly about the patriarchal bias of early Christian texts. However, she is more critical of the less than nuanced use of a 'History of Religions' approach to claim that it was the Graeco-Roman influence which brought about this silencing of women and that the Jewish roots were more women-friendly. In Irigaray's view, such an opposition is too simplistic. Each tradition contained patriarchal strands. But Irigaray's more searching criticism relates to the fact that Schüssler Fiorenza seems more interested in demonstrating the equality of women

with Jesus' male disciples than in claiming for women 'an equal
share in the divine'.[64] Irigaray wants to know what the incarnation
of Jesus Christ might tell us about the divine. In a rather sharp
comment, she exclaims that, 'sociology quickly bores me when
I am expecting the divine'.[65] Will a male Jesus allow patriarchal
structures to be displaced in order to create space for new ways
of conceiving and being which enable women to be subjects as
women? The significance of Irigaray's question is that it brings
the question of divine disclosure centre-stage. Irigaray goes on
to reflect about the way in which language about the Holy Spirit
subverts patriarchal structures. But even though she is so critical
of Schüssler Fiorenza's work, she still argues that 'the notion of
a Holy Spirit as the pure product of patriarchal culture seems
erroneous in view of Jesus' personality. His behaviour toward
women, in conjunction with his personal qualities, is evocative
of a resistance to patriarchy'.[66] In spite of her criticisms, Irigaray
is still appealing to Schüssler Fiorenza's account of the historical
Jesus to sustain her argument.

In each of these patterns of resistance, whether liberationist
or feminist, we see repeated appeals to more conventional forms
of historical criticism and literary theory. Their distinctiveness
lies in the way in which they alert the reader to the ideological
bias at work within the text or within an interpretation of a
text. However, the difficulty comes when a text is so difficult
that it results not so much in a hermeneutic of suspicion as
outright rejection. For example, Cheryl Exum[67] points out that
the language used in Ezekiel and Hosea which describes an act
of sexual violence in which God is the perpetrator and Israel,
personified as a woman, is the object, is particularly problematic.
She asserts that such language cannot simply be dismissed as a
metaphor. It cannot be the case that gender relations are rendered
less problematic if described metaphorically rather than literally.
Nor is the prospect of reconciliation following this act of violence
a solution to the pattern of sexual abuse described in the text.
The submission of a faithful wife only serves to emphasize the
patriarchal hierarchy. Similarly, Schüssler Fiorenza argues that
not all the traditions that we find in scripture are meaningful
or relevant for Christian communities today. Others seek to
minimize the offence, arguing that it is necessary to look for
alternative metaphors to describe divine-human relationships.

Others suggest that it is worth keeping these texts in the canon not to legitimate or authorize their theological perspective, but to challenge readers to confront difficult questions. So, for example, Ellen Davis argues that no biblical text should be repudiated as a potential source of edification for the church: 'When we think we have reached the point of zero edification, then that perception indicates that we are not reading deeply enough; we have not probed the layers of the text with sufficient care'.[68] And yet, I suspect that scholars like Cheryl Exum read the scandalous imagery of Ezek. 16 and 23 all too carefully. My own view is that our resistance to such texts is entirely justified. It is a reminder that the Bible has been read by Christians in the course of the centuries to authorize violence, discrimination and injustice. Our resistance to these texts should be an occasion of repentance in the hope that we may yet discover the subversive emancipation of the gospel. It is only in that sense that these texts might ever be regarded as a source of edification.

9 *Performance*

Such an observation suggests that the point of divine disclosure lies not so much in any intrinsic property of scripture, but in the way we respond to the act of reading or interpreting the text. This is the starting point of an essay by Nicholas Lash, in which he observes that when we open a copy of the New Testament, 'all that we *see* is a set of black marks on white paper'.[69] Confronted by these black marks on white paper, we try to make sense of them and to interpret them. Thus the reader has an active rather than a passive role in the task of interpretation. Moreover, depending on the kind of text, we will make all sorts of decisions about how it may be used. So, for example, a group of people on a hike may be interpreting a map in one hand while carrying a compass in the other, an engineer might be looking at a circuit diagram to mend a television set, but 'it would be silly to sing railway timetables, rather than use them to catch trains'.[70] So when four musicians look at the score of one of Beethoven's string quartets, they not only read it and interpret it, they also perform it. Their performance is a creative act. A performance can be flawless but unimaginative, or it can release a profound sense of passion and energy. Similarly, when a group of actors interpret a text like *King Lear*, they perform it, and their performance can reveal things that neither the actors nor the audience has seen before. Such interpretation is quite different from the rather technical attempt to research the manuscripts of Beethoven's original score or to resolve the inconsistencies in the transmission of the script of *King Lear*. While such scholarship has value, Lash makes the point that when considering questions of biblical hermeneutics, we think about the interpretation of scripture in this technical, scholarly sense rather than in the wider sense of the text being interpreted and performed. And when a score is performed or a script enacted, no single interpretation is final or definitive in the sense of bringing the possibility of further performances to an end.

These analogies provide the necessary backdrop to the consideration of the interpretation of scripture. While Lash concedes that not all the texts of the New Testament are stories, when they are taken together, they 'tell the story' of Jesus and the early church. Thus the fundamental form of Christian interpretation of scripture is not the kind of technical scholarly exercise of reconstructing the original meaning of the text, important as that may be, but 'the life, activity and organisation of the Christian community, construed as performance of the biblical text'. For Lash, this is best illustrated in the celebration of the Eucharist, when the Christian community responds through interpretative performance to the words 'Do this in remembrance of me'. In the Eucharist, our interpretation of scripture takes the form of an embodied dramatic enactment: 'Here, that interpretative performance in which all our life consists – all our suffering and care, compassion, celebration, struggle and obedience – is dramatically distilled, focussed, concentrated, rendered explicit'.[71] When we listen to the story of Jesus in the Liturgy of the Word, we do this not so that the words may simply be remembered but in order that this story 'may be *performed* in the following of Christ'. And yet, the difficulty lies in being able to determine the quality of the performance. In the end, Lash suggests that the determining factor lies in 'the quality of our *humanity*' but he recognizes that this criterion admits no final definitive answer.

The lack of finality associated with this emphasis on performance is picked up by Frances Young in *The Art of Performance* and by Samuel Wells in *Improvisation*. Young employs the idea of performance to explore the dynamics of biblical interpretation. She expands on the musical metaphor employed by Lash to suggest a more comprehensive understanding of the inspiration of scripture. Inspiration relates not just to the original writers being inspired by God, as the Lausanne Covenant would insist. It also relates to the inspiration of those performing the score. Sometimes we can witness a performance, which is inspiring and inspired. At other times, we may be disappointed. When we draw the analogy with the interpretation of scripture, we begin to understand that a performance, which is inspiring or inspired, is a sign that the Holy Spirit is at work. But Young extends the musical metaphor much further. She points out that originally, it was a convention in playing a concerto to add a cadenza. This was a form of improvization, in which the concerto was brought to a climax as a soloist took a particular cadence or passage from the concerto and began to improvize on it. There is a display of virtuosity and skill, but the soloist must draw on the given score, bringing out its hidden themes and exhibiting its style. Young uses this analogy to talk about the relationship between the Bible and good preaching: 'Just playing the old classic without a cadenza is like reading the lessons without a sermon . . . only the preaching enables proper development of the classic themes for a new situation'.[72] For Wells, this vision of improvisation is too limited. Young gives the preacher an opportunity to improvize, but she does not consider the way in which improvization may be an essential element of all Christian discipleship. In Wells' view, while performance provides a useful way of thinking about the embodied, communal way in which the Church responds to the scriptures, the problem is that such a perspective lends itself to the idea that the Bible is simply a script (like the script of a play) and all we need to do is perform it. Wells says: 'This expectation is quite clearly an inappropriate one. The script does not provide all the answers. Life throws up circumstances that the gospel seems not to cover. If performance of a script is regarded as the paradigmatic form of discipleship, a great deal of disappointment or doublethink is likely to result. It cannot simply be a matter of performing the same story in new circumstances'.[73] In other words, Christians continue to encounter situations in the modern world for which there is no reassuring script to which they can appeal. Like Young, he suggests that Christian discipleship demands more than repetition and performance. It demands also the capacity to improvize. The important point about improvization is that it involves a tremendous amount of discipline. Actors who improvize on the stage are informed by years of training and experience: 'they learn to act from habit in ways appropriate to the circumstance'.[74] One might make the same observation of musicians as well. For Wells, theological ethics has exactly the same goal. The habits of Christian discipleship are shaped and formed by worship and the reading of scripture in the context of a Christian community. The way in which we respond to a given situation will often simply be a question of character, a character formed and shaped by the reading of scripture.

Scripture, Theology and Divine Disclosure

What makes these patterns of interpretation *theological?* One of the striking things about this analysis is that it demonstrates that attempts to define the *theological* interpretation of scripture over and against literary or historical approaches will often ignore some of the key influences that have fashioned the theological imagination. Each of these approaches draws on the insights of historical criticism, literary theory, or recent developments in hermeneutics, in some shape or form. In this respect, these theologians follow in the footsteps of earlier Christian interpreters, who also employed the established conventions of historiography and literary theory in their reading of scripture. However, the distinctiveness of a *theological* interpretation lies in the fact that their exegetical insights intersect with a series of theological commitments, the most significant of which is that scripture 'is a site of God's self-revelation'.[75] This is the point at which some of the real differences between these approaches begin to emerge. For some, divine disclosure is defined in relation to an intrinsic property of the text: the doctrine it teaches, the history it records, the memory it treasures, the story it tells or the testimony it contains. In such instances, divine disclosure may be indirect. It may have a secondary role in relation to the primary mode of God's self-revelation in the person of Jesus Christ. For others, divine disclosure is circumscribed by a pattern of interpreting the text: the canon or the tradition. For others, divine disclosure is located in an encounter with the text: resistance or performance. But however tempting or reassuring it may appear to be, we should not for a moment imagine that the divine mystery will be disclosed through the application of a particular method or technique. In the *theological* interpretation of scripture, any 'method' or 'technique' needs to leave itself open to divine agency.

To consider the question of divine agency brings us up against a significant problem, a difficulty which we have encountered already in previous chapters. This is the tendency to think that *revelation* is a thing, an object or a proposition. In an important essay on 'Revelation', John Montag points out that this modern concept of revelation bears little resemblance to the way in which St Thomas Aquinas thought about revelation. In the modern world, the notion of 'revelation' has been reified to become the subject matter of theology in the way that 'numbers' are the subject matter of arithmetic and 'living things' are the concern of biology. This is an extraordinarily limited and distorted understanding of revelation. Montag points out that revelation does not refer to 'a supplementary packet of information about "facts" which are around the bend, as it were, from rational comprehension or physical observation'.[76] He draws out the differences between the thought of Thomas Aquinas and that of the Spanish Jesuit Francisco Suárez (1548–1617) in their differing understandings of the mediation of revelation. In Montag's view, 'Thomas never had cause to reify the mediation into words or propositions through which God hands over "things to be believed". Nor does Thomas separate the moment of belief or assent from some prior moment of apprehension. We have seen, too, that for Thomas, revelation takes place in the judgement and understanding, as part of the assent of faith. Revelation does not occur "on its own", as if it were a thing apart, before becoming part of human thought and experience'.[77] Thus modernity's tendency to make 'revelation' into an object has meant that it has been isolated from the 'reason' of the human subject. Consequently, the distinction between revelation and reason is simply assumed as a self-evident truth in modern theology. Theologians and biblical scholars are then required to make a choice between revelation and autonomous reason. And yet, Montag insists that this is a distortion. Revelation refers to an unveiling, an act of disclosure, in which the human subject is an active participant rather than a passive observer. If there is no-one to discern the revelation, then no revelation has taken place. Nothing has been unveiled. So 'revelation' is characterized by a relationship of communion and communication. This means that the reason of the human subject is not to be set over and against revelation. Reason is an essential element in the act of revelation. Divine disclosure does not displace or dispense with our capacity to reason. It evokes in us a greater intensity: we apprehend, we question, we discern, we contemplate the unfolding of the divine mystery. The use of the term 'mystery' is deliberate. It is no obfuscation. As Herbert McCabe, the Dominican theologian, asserts: 'mysteries are not for concealment but for revelation; it is because the revelation is so important and so profound that we have to work to understand it'.[78] Like someone watching a performance of a play like *Macbeth,* we must allow the play to take us into its mystery. We discover that in seeing it once, we have not begun to exhaust its meaning: 'To understand *Macbeth* is to reach into depths within ourselves which we did not suspect we had'.[79]

All of this depends upon the recovery of the sense that revelation is the self-disclosure of the triune God and that human beings are participants in the triune life of God. As such, we become agents in the gracious communication of God's life. This pattern of divine communication is by no means limited to the Bible. Nevertheless, it does provide the necessary starting point for thinking about the way in which God communicates through scripture. Revelation both transcends and includes Scripture. The authors, redactors, readers and interpreters of scripture all have a part to play as agents of divine communion and communication. Divine agency is not to be limited to the moment that the author wrote things down, or the closure of the canon, or the publication of a new translation, or the act of reading a passage in the context of Christian worship. We can identify an element of divine agency each step along the way.

In asserting that there is an element of divine agency in the writing, translation, canonization and interpretation of these texts, it is important to resist the temptation to 'divinise' the scriptures themselves. In *Holy Scripture: a dogmatic sketch,* John Webster rightly takes Karl Barth to task for applying the analogy of the 'hypostatic union' to the Bible. Barth asserted that Holy Scripture was 'like the unity of God and Man in Jesus Christ'.[80] Webster points out that this analogy needs to be viewed with caution: 'Like any extension of the notion of incarnation . . . the result can be Christologically disastrous, in that it may threaten the uniqueness of the Word's becoming flesh by making "incarnation" a general principle or characteristic of divine action in, through or under creaturely reality'.[81] Webster insists, rightly, that the Word made flesh and the scriptural word are in no way equivalent. To claim such an equivalence runs the risk of making the Bible into an idol. It would be quite inappropriate to speak in terms of the 'divinity' of scripture. Nevertheless, it is possible to speak of 'the mystery of human words *as* God's Word'. For Webster, this mystery depends chiefly on the notion of sanctification – only this preserves the creaturely reality of both scripture and humanity. In Webster's view, the distinction between the human and the divine must be preserved at all costs. My own view is that this mystery depends on the discovery of a more dynamic understanding of the relationship between reason and revelation and the co-inherence of nature and grace. There is a rich vein in the Christian theological tradition, including Scripture itself, that speaks of our participation in the triune life of God. John the evangelist, with his language of 'remaining' or 'abiding' in Christ, points to the reality that we are creatures who are called to abide in the life of God (Jn 15.5–10). The Pauline tradition constantly reminds us that we participate in the death and resurrection of Jesus Christ. We are drawn into the grace of the Lord Jesus Christ, the love of God and the fellowship of the Holy Spirit (2 Cor. 13.14). We find further exploration of the theology of participation in the writings of the early Church fathers. It is also as aspect of the tradition that has become a source of considerable fascination in contemporary theology. As one spiritual writer puts it, we are 'creatures who can only truly become ourselves by going beyond ourselves, can only become fully human by finding ourselves in God. There is within our nature an infinite and unbounded capacity for God'.[82]

Participation in the triune life of God provides the proper context for consideration of the doctrine of the inspiration of scripture. It is particularly important to emphasize that this involves a much more dynamic understanding of inspiration than just rather woodenly observing that the original authors were 'inspired'. As Robert Jenson observes, 'How . . . can the productions of some civil servant in the Jerusalem court, in part cribbed from Egyptian models, be God's "wisdom" for my life? Not because the Spirit provided exactly the words he one day wrote, thereby guaranteeing their wisdom and power independently of all subsequent history. Rather because the whole event, from that civil servant's memorizing Egyptian and other wise maxims in his youth to his rethinking them in maturity, to the accidents of collecting and editing and preserving, to the way in which we attend the Old Testament reading some Sunday morning, is drawn on by the Spirit's freedom'.[83] Such a dynamic account of inspiration is important for three reasons: first, it overcomes an uneasy dualism between divine and human agency in which one competes against the other; secondly, it embraces the active role of the interpreter in questioning, understanding and contemplating the biblical text and thirdly, it enables us to see that our encounter with the divine mystery cannot be separated from our participation in the triune life of God. Moreover, in this encounter, there lies the hope and the promise of our sanctification – for as Isaiah discovered, when we encounter the divine mystery, we may find that we are overwhelmed and transformed by the holiness of God (Isa. 6.1–13). It is in this sense that Christians can speak of *Holy* Scripture.

CHAPTER FIVE

Calling the Shots

In his *Commentary on Daniel,* Theodoret of Cyrus suggests that if it were easy for everyone to explain and understand the words of the divine prophets, then we might dispense with the need for commentaries and commentators. No guidance would be required. We would be able to rely completely on the perspicuity of scripture. We would sit down, read the book and the prophetic message of a book like Daniel would be abundantly clear. Theodoret recognizes, however, that the words of the prophet demand far more of us than that. He recognizes that the text can be obscure and that it can be the source of some perplexity to the person reading it. This is why we can benefit from the guidance of a commentary. In describing the role of the biblical commentator, he goes on to use the arresting image of a pearl diver. To engage properly with scripture, he says that one must get beyond the surface of the letter and penetrate to the depths. There the commentator will 'light upon the pearl of the contents hidden there'.[1]

This image of diving for pearls appears to have had a special resonance in early Syrian Christianity. It is an image which Ephrem the Syrian returns to again and again in his poetry. In one of his poems, there is an elaborate play on the Syriac word *schlihe*. It has several meanings: first, the word can mean 'stripped naked'. The word has a twofold resonance: it describes either the pearl divers, diving to the depths of the sea, or those being baptized, stripped of their clothes at baptism. Secondly, the word means 'apostles' or 'those sent'. In one of Ephrem's poems, men stripped bare dive down and draw up the Pearl, which is Christ. And Ephrem makes the point that it was not kings who first presented Christ to humanity, 'but men stripped, symbols of the apostles, poor Galilean fishermen'.[2]

The distinction between the letter and the spirit, from which Theodoret draws his distinction between the surface and the depths, comes from 2 Cor. 3.6. In *Chapter 1*, we noted Margaret Mitchell's description of this passage as the 'Magna Carta of allegorical interpretation'[3] in the Christian tradition. The complex schemes beloved of patristic and medieval exegetes, with their fourfold scales of meaning from the literal and the moral to the allegorical and the spiritual, have generated a vast tradition of biblical commentary. In surveying this material, Henri de Lubac notes that scripture is 'undecipherable in its fullness in the multiplicity of its meanings'. It is like a vast sea or an ocean of mystery: '(Scripture) will always have new mysteries to teach us, and the grandeur of these mysteries will always exceed us. This is the way with anything that is divine'.[4] And yet, the text at times appears to buckle under the weight of these proliferating interpretations. In this context, the analogy of someone diving for pearls is an instructive one. George Steiner notes that 'deep-sea divers tell of a certain depth at which the human brain becomes possessed of the illusion that natural breathing is again possible. When this happens, the diver removes his helmet and drowns. He is inebriate with a fatal enchantment called *le vertige des grandes profondeurs,* "the vertigo of the great depths". Masters of scholastic reading and explication knew this dizziness. Hence the systematic and legislative attempts at agreed finality'.[5]

The previous chapter has outlined nine different ways in which theologians have attempted to systematize or articulate the *theological* interpretation of scripture. These attempts to resist the 'fatal enchantments' of proliferating interpretations and to arrive at an appropriate and consistent pattern of construal have generated considerable debate and provoked a number of questions. As David Kelsey noted in *The Uses of Scripture in Recent Theology*, this diversity is caused in part by a range of different understandings of the authority of scripture: so, for example, we can see the clear blue water between the respective positions of John Stott and Elizabeth Schüssler Fiorenza in thinking about the question of biblical authority: if the *discrimen* one adopts in searching the scriptures is about seeking 'proof', one is going to read a passage like 1 Cor. 14.34–35 on the role of women very differently from a reader who adopts a strategy of 'resistance'. Similarly, a Protestant who adopts a 'canonical approach', with a clearly defined canon that excludes the Apocrypha, is going to be less sympathetic to a Roman Catholic, who draws on 2 Macc. 12.43–46 to explain the fact that the practice of praying for the dead forms an authentic part of the 'tradition'. At other points, these patterns of construal may not be entirely mutual exclusive. We have noted that there are overlaps between 'narrative' and 'testimony', and between 'narrative' and 'performance'. We can see a number of points where the interactions between theologians mutually inform and enrich their different ways of interpreting scripture. In these circumstances, we may be able to see considerable common ground between them. However, when we begin to explore the way in which a narrative understanding can sometimes fall prey to the temptation to reduce scripture to a single story, we also begin to see the clear differences with the 'dialogical' character of Brueggemann's emphasis on 'testimony'. In spite of the potential overlaps, divergences still remain.

Clear differences in these patterns of construal begin to emerge when we start to consider specific theological and ethical questions. More significantly, these patterns of construal bring into sharp relief some of the ongoing conflicts and disagreements within the life of the Church, particularly when those conflicts and disagreements are focussed around the interpretation of scripture. One of the profound difficulties in the life of the contemporary Church is that when these disagreements emerge, it is not always clear that a simple appeal to scripture will serve to authorize a particular theological or ethical proposal. This is not always a straightforward way of securing agreement. As David Kelsey points out, 'a theologian who marshals his proposals under the emblem "Let theology accord with scripture" does not thereby announce that he has made a methodological decision, but only that he has taken on an awesome array of methodological problems'.[6]

Theologians can explore the density of meaning within the scriptures. They can search out its mysteries and fathom its depths. But there comes a point in the interpretative enterprise when commentators can say that the text can mean *this* and *this*, but it cannot mean *that*. When profound disagreements about the interpretation of scripture emerge in the life of the Church, it is not always clear how these disagreements might be resolved. Two different commentators can interpret a text in radically different ways, each believing profoundly that in their engagement with the text they are seeking to discover God's will and truth for the church and for humanity. But however generous or gracious the conversation partners may be, both of them cannot always be right. There is a disagreement. Some kind of resolution is required. In such circumstances, how do we establish agreement? When we seek to authorize our theological proposals, to what kind of authority do we appeal? To scripture alone? To scripture and tradition? To what extent is scripture to be regarded as 'normative' for defining Christian doctrine or fashioning Christian identity? Who exactly calls the shots?

The Authority of Scripture

In *Chapter 2* we saw that the Protestant Reformation in the sixteenth and seventeenth centuries emerged out of a significant development in the reading and interpretation of scripture. Theologians and Biblical scholars returned to the Biblical texts in their original languages. They contrasted what they found in scripture with the life of the contemporary Church. The differences, which they discovered, motivated their zeal for reform. For the Reformers, it was axiomatic that the Bible disclosed the Word of God. A proper understanding of the Word of God was all that was necessary for the guidance of Christian faith. Christians who listened carefully to the Word of God in the Bible and used all their ability to read and study the texts of the Bible would find that nothing else was required. As Luther declared at the Diet of Worms: 'Unless I am convinced by the testimony of the Scriptures or by clear reason . . . I am bound by the Scriptures I have quoted'. Thus the principle of *sola scriptura* (Scripture alone) came into being.

In response to the theological programme of the Protestant Reformation, Roman Catholic theologians assembled at the Council of Trent (1545–63). They confirmed the two-source theory according to which both Scripture and Tradition together provide the sources for authentic Christian faith and theology. Thus, they contradicted the Reformers' insight that only the Bible provided a clear, coherent and sufficient guide for Christians to understand God's word and will. According to Tridentine theology, the traditions of the Church also formed an essential source for authentic Christian faith. The Magisterium (the teaching authority of the Church) remained the ultimate judge as to whether or not a particular interpretation of a biblical text was 'orthodox', i.e. in line with the officially defended understanding of the Church.

As the argument gathered pace, a number of Protestant theologians, who saw themselves as successors to Luther and Calvin, developed the doctrine of the verbal inspiration of scripture. The Bible had been dictated word for word by the Holy Spirit. It presented a compendium of Christian doctrine. This teaching was to be regarded as infallible because it was dictated by the Holy Spirit. The Bible was the Word of God. It taught a set of doctrines about God and about the world. No-one claiming to be a Christian should doubt the truthfulness of any part of the biblical text. Assent to these doctrines as revealed in scripture was demanded of every person who claimed to be a Christian. Intriguingly, Luther and Calvin did not themselves make this naïve identification of the words of scripture with the Word of God. Certainly, for Luther, the text is not the Word of God, rather it discloses the Word of God to the faithful interpreter or listener. But those who took on the mantle of these leading Reformers betrayed, somewhat ironically, one of the essential aspects of the Protestant Reformation, namely the freedom of every Christian critically to study the biblical texts in the vernacular. The Christian was not to interpret the text and thereby encounter the Word. The Christian was to receive and accept the Word as it was written down in black and white.

Such a rigid Biblicism was incapable of conversation with natural science and any alternative account of the world. It reinforced the distinction between revelation and reason. As time continued, and as advances in the sciences and the arts were made, this distinction became more and more marked. Isolated from a more nuanced tradition of reading and interpretation, and setting its stall in opposition to the world of scientific discovery, the authority of scripture came more and more into question. We see the legacy of this worldview in the attitudes of modern fundamentalism. Indeed, a commitment to the doctrine of biblical inerrancy is one of the defining features of Christian fundamentalism. Of course, contemporary Christians who wish to assert the centrality of scripture in determining the faith and morals of the Church are not all fundamentalists. But the difficulty for many of them is that the rhetoric of biblical inerrancy and biblical infallibility has accentuated the sense that the Bible possesses only a residual authority. Its authority has been contested and disputed to such a degree that the claims of biblical inerrancy are no longer perceived as intellectually honest or credible. Is it still possible to speak of the 'authority of scripture' in a way which is compelling and persuasive?

In a series of lectures given at the University of Oxford, John Barton made a major contribution to this debate. In *People of the Book? The Authority of the Bible in Christianity,* Barton argued that Biblicism – and the corresponding crisis of authority it provoked – was partly a consequence of attributing an inappropriate kind of authority to the Bible. He was particularly dissatisfied with the naiveté of Biblicist understandings of the authority and inspiration of the Bible. He set out from the beginning to plan a raid on Biblicist and fundamentalist arguments in order to construct a theory of biblical authority, which we need not be fundamentalists to hold.

Barton argues that there has always been a tension within the Christian Church between the new Christian faith and the old scriptures of Jewish belief. His evidence for this argument lies within the New Testament and the early Church Fathers, particularly Irenaeus of Lyons. He goes on to assert that 'Christians are people who have a book, in order to be able to proclaim their freedom from it; yet the character of that freedom is deeply shaped by the book from which they have been freed, and it is the God who gave the book who also gives the freedom'.[7] Thus Barton's exploration of the concept of authority begins with this assertion of freedom. He makes the points that any attempt to define or propose what we mean by the word *authority* has to be set out in the light of the fundamental insight that Christians proclaim a God who sets us free from the bondage of fear and sin and poverty. It is intriguing to note that when the people were astounded at Jesus' teaching in the synagogues 'because he spoke with authority' (Lk. 4.32), Jesus has just quoted a series of texts from the prophets about proclaiming good news to the poor, release to the captives, recovery of sight to the blind and freedom for the oppressed. It is in the context of proclaiming freedom that the authority of Jesus is recognized. This observation provides a telling counterpoint to those who might be tempted to use the scriptures for authoritarian ends: when we appeal to the authority of scripture, are we appealing to an injunction or a story that offers the possibility of freedom and liberation, or are we colluding with the forces of oppression and slavery? Barton applies three simple tests to the notion of biblical authority. He suggests that we can think of the Bible as 'evidence', as 'a source of correct theology' and as 'a classic' of literature. First, Barton looks at the Bible as *evidence*. Barton appeals to the writings of Irenaeus. These writings reveal that for Irenaeus the important thing about the Gospels is that they provide a reliable historical source. He may not have appealed to the same conventions of historical scholarship, but he finds in scripture real and authentic testimony about Jesus Christ. Thus the authority of the Gospels is treated as being the authority of the apostles who are supposed to have written them: it is as these men's testimony that the Gospels are to be believed. To put this in a wider sense, the Bible has authority because it is the earliest and most compelling evidence about Jesus: 'The authority of the New Testament for modern believers is not that it enables them to be supernaturally sure of alleged events which they would otherwise entertain well-founded doubts about. On the contrary, the New Testament is authoritative because it provides at least some of the early evidence with which it is possible to judge how far the Christian faith really does have a secure historical foundation'.[8]

The second element in Barton's argument sees the authority of the Bible as a source book for correct theology. To call the Bible theological evidence is to say that Christians can appeal to it for insight into the nature and purposes of God. As David Kelsey suggests, we can speak of the Bible being used to 'authorise' a theological statement or assertion. This can range from 'proof-texts' to some of the more extended forms of the theological interpretation of scripture which we have explored in the previous chapter. The basic point is that the Bible gives expression to a relationship between ourselves and God. Significantly, that relationship would have existed and would have continued even if the Bible had never been written. Again this is a point made by

Irenaeus, 'Even if the apostles had not left us any writings, would it not be necessary to follow the course of the tradition which they handed down to those to whom they committed the churches?' The Bible serves to authorize the faith that has been handed down through the centuries.

Finally, Barton describes the Bible as a 'classic' of literature. Like any classic text, it possesses a certain authority. It has a timeless quality which speaks to each and every generation. Barton borrows from George Steiner four stages of analysis which tell us whether a text is a classic or not: the first stage is an act of trust towards the text. It rests on an assumption that there is something worth understanding. We may find with some texts that this is a mistake. Some texts will only enable us to plumb the depths of shallowness. The second stage comes when we recognize that there is more here than meets the eye. Then we question the text, we subject it to scrutiny and try to grasp its meaning. The third stage is when we attempt to appropriate it into our own way of thinking. And yet, if the text is to resist being completely appropriated and manipulated by us, then there must be a fourth stage: the reader recognizes that the text possesses an integrity of its own. It will neither totally resist an alien culture not be subsumed by it. If the text possesses this kind of resistance and integrity, then it is a 'classic'. Barton argues that the Bible conforms with this definition of a classic. In this respect, it possesses authority.

In each of these senses, the Bible is recognized as having authority, but that authority is carefully circumscribed. The significance of Barton's argument lies in the fact that he locates the authority of scripture in specific features of the text: it presents evidence, it provides a resource, it constitutes a 'classic'. In each case, Barton's concern is to demonstrate that the authority of scripture arises out of a commitment to *truth*: the Bible provides evidence about Christian origins that we can trust, it challenges us with profound questions about God and humanity, and it has something fresh to say to each and every generation. As Barton puts it simply and succinctly, 'Truth plain and simple is better . . . than infallibility'.[9]

Tom Wright adopts a similar approach in raiding Biblicist arguments in order to present a coherent account of the authority of scripture. He argues that claims about the 'authority of scripture'

need to be considered in the light of what scripture itself says
about questions of authority. He begins by acknowledging that
in Rom. 13.1, St Paul declares that all authority is from God. He
notes that Jn 19.11 records that at his trial Jesus responds to Pilate
with the words, 'You would have no power over me unless it had
been given you from above', and that in Matthew's account of
the great commission, Jesus says, 'all authority in heaven and on
earth has been given to me' (Mt. 28.18). Wright argues that these
texts demonstrate that the phrase 'the authority of scripture' only
makes sense as a shorthand for speaking of 'the authority of the
triune God, exercised somehow *through* scripture'.[10] Moreover,
scripture points beyond itself to the Word made flesh: 'When John
declares that "in the beginning was the word", he does not reach a
climax with "and the word was written down" but "and the word
became flesh"'.[11] The Epistle to the Hebrews contains a similar
statement when it says: 'Long ago God spoke to our ancestors in
many and various ways by the prophets, but in these last days he
has spoken to us by a Son' (Heb. 1.1–2). The incarnation is God's
Word to us. Moreover, the testimony of Jn 8.39–40 suggests that
Jesus is the one who speaks the truth from God.

In presenting this anthology of texts, Wright is constructing
a very similar form of argument to Barton. He is using a series
of texts from scripture to provide *proof* to demonstrate that any
reference to 'the authority of scripture' must be a shorthand
for 'the authority of God *through* scripture'. Wright employs a
familiar Biblicist form of argument in order to subvert it and
present a more nuanced account of the authority of scripture. He
is suggesting that those who attribute an inappropriate kind of
authority to the Bible do not take sufficiently seriously what the
Bible says about its own authority. It has far more to say about the
authority of God. Moreover, he recognizes that the question of
authority is ultimately bound up with the question of truth.

But in what sense is the authority of God exercised *through*
scripture? For Wright, God's authority is best understood within
the context of the Kingdom of God. He recognizes that there is a
tension implicit in this statement. When the biblical writers speak
of the sovereignty of God, they are acknowledging the sense in
which God has always been sovereign over creation *and* at the
same time they are describing their belief that God's kingdom is
breaking afresh into a world dominated by sin, corruption and

idolatry to transform and renew the whole of creation. So what exactly is the role of scripture in this process of transformation and renewal? In response to this question, Wright asserts that 'scripture is there to be a means of God's action in and through us'.[12] For Wright, this divine action refers to the Holy Spirit at work as people read, study, teach and preach scripture. The purpose of this divine action is 'to energize, enable and direct the outgoing mission of the church'.[13]

There are clear resonances here with my observations in the previous chapter about the central importance of our participation in the triune life of God. If this is the starting point for the theological interpretation of scripture, it is also the starting point for talking about the authority of scripture. And yet, Wright is cautious about suggesting that this means that the Bible is simply a devotional aid. He recognizes the importance of scripture 'as the fuel and raw material of personal prayer, adoration, meditation and so on',[14] and he can attest to the value of spiritual practices like *lectio divina,* the Evangelical 'quiet time' and the spiritual exercises of Ignatius of Loyola. Nevertheless, he is anxious about confusing devotion with authority. He realizes that all sorts of things happen in prayer, and that even as we reflect on a passage of scripture, human beings still have an extraordinary capacity for self-deception and deceit. The devotional reading of scripture needs to be accompanied by the reading of scripture in the context of public worship and by demonstrating that the teaching and preaching of scripture lies at the heart of the Church's life. These are the practices which attest to the fact that a Christian community takes the authority of scripture seriously. It is a perspective also shared by Robert Jenson: 'The churches most faithful to Scripture are not those that legislate the most honorific propositions about Scripture but those that most often and thoughtfully read and hear it'.[15]

Scripture and the Church

The authority of scripture rests not so much on an intrinsic characteristic of the text as on the way in which a particular community reads and construes it. Partly as a response to the hermeneutical explorations of Hans-Georg Gadamer and Stanley Fish, theologians have come to recognize that the hermeneutic of the community engaged in reading, its self-understanding and identity are crucial elements in the interpretative process. Determining what might be a valid reading depends not so much on some inherent aspect of the text itself, but on the identity of the one who is doing the reading – the interpreter, the commentator. We see this emphasis in particular in two important and significant contributions to the theological interpretation of scripture: Stephen Fowl, *Engaging Scripture*, and Francis Watson, *Text, Church and World*. Fowl begins with the assertion that 'the Bible, for Christians, is their scripture. As scripture, the Bible provides a normative standard for the faith, practice, and worship of Christian communities'.[16] He presents a 'performative' understanding of the Church's interpretation of scripture. Christians are called 'not merely to generate various scriptural interpretations but to embody those interpretations as well'.[17] Scripture 'functions as a normative standard for faith and practice'. Implicit in these statements is a basic assumption that scripture is authoritative for Christians. However, when he considers the authority of scripture in more detail, he acknowledges that the assertion 'scripture is authoritative' is not an assertion about a property of the text: 'Christians should best understand claims about scripture's authority as establishing and governing certain networks of relationships'.[18] From Fowl's essay, it is clear that he has in mind a number of textual relationships, including the relationship between the canonical form of scripture and its pre-history (this includes some of the ecclesial disagreements over the contents of the canon), as well as the relationship between the Bible and other texts in the tradition that offer interpretative remarks about scripture (this includes Irenaeus of Lyons' articulation of the 'Rule of Faith'). Fowl suggests that this rule sets out 'boundaries within which interpretation must operate if Christians are to read scripture properly'.[19]

This argument alerts us to two significant issues: first, when Christians read scripture, their interpretation is informed by a series of practices (for example, baptism and eucharist) and a body of doctrine; secondly, their engagement with scripture is 'part of the prior and ongoing life of a particular tradition'.[20] The 'doctrinal emphasis' characteristic of Fowl's work in *Engaging Scripture* reflects the debate generated by Francis Watson's *Text, Church and World*. The idea that Christian doctrine 'has a hermeneutical function' in the interpretation of scripture was central to Watson's argument. He wrote in order to present a more fruitful conversation between the disciplines of biblical studies and systematic theology. He was suspicious of biblical scholarship's commitment to 'secularity'. He argued that it was necessary to interpret scripture *theologically*. Like Fowl, he held to the conviction that 'the primary reading community within which the biblical text is located is the Christian church'.[21] If one were to engage in a theological reading of scripture and if that theology were to be 'Christian', then 'the ecclesial community must be seen as its primary point of reference'.[22] Those engaged in the theological interpretation of scripture had a responsibility to the community of faith. He argued that the theological interpretation of scripture also contained resources for criticism and reflection which did not simply rely on the conventions of literary theory and historical criticism. Scripture contained within it a capacity for 'self-criticism'. To sustain this assertion, Watson pointed to the distinction between 'Law' and 'Gospel' in the writings of Paul. He extrapolated from this antithesis the following statement: 'Since theological interpretation must distinguish the law from the gospel within the biblical text, the decision to work with the canonical form does not render the text immune from criticism'.[23] Watson conceded that there was a certain amount of fluidity about this distinction, and that the judgements offered by those engaged in theological interpretation would require discrimination and discernment. Above all, he asserted that this pattern of discernment needed to take place 'in dialogue with others'. For Watson, this dialogue referred not only to the ecclesial community but also to those beyond it, the 'world'. One can see some significant overlaps with later developments in the canonical approach of Brevard Childs in Watson's thinking. Both emphasize the final canonical form of the text. Both argue that biblical interpreters have a responsibility to the community of faith. They part company at this point: while Childs is content that the community of faith has all the resources it needs to interpret the text as sacred scripture, Watson recognizes that 'insights originating in the secular world outside the Christian community can have a positive role in assisting the community's understanding of holy scripture'.[24] Through a detailed exploration of what the Bible says about the role of the Spirit within the world, Watson argued that these insights originating in the secular world were animated by the Holy Spirit. This was one of the ways 'in which the Spirit leads the community out of distorted and inadequate positions into all the truth (cf. Jn 16.13)'.[25]

In spite of the generosity of Watson's argument, Philip Davies, an avowedly 'secular' critic, did not exactly see himself engaged in this kind of enterprise. While he was happy to concede that the religious institutions of Judaism and Christianity had a claim on their bibles, he was conscious of the fact that the books of scripture were also read by readers who would not necessarily think of themselves as engaged in an 'ecclesial reading'. Moreover, he argued that 'there is no realistic hope of imposing an ecclesial interpretation outside the ecclesial domain'.[26] For Davies, 'confessional discourse' had no place in the context of the academy. It was to be resisted at all costs. And yet, Davies forgets the extent to which the 'criticism', which characterizes the life of the academy has been shaped by theological debate and controversy. These debates have served to animate the development of critical inquiry. At almost every turn, they have been informed by the methods of historical criticism and literary theory.

Watson's claim that the Christian church was the 'primary reading community' of the biblical text sounded too proprietorial to Davies. It provoked in him the rather curmudgeonly question: 'Whose Bible is it anyway?' The irony is that Watson had accepted – willingly – that there were other interested parties engaged in the interpretation of the Bible. He was also keen to explore ways in which the ecclesial community might reflect on this phenomenon from a more theological perspective. Indeed, one of the most delicate questions in the theological interpretation of scripture is the issue of recognizing that the books of the Hebrew Bible are shared between Jews and Christians. Indeed, there are also a number of Jewish scholars – Amy-Jill Levene and Daniel Boyarin – who have made a significant contribution to New Testament studies. Moreover, the practice of 'scriptural reasoning' in which Jews, Christians and Muslims read their respective scriptures together has offered opportunities for those engaged in the theological interpretation of scripture to learn from the insights of people of other faiths. Watson is quite right to emphasize the importance and significance of engaging with insights that are generated beyond the confines of the ecclesial community and to recognize that the Holy Spirit may well be at work in them.

A rather more telling criticism of Watson's book, however, came from Christopher Rowland. While Rowland welcomed the fact that Watson had sought 'to establish a theologically credible biblical hermeneutic, no longer grounded in the obsolescent verities of a hegemonic historicism, but in the richness of Trinitarian theology',[27] he wondered if the book sometimes drifted into 'a stratospheric idealism away from the real world of conflict and contradiction'.[28] Put simply, Rowland wants to know whose theology and whose church Watson was speaking for. Indeed, Watson does not spell this out. In his response to Rowland, he resists any further disclosure: he regards such biographical details as irrelevant. He is not writing an autobiography. Consequently, his book addresses the life of an ecclesial community at a more theoretical level. It presents a very different kind of prospectus from some of the reports and studies of biblical interpretation commissioned by churches in recent years: for example, *The Interpretation of the Bible in the Church* (1993) published by the Pontifical Biblical Commission of the Roman Catholic Church, *A Lamp to my Feet and a Light to my Path: The Nature of Authority and the Place of the Bible in the Methodist Church* (1998), and the *Windsor Report* (2004) commissioned by the Anglican Communion.

These reports were often commissioned to respond to particular issues or concerns in the life of an ecclesial community: the hermeneutics of liberation theology, the baptism of infants, the role of women in ministry, the use of inclusive language, environmental justice, the remarriage of divorced persons, or issues in human sexuality. It would be easy to assert that Watson's failure to address the contingencies and conflicts of a particular ecclesial community in wrestling with the authority of scripture speaks of a more general 'ecclesial deficit' in his work. One might lay this charge at the feet of most of the theologians described in the previous chapter. My own view is that critics ought to be cautious about presenting such a charge. One of the characteristics of the study of ecclesiology is that there is often a tension between the church as an institution, which we experience, and the church as an eschatological reality, which is a gift from God. Watson finds himself caught in the strings of this tension. When he speaks of the Church as an ecclesial community, he does not disclose his confessional sympathies explicitly. In this respect, his writing reflects the conventions of the systematic theologian rather than those of the practical or ecumenical theologian. As Stephen Fowl remarks, 'recognition of and attention to the purposes for which Christians interpret scripture seem to play little role in the body of the text. Neither do the particular shape and practices of real Christian communities play a significant role. This results in a book that reads very much like a contemporary systematic theology'.[29] Rather waspishly, he notes that Watson's commitment to an 'interdisciplinary' approach only serves to traverse the disciplines of biblical studies and systematic theology.

Stephen Fowl's exploration of the theological interpretation of scripture leads very quickly from an emphasis on the significance of the community engaged in reading the text to the assertion that this community embodies a tradition of reading and interpretation through its ongoing reflection and practice. This reinforces the sense that confessional loyalties are significant. They shape the way in which a particular theologian will approach the relationship between scripture and tradition. One of the recurring motifs of the arguments over the relationship between scripture and tradition relates to the question of which of these has priority. Luther's assertion of the principle of *sola scriptura* suggests that Scripture always had priority. For the Reformers, scripture disclosed the Word of God. It was therefore prior to and independent of the Church: the proclamation of the Word of God created the Church. The difficulty with this assertion is that the earliest Christians worshipped God, celebrated the presence of the risen Christ and established churches across the Mediterranean world without so much as a copy of the New Testament.[30] Indeed, the writings, which make up the Old and New Testaments of the Christian scriptures, emerged in a variety of different contexts over a long period of time. This suggests that there is a more complex relationship between scripture and tradition. The Church seems to have exercised some considerable influence over the creation of the canon. Thus in considering the relationship between scripture and tradition, we are left wrestling with the celebrated dilemma: which came first, the chicken or the egg?

While we might expect Protestant theologians to hold rigidly to the principle of *sola scriptura* and Roman Catholic theologians to defend the two sources of scripture and tradition, the truth is that the documents of the Second Vatican Council contain some surprises. The Constitution *Dei Verbum* presents a rather fascinating revision of the two-source theory: 'Scripture is, as it were, the soul of theology'. As Karl Rahner points out in *Foundations of Christian Faith*, 'the Second Vatican Council refused to make tradition a second source for us today which exists by itself alongside scripture, a source which testifies to individual, material contents of faith which have no foundation at all in scripture. However much the more precise relationship between scripture and tradition still needs a great deal of further theological clarification, it is perhaps obvious from what has already been said earlier that the "scripture alone" of the Reformation is no longer a doctrine which distinguishes and separates the Churches'. And yet, although this Constitution was enthusiastically endorsed by the young Professor Josef Ratzinger when it was first published, the former Pope has disclosed that as an adviser to the Council he was rather more cautious at the time it was being drafted. In particular, he perceived a weakness in its theology of revelation. For Benedict, revelation is a living reality which cannot be enclosed in or defined by a text. In his view, tradition is 'that part of revelation that goes above and beyond scripture and cannot be comprehended within a code of formulas'.[31] These words suggest a more dynamic relationship between scripture and tradition in the life of the Church. Indeed, the idea that tradition 'goes above and beyond' scripture appears to hint at a reconfiguration of the authority of scripture in relation to the tradition. It sounds very much like a subtle restatement of the two-source theory of scripture and tradition.

Attempting to assert the priority of either scripture or tradition is one of those arguments, which is unlikely to be resolved in our lifetime. I am not convinced that it is entirely helpful to settle the argument in these terms. There is an important sense in which both scripture and the church are 'mutually constitutive' of one another. This does not mean that they can be collapsed into one another or that they are identical. It might be more helpful to think of the relationship between scripture and the church in terms of the strands of a double helix. Each of the elements remains distinct but they share a number of characteristics. So how might we describe the characteristics shared by both scripture and the Church?

In the Nicene Creed, the church is described as 'one, holy, catholic and apostolic'. These traditional marks of the church describe what it is the vocation of the Church to be. We see intimations and signs of these characteristics in our experience of the church, but there is also a sense in which they are only partially reflected in the life of the church. We affirm the unity of the church, but we also acknowledge that that unity continues to be vitiated by the divisions among Christians. We attest to the holiness of the Church, and yet at times it appears to be completely compromised. We can bear witness to the catholicity of the church, and yet there are times when institutional racism and sexism have compromised its witness to the universality of God's offer of salvation. We can speak of the apostolicity of the church, and our common life can be consumed by profound disagreement about the way in which our faithfulness to the mark of apostolicity can be expressed. When we describe these marks of the church, we are describing an entity which is caught between the 'already' and the 'not yet' of eschatological fulfilment. We are describing the vocation of the Church. These words describe a future hope.

The value of acknowledging this tension is that it addresses some of the underlying issues in the debate between Francis Watson and Christopher Rowland. It enables us to consider carefully the way in which our use of these terms in relation to the church embrace both the present reality of the church as we experience it and the future ideal for which we may dare to hope. But I also want to go one step further. I want to suggest – tentatively – that these distinctive marks of the church characterize our interpretation of scripture. They remind us of the authentic marks of the theological interpretation of scripture in the life of the Church.

When we read the scriptures, we are reminded of the apostolic witness of the first apostles. We are reminded of their testimony, testimony that is animated by faith and trust in God. This emphasis on apostolic testimony stood at the heart of the teaching of Irenaeus of Lyons. When we read the scriptures, do we take the mark of *apostolicity* seriously? Are we willing to pay attention to the faith which animated this apostolic testimony? Are we willing to engage with the methods of historical criticism truthfully and honestly? Similarly, it is helpful to think of the theological interpretation of scripture in the light of the *catholicity* of the scriptural witness.

And yet, this is a term, which is often misunderstood. It is a word which has a much broader resonance than the 'tribalisms' of the contemporary Church would perhaps suggest. In the eighteenth of his lectures to catechumens, Cyril of Jerusalem identifies five meanings for the word as applied to the Church: first, it is *catholic* or universal in the sense that it extends over the whole world; secondly, it teaches universally and completely the whole truth; thirdly, it makes holiness possible for every kind of person; fourthly, it treats and heals all the sicknesses and sins of human beings; and finally, it displays the fullest possible variety of human virtue and spiritual gift. Cyril's five definitions point to the great variety and complexity of human reality. We can speak of the *catholicity* of scripture in two different ways: first, we can respond to the universality of Cyril's vision simply by noting the continuous and continuing enterprise of translating the scriptures into every single language on the planet. This programme of translation is a constitutive element of the ongoing mission of the Church. Secondly, when we read the scriptures with a *catholic* sensibility, we are committing ourselves to recognize the way in which scripture continues to animate and transform human culture. As Marie-Dominique Chenu suggests, scripture offers not only the resources for fashioning Christian identity. It also offers a point of mediation between human culture and divine truth. The language and imagery of the Bible embrace the full range of human longing and experience, and it provides the resources to enable us to speak about it in the light of the Word of God. This involves telling the whole truth about God and the whole truth about ourselves as human beings, men and women. Of course, telling the whole truth takes time. It is not simple or straightforward. It is sometimes painful, sometimes rather chaotic. It is an enterprise which takes a lifetime. It speaks implicitly of struggle and bewilderment, as we engage in an almost endless labour of interpretation. But it also speaks of the passion, joy and delight as we attempt to articulate our response to God's call. Moreover, to speak of the *holiness* of scripture is to acknowledge that in reading scripture we may find ourselves participating in the triune life of God. People may read the Bible for all sorts of different reasons and with a host of different interests, but to acknowledge the *holiness* of scripture is to express a willingness to read it theologically. In doing so, we may embrace a wide variety of different patterns of construal, but whatever the method or technique we adopt, to acknowledge the *holiness* of scripture is to recognize that scripture is a site of divine disclosure.

But of course, while these three traditional distinct marks of the Church – apostolicity, catholicity and holiness – describe the vocation of the Church and while we may be ready to acknowledge that they are reflected in our reading of scripture, the fact remains that when Christians say the Nicene Creed, they say, 'We believe in *one*, holy, catholic and apostolic Church'. What does the vocation of the Church to be *one* tell us about the way in which the church reads scripture?

Conflict, Consensus and Conversation

The Gospel of John tells us that Jesus prayed that his disciples 'may be one' (Jn 17.11). The painful reality is that this unity continues to elude the churches. Moreover, competing interpretations of scripture often contribute to this lack of unity. Augustine acknowledged in Book 12 of his *Confessions* that this was a reality that he had to grapple with in his own time and context. He sought to show that much of the time different interpretations of scripture were not necessarily mutually exclusive. He was willing to countenance the idea that there might be 'a diversity of truths'. Nevertheless, he also concedes that there were also interpretations which were not true. Inevitably, in such situations, conflict is likely to arise. How do we begin to tackle and resolve the interpretative conflicts that have emerged in the course of Christian history and which persist even to this day? There are, I think, two principal strategies for addressing interpretative conflict in the life of the church: consensus and conversation.

Consensus is an attractive word and perhaps an attractive prospect. Certainly, the desire for a shared consensus appears to have unity as one of its main concerns. We see an emphasis on a consensual approach to resolving disputes in various forms of church government: synods, conventions, conferences and councils. There is the recognition here that there may be a place for slightly divergent readings of scripture, but there is also a need to refute and exclude deviant and heterodox readings of scripture. It is at this point that people start looking for criteria of validity, particular rules to which we can appeal to decide whether something is an appropriate reading or not. We see precisely this approach in *The Interpretation of the Bible in the Church*, published by the Pontifical Biblical Commission of the Roman Catholic Church in 1993. This document refers to the 'limits of actualisation' in the interpretation of the Bible. The first limit or criterion they proposed was *the avoidance of tendentious interpretations.* Immediately, we are confronted with the problem of tactical definition. How does one define a 'tendentious' interpretation? It appears that the Commission has in mind those readings which 'instead of being docile to the text make use of it only for their own narrow purposes (as is the case in the actualization practised by certain sects, for example Jehovah's Witnesses)'. In spite of the rhetoric at this point, it seems clear that the Commission is suggesting that an interpretation should be capable of argued defence and patient of reasoned elaboration. This would mean appealing to a host of different historical and literary critical methods of interpretation. The second criterion proposed is *an interpretation at variance with the fundamental orientations of the biblical text.* An interpretation of scripture should respect the integrity of the text. This means that from a theological perspective, purely secular readings of the text, which have absolutely no interest in the question of God, are problematic. They ignore the fundamental orientation of the text. And yet the interesting point for discussion here is whether those engaged in the theological interpretation of scripture can learn from those committed to a non-theological or purely secular reading of the text. Little space is left for such a conversation. The third criterion proposed by the Commission was *consistency with evangelical justice and charity.* The members of the Commission wanted to insist that the use of the Bible to justify racial segregation, anti-Semitism or sexism whether on the part of men or of women should be rejected.

The latter point made by the commission in relation to sexism raises an interesting question. In drafting an earlier section in the report on feminist approaches to the interpretation of scripture, it is clear that some disagreement arose about the wording of the final paragraph of this section. Members of the Commission had to take a vote, and the section includes the following footnote: 'Out of nineteen votes case, the text of this last paragraph received eleven in favour, four against and there were four abstentions. Those who voted against it asked that the result of the vote be published along with the text. The commission consented to this'. It is not clear from the report whether the Commission voted on every paragraph, or whether a vote was the only way of containing the conflict that had emerged at this point. However, it is clear that this little footnote enables us to see one of the problems with a consensual approach. The language of consensus can often be used to conceal the voice of a minority or the power dynamics and ideological processes at work within a community. Four people voted against the inclusion of this paragraph, and four people abstained. It is not clear what their concerns were, and it is unlikely that we will ever know. But it is instructive that even in a document that presents a series of 'limits of actualisation' for the interpretation of scripture, the participants were not able to come to a common mind about the wording of their report.

Greater transparency might be offered by the introduction of another strategy, namely, conversation. For David Tracy, a conversation need not be a confrontation or a debate. He describes it as 'questioning itself'. Good questions lie at the heart of a fruitful conversation. Tracy's basic concern is to recognize our capacity for distorting meaning both in communication and in interpretation. The concept of conversation does not imply either an easy consensus or an agreement to differ. Conversation implies a willingness to resist what one perceives as the distortions in the other's communication and interpretation. The model of conversation rests on some hard rules: 'say only what you mean; say it as accurately as you can; listen and respect what the other says, however different or other; be willing to correct or defend your opinions if challenged by the conversation partner; be willing to argue if necessary, to confront if demanded, to endure necessary conflict, to change your mind if the evidence suggests it and if your integrity demands it'.[32] Of course, 'conversation' might be regarded as far too genial a metaphor for some profound differences and real conflicts in the life of the church. Nevertheless, it is a metaphor which alerts us to the importance of communication. We do not always communicate and speak clearly. We are not always alert to the fact that our acts or thoughts may be grounded in prejudice, or willing to allow that our prejudices need to be open to critical analysis. Moreover, asking serious questions of both the text that we are reading, of our conversation partners and of ourselves, can

offer the starting point for recognizing that our interests in the
text may be motivated not simply by the desire for understanding,
but also be power, fear and anxiety. Such conversation is about
unmasking the prejudices and resisting the distortions of the
conversation partner. In this respect, it is motivated by a profound
commitment to truth.

Consensus and conversation are by no means mutually
exclusive, and the emphasis given to one in relation to the other will
depend largely on questions of ecclesial governance and decision-
making. But in a sense there is nothing new about hermeneutical
and interpretative disagreement. In the ancient world, all sorts
of disagreements emerged about the interpretation of texts,
particularly legal texts. In *Hermeneutics and the Rhetorical
Tradition*, Kathy Eden points out that teachers of rhetoric found in
the concept of 'equity' a useful way of balancing the letter of a text
and the needs of a new situation, for adapting and accommodating
the original text to new and unforeseen circumstances. One of the
ways in which those who had benefitted from a good rhetorical
education would do this was by appealing to 'the whole' or to 'the
spirit' in order to resolve a dispute about a specific controversial
passage within a text. Eden argues that Augustine sees love
or *caritas* as a Christianised form of equity: '*caritas* . . . is the
summa of all scriptural teaching (cf. 1.35.39)'. It revealed the
true intention of the written words of scripture, and expressed
the purpose of the whole witness of scripture, rather than just a
single part: '*caritas* represents the Christianization of *aequitas,* or
equity. Like equity, charity corrects the rigidity of the law – here
Jewish law – by judging the agent's intentions rather than his or her
actions. Like equity, charity accommodates human weakness, not
only measuring any single event against the quality of our lives as
a whole but also pitying and pardoning errors'.[33] In other words,
the capacity to foster love is the true test of faithful and truthful
biblical interpretation. Margaret Mitchell argues that this principle
of charity finds it origins and antecedents in the writings of St Paul
the Apostle: 'Everything, beloved, is for the sake of building you
up' (2 Cor. 12.19).

In his exploration of the nature of biblical interpretation,
Augustine insists that beyond the complexity of the rhetorical
techniques and devices which we might employ in reading
scripture, the whole purpose of the law and the fulfilment of

the holy scriptures is to love God and to love your neighbour as yourself.[34] If we were to extend Augustine's insights and consider the strategies of consensus and conversation in the light of the demand of charity, we can see an allusion to this demand in the Pontifical Biblical Commission's insistence on *consistency with evangelical justice and charity*. This alerts us to the fact that great care must be taken in determining what the particular 'limits of actualisation' or the appropriate criteria for the theological interpretation of scripture might be. The tradition suggests that 'charity' or 'love' is an essential virtue in this enterprise. Moreover, however 'genial' the metaphor of conversation may be, we can also see that constructive conversation demands the virtue of charity. If we always seek to think the worst of our conversation partners, or to trip them up, or to dismiss whatever they say, we will probably reveal that we have little to share about what it means to love our neighbours as ourselves. We may need to discover a more irenic way of exploring the way in which Christians reconcile their differences in the reading and interpretation of scripture than simply posing the question, 'Who calls the shots?' Like Theodoret of Cyrus, we may discover that in order to fathom the depths and discover the riches of what the scriptures have to offer, we may need the help of those around us. The theological interpretation of scripture is not something that we can arrive at on our own. We need conversation partners. We need others to ensure that we do not succumb to the 'vertigo of the depths'.

CHAPTER SIX

Conclusion

In the measure that our mind is renewed by meditation on Scripture, the very face of Scripture begins to be renewed, and the beauty of the holier meaning somehow begins to grow with our own growth.

JOHN CASSIAN[1]

I am conscious of the fact that a number of books have been published about biblical hermeneutics in recent years. Indeed, one might be forgiven for asking whether we really need another one. In a sense, this observation demonstrates that there is a need for a volume of this kind. The theological interpretation of scripture has become a rather bewildering and perplexing field of study. In this volume, I have attempted to present a brief survey of the principal issues and the contributions made by some of the most influential voices. My purpose has been to enable readers to approach the theological interpretation of scripture with much greater confidence.

But what does the theological interpretation of scripture look like in practice? This is a serious question. When theologians start speaking of the 'obsolescent verities of hegemonic historicism' or of 'the modernist critical excesses of the twentieth century', one might imagine that this means that the theological interpretation of scripture is about nothing other that the rejection of 300 hundred years of scholarly inquiry. We can forget everything that our forebears learned through the lens of historical criticism and literary theory. All we need to do is inhabit the citadel of Nicene orthodoxy and we will have all the resources we will ever need for the theological interpretation of scripture.

This illustrates the dangers of overstating the case. Few if any of the critics who have made the statements quoted in the previous paragraph would concur with the idea that historical criticism is dispensable in the reading and interpretation of scripture. Indeed, I have argued that the tools of historiography and literary criticism have been indispensable from the very beginnings of biblical interpretation. But I have also argued that if the idea that scripture is a site of divine disclosure is to be taken seriously, then we need to recognize that those engaged in the theological interpretation of scripture are called to participate in the Trinitarian life of God. The Bible is not 'Scripture' in and of itself. It becomes 'Scripture' when we read it in the power of the Holy Spirit and encounter the Word of God. Does this mean that cultivating the devotional reading of scripture, such as the monastic practice of *Lectio divina* or the 'spiritual exercises' of Ignatius Loyola, is all that is required for readers to recover the practice of reading scripture theologically?

To pose the question in this way draws attention to a profound tension in Western consciousness between criticism and the imagination. We find further illustration of this tension in a recent book by Dale Martin on the *Pedagogy of the Bible: An Analysis and Proposal*. Martin is concerned about the woeful lack of biblical literacy among preachers and clergy, and about the fact that many well educated Christians have not been taught to think theologically in an adult way. For Martin, the problem is that 'most theological students are not taught theological hermeneutics – that is, they are not taught in explicit and self-conscious ways how to interpret Scripture Christianly'.[2] Martin presents a series of proposals about the teaching of the Bible in theological education. In his survey of ten seminaries in North America, he notes the pre-eminence given to historical criticism in biblical interpretation, but he also laments the lack of awareness of more recent developments in the fields of hermeneutics and literary theory. Moreover, in his visits to interview faculty and students, he discerned a poor grasp of theological hermeneutics, an inability to make connections between biblical knowledge and theological argument and a failure to integrate biblical studies with other areas of the curriculum.

Martin proposes that scripture should be at the heart of a seminary's curriculum. He notes Dom Jean Leclercq's insistence that the centrality of Scripture was not invented at the end of the middle ages – the principal task of the patristic tradition 'was to transmit and explain the Bible'.[3] He argues that theological education needs to reclaim this heritage – and some of its practices as well. This includes learning to encounter scripture through worship and the liturgy, and cultivating devotional practices like *Lectio divina* and the 'spiritual exercises'. He suggests that students might be introduced to the practice of *Lectio divina* before 'encountering the more technical method of historical criticism or other critical approaches to the Bible'. This would serve to enable seminarians to imagine Scripture differently and 'to imagine Christian ways of reading and interpreting Scripture that move beyond modernist methods'.[4] But he does not suggest that an understanding of historical criticism, literary theory and hermeneutics should be dispensable. Indeed, Martin insists on the continued relevance of historical criticism and the need for seminarians to be familiar with modern techniques of exegesis. Intriguingly, he sees the value of historical criticism in challenging students who arrive at seminary with an approach to biblical interpretation, which is self-serving:

> Churches often tame Scripture or ideologically construe its meaning so that it affirms rather than challenges their beliefs, prejudices, and even complicity with oppressive powers. In less ominous cases, students simply read Scripture so that it teaches rather innocuous but uninteresting platitudes and easy pieties. The interpretations furnished by historical criticism, as many professors will attest, may serve as leverage to dislodge harmful or simply boring appropriations of Scripture, hasty accommodations of the text to our own culture.[5]

And yet one of the difficulties with Martin's argument is that he supposes that 'criticism' is the preserve of the biblical critic while Christian theology will benefit from a greater use of the 'imagination' in appropriating scripture. There is an underlying assumption about the relationship between 'criticism' and the 'imagination', which demands further scrutiny.[6] In distinguishing between 'historical criticism' and 'confessional piety,' he may in fact be reinforcing a sense of dislocation between the theological interpretation of scripture and the practice of historical criticism.

A more promising way of overcoming the dislocation of historical criticism and a more overt theological interest in biblical interpretation might be to approach the question with some of the insights offered by Pierre Hadot. One of the central themes of Hadot's thought is that modern commentators have a tendency to project modern constructions of the discipline of philosophy on their reading of ancient philosophical texts. It is easy to assume that philosophy is something akin to Western analytical philosophy, which rarely gets past questions of logic and epistemology. Drawing in particular on the writings of Philo of Alexandria, Hadot argued that ancient philosophy had a much broader canvas in view. Philosophy in the ancient world was not a theoretical or abstract construct. It was a 'method for training people to live and to look at the world in a new way'.[7] Philosophy was 'a way of life'.[8] Like Martin, he quotes the writings of Jean Leclercq: 'As much as in antiquity, *philosophia* in the monastic Middle Ages designates not a theory or a way of knowing, but a lived wisdom, a way of living according to reason'.[9] The pursuit of wisdom not only offered peace of mind and a particular way of addressing questions of moral conduct, but it enabled the student to discover 'the art of living'.[10] It offered the student the possibility of personal transformation. The student discovered the art of living in a series of 'spiritual exercises'.

Hadot's use of the term 'spiritual exercises' aroused some controversy. But his rationale for using this particular phrase was precisely that it embraced not only the intellect but also the imagination. Hadot noted that the first century Jewish writer, Philo of Alexandria, offered two different lists of these spiritual exercises in two different works: *Who is the Heir of Divine Things* and *Allegorical Interpretations*.[11] In *Who is the Heir,* Philo describes the following forms of *ascetic practices* or *spiritual exercises:* inquiry, examination, reading, listening, attentiveness, self-mastery and indifference to indifferent things. The other list includes reading, meditation, therapies of the passions, remembrance of past things, self-mastery and devotion to duty. Inevitably, the lists reflect Philo's debt to Stoic philosophy, but two things emerge clearly from

Hadot's analysis: first, these practices engage both the intellect and the imagination; secondly, *reading* is an essential element of both lists. The close and intensive reading of the foundational texts of a philosophical school was supposed to embrace all the intellectual, analytical and imaginative gifts at the reader's disposal. Hadot recognizes that there are striking parallels between these practices in the philosophical schools and the patterns of ecclesial life in late antiquity. For Christians of late antiquity, Christianity was a form of philosophy. The distinction between philosophy and theology emerged much later in the course of the middle ages. Moreover, Hadot argues that the cultivation of 'spiritual exercises' in the Hellenistic schools was the direct antecedent of the 'spiritual exercises' of Ignatius Loyola.[12] And yet, modern accounts of the 'spiritual exercises' of Ignatius Loyola would hardly associate them with 'a critical approach' to biblical interpretation. Ironically, premodern accounts of these spiritual exercises would not have recognized such a distinction. In fact, for ancient commentators, a commitment to the practice of *askesis* would have embraced the kind of resistance to 'uninteresting platitudes and easy pieties' which Martin reserves for a more critical approach. When early Christian commentators used the tools of ancient literary criticism, they did not decide that they were no longer thinking *theologically*. While Martin is right to be concerned about the quality of teaching and learning in seminary education, perhaps 'the expansion of the Christian imagination', which he seeks, involves the discovery and the use of the techniques of historical criticism. Thus it may be that the critical reading of scripture is as much of a 'spiritual exercise' as the kind of reading that characterizes the devotional practices mentioned earlier in this chapter. Indeed, there are some intriguing parallels between the desire for a more 'dispassionate objectivity' characteristic of modern biblical criticism and the ascetic practices and spiritual disciplines of the Christian tradition which serve to challenge our capacity for self-absorption and self-interest. As Rowan Williams has observed, 'spiritual disciplines are invariably methods of challenging the assumption that I – my conscious, willing ego – stand at the centre of all patterns of meaning. Silence, fasting, receiving the sacraments, confession and penance, even listening to a sermon, have all been listed as spiritual disciplines, because they all direct themselves to this "decentring" exercise, without which, the Christian believes, the impact of the true God upon us will always be muted, perhaps stifled, by our own scripts and dramas'.[13] There is an important connection between these ascetic practices and the dislodging of 'harmful or simply boring appropriations of Scripture'. Hadot's description of 'spiritual exercises' may in fact enable us to explore a greater degree of integration between criticism and the imagination. When Cassian speaks of the renewal of our minds, he is describing not just the imagination but also our capacity for criticism, including self-criticism. He is describing our capacity for self-awareness.

The way in which Hadot speaks of philosophy as 'a way of life' should also challenge us to reflect on the vocation of the theologian. Theology has been construed all too often as primarily a matter of ideas: when we think of theology, we think of something abstract, conceptual and theoretical. And yet, Hadot's description of 'spiritual exercises' should enable us to see that the richness of our theological vision is made manifest in lives of holiness and sanctity. Christian discipleship is as much about reflecting the way of Christ as it is about reflecting the mind of Christ. And Scripture serves to challenge, provoke and even perplex us in this task. It presents us with the mirror of charity. The challenge is this: as we read these words, do we see our reflection there?

> Beloved, let us love one another, because love is from God; everyone who loves is born of God and knows God. Whoever does not love does not know God, for God is love. God's love was revealed among us in this way: God sent his only Son into the world so that we might live through him. In this is love, not that we loved God but that he loved us and sent his Son to be the atoning sacrifice for our sins. Beloved, since God loved us so much, we also ought to love one another. No one has ever seen God; if we love one another, God lives in us, and his love is perfected in us. (1 Jn 4.7–12)

NOTES

Preface

1 Jean Leclercq, *The Love of Learning and the Desire for God* (trans. Catherine Misrahi; New York: Fordham University Press, 1961), p. 5.

Chapter One

1 Augustine, *Confessions* 8.12.29.

2 Athanasius, *Life of Antony* 2.

3 Henry Chadwick, *Augustine* (Oxford: Oxford University Press, 1986), p. 3.

4 William Lamb (ed.), *The Catena in Marcum* (Leiden: Brill, 2012), p. 259.

5 Richard Dawkins, *The God Delusion* (London: Bantam Press, 2006), p. 242.

6 Bertrand Russell, *Why I Am Not a Christian* (London: Routledge, 2004), p. 15.

7 Henry Chadwick, *Saint Augustine Confessions* (Oxford: Oxford University Press, 1991), p. xxiv.

8 Augustine, *Confessions* 12.2.3.

9 Augustine, *Confessions* 12.31.42.

10 Augustine, *On Christian Teaching* Prologue 3.

11 Heraclitus, *Homeric Problems* 1.1.

12 Heraclitus, *Homeric Problems* 21.3.

13 Robert Lamberton, *Homer the Theologian: Neoplatonist Allegorical Reading and the Growth of the Epic Tradition* (London: University of California Press, 1989), p. 20.

14 Pierre Hadot, *Philosophy as a Way of Life* (ed. Arnold I. Davison; trans. Michael Chase; Oxford: Blackwell, 1995), p. 73.

15 Augustine, *On Christian Teaching* 2.1.1.

16 Augustine, *On Christian Teaching* 2.10.15.

17 Augustine, *On Christian Teaching* 2.6.7.

18 Gregory, *Homilies on Ezekiel* 1.6.1.

19 Gregory, *Homilies on Ezekiel* 1.6.2.

20 Margaret Mitchell, *Paul, the Corinthians and the Birth of Christian Hermeneutics* (Cambridge: Cambridge University Press, 2010), p. 70.

21 Gregory, *Homilies on Ezekiel* 1.6.14.

22 Gregory, *Homilies on Ezekiel* 1.6.10.

23 Gregory, *Homilies on Ezekiel* 1.6.9.

24 Gregory, *Homilies on Ezekiel* 1.6.8.

25 Ibid.

26 Ibid.

27 Quoted in Henri de Lubac, *Medieval Exegesis: the Four Senses of Scripture* (trans. Mark Sebanc; vol. 1; Edinburgh: T&T Clark, 1998). As de Lubac points out, the verse is often mistakenly attributed to Nicolas of Lyra. He suggests that it is more likely to have come from Augustine of Dacia.

28 Maimonides, *The Guide for the Perplexed* (trans. M. Friedländer; New York: Dover, 1956), p. 2.

29 Eusebius, *Preparation for the Gospel* 15.9.13 (quoted in Charles Schmitt, 'Aristotle as a Cuttlefish: The Origin and Development of a Renaissance Image' in *Studies in the Renaissance* 12 (1965), pp. 60–72).

30 Charles Schmitt comments on the delicious irony that writers who drew a comparison between Aristotle and a cuttlefish were drawing on Aristotle's own research into the behaviour of cuttlefish (Schmitt, 'Aristotle as a Cuttlefish', p. 72).

31 Søren Kierkegaard, *Attack upon Christendom,* (trans. Walter Lowrie; Princeton: Princeton University Press, 1968), p. 197.

32 Hugh Pyper, 'The Offensiveness of Scripture', Conference Paper at *The Society for the Study of Theology* in Manchester, 2011.

33 Søren Kierkegaard, *The Sickness Unto Death: A Christian Psychological Exposition for Upbuilding and Awakening* (ed. and trans. Howard V. and Edna H. Hong; Princeton: Princeton University Press, 1980), p. 116.

34 Ibid., p. 38.

35 Russell Reno, *Editorial Preface*, Brazos Theological Commentary Series, p. 12.

36 George Steiner, *No Passion Spent* (London: Faber and Faber, 1996), p. 36.

37 Augustine, *On Christian Teaching* 1.36.41.

Chapter Two

1 Hadot, *Philosophy as a Way of Life*, p. 52.

2 Justin, *First Apology*, 66.3, 67.3 and Justin, *Dialogue with Trypho the Jew*, 100.4, 101.3, 102.5, 103.6, 104.1.

3 Irenaeus, *Against the Heresies* 8.1.

4 Irenaeus, *Against the Heresies* 3.4.

5 Irenaeus, *Against the Heresies* 3.5.

6 Tacitus, *History* 5.9.

7 Origen, *Against Celsus* 2.72.

8 Porphyry, *Against the Christians* Fr. 11, 9, 10, and 49.

9 Arnaldo Momigliano, 'Pagan and Christian Historiography in the Fourth Century AD', in *The Conflict between Paganism and Christianity in the Fourth Century* (ed. Arnaldo Momigliano; Oxford: Oxford University Press, 1963), p. 90.

10 Origen, *Against Celsus* 1.45, 1.49, 1.55, 2.3, 2.30, 2.31. Origen's engagement with Celsus is complicated by the fact that in many passages Celsus adopts the fictitious persona of a Jew.

11 Richard Hanson, 'Biblical Exegesis in the early Church', in *The Cambridge History of the Bible* (ed. P. R. Ackroyd and C. F. Evans; Cambridge: Cambridge University Press, 1970), p. 412.

12 Maren Niehoff, *Jewish Exegesis and Homeric Scholarship in Alexandria* (Cambridge: Cambridge University Press, 2011), p. 95.

13 William Lamb, (ed.), *The Catena in Marcum: A Byzantine Anthology of Commentary on Mark* (Leiden: Brill, 2012), p. 402.

14 Theodore of Mopsuestia, *Commentary on Galatians* 75.

15 Frances Young, *Biblical Exegesis and the Formation of Christian Culture* (Cambridge: Cambridge University Press, 1997).

16 Kathy Eden, *Hermeneutics and the Rhetorical Tradition* (New Haven: Yale University Press, 1997), p. 55.

17 Brian Cummings, *The Literary Culture of the Reformation: Grammar and Grace* (Oxford: Oxford University Press, 2002), p. 20.

18 Eden, *Hermeneutics and the Rhetorical Tradition*, p. 73.

19 Jonathan Sheehan, *The Enlightenment Bible: Translation, Scholarship, Culture* (Oxford: Princeton University Press, 2005), p. 4.

20 Christopher Hill, *The English Bible and the Seventeenth-Century Revolution* (London: Penguin Books, 1994), p. 421.

21 G. E. Lessing, 'On the Proof of the Spirit and of Power', in *Lessing's Theological Writings* (ed. and trans. Henry Chadwick; Stanford, CA: Stanford University Press, 1956), p. 52.

22 John Sandys-Wunsch and Laurence Eldredge, 'J.P. Gabler and the Distinction between Biblical and Dogmatic Theology: Translation, Commentary, and Discussion of his Originality', *Scottish Journal of Theology*, 33(2) (1980), pp. 134–35.

23 Ibid., p. 138.

24 Ernst Troeltsch, 'On the Historical and Dogmatic Methods in Theology' [1898] published in *Gesammelte Schriften* (vol. 2; Tubingen: Mohr Siebeck, 1913), pp. 728–53.

25 William Wrede, 'The Task and Method of New Testament Theology So-called', in *The Nature of New Testament Theology* (ed. Robert Morgan; London: SCM, 1973), p. 69.

26 Ibid., p. 73.

27 Albert Schweitzer, *The Quest of the Historical Jesus: A Critical Study of its Progress from Reimarus to Wrede* (English Translation; London: A&C Black, 1954), p. 397.

28 James Barr, *Holy Scripture* (Oxford: Clarendon, 1983), p. 108.

29 N. T. Wright, *The New Testament and the People of God* (London: SPCK, 1992), p. 35.

30 Ibid., p. 97.

31 Markus Bockmuehl, 'Compleat History of the Resurrection: A Dialogue with N.T. Wright', *JSNT* 26(4) (2004), p. 502.

32 Ibid., p. 503.

33 Joseph Ratzinger, *Jesus of Nazareth: From the Baptism in the Jordan to the Transfiguration* (London: Bloomsbury, 2007), p. xiii.

34 Ibid., p. xvii.

35 Ibid., p. xviii–xix.

36 Ibid., p. xix.

37 Raymond E. Brown, *The Birth of the Messiah: A Commentary on the Infancy Narratives in the Gospels of Matthew and Luke.* (London: Chapman; New Updated Edition, 1993), p. 702 (fn. 314).

38 Ibid., p. 704.

39 Joseph A. Fitzmyer, *Romans* (The Anchor Bible Commentary; vol. 33; London: Chapman, 1992), p. 408.

40 Ibid.

Chapter Three

1 Hadrian, *Introduction to the Sacred Scriptures (Isagoge ad scripturas sacras)* (Patrologia Graeca 98.1273A–1312B).

2 Augustine, *On Christian Teaching* 3.29.40.

3 *Teachings of the Apostles (Didascalia apostolorum)* 2.1.6.

4 Bede, *On Figures and Tropes* 1 (CCSL 123A:142–171, ed. C. B. Kendall), pp. 142–43.

5 Benjamin Jowett, 'On the Interpretation of Scripture', in *Essays and Reviews* (ed. Frederick Temple et al.; London: Longman, Green, Longman and Roberts, 1861), pp. 371–72.

6 Ibid., p. 404.

7 These quotations come from a number of Westcott's letters (dated 1861) in the Westcott House archive. The letters are addressed to Professor Arthur Stanley, the Regius Professor of Ecclesiastical History in the University of Oxford. A broad churchman with a generous disposition, Stanley had sought to prevent the formal condemnation of Newman and the leaders of the Oxford Movement after the publication of the infamous Tract 90. Westcott thought that Stanley would be just as sympathetic to the plight of the writers of *Essays and Reviews*.

8 Robert Alter and Frank Kermode (eds.), *The Literary Guide to the Bible* (London: Collins, 1987), pp. 2–4.

9 Robert Alter, *The Art of Biblical Narrative* (London: Allen and Unwin, 1981), pp. 12–13.

10 David Clines, 'Story and Poem: The Old Testament as Literature and as Scripture', *Interpretation* 34 (1980), p. 119.

11 David Gunn, *The Story of King David: Genre and Interpretation* (JSOT Supplement Series, 6; JSOT Press, Sheffield, 1978), p. 111.

12 J. Cheryl Exum, *The Song of Songs* (The Old Testament Library; Louisville: Westminster John Knox, 2005), pp. 76, 1, 3, 17, 19.

13 Ibid., p. 82.

14 David Rhoads, *Reading Mark, Engaging the Gospel* (Minneapolis: Fortress Press, 2004), p. 4.

15 Stephen Moore and Yvonne Sherwood, *The Invention of the Biblical Scholar: A Critical Manifesto* (Minneapolis: Fortress Press, 2011), p. 110.

16 Frank Kermode, *The Genesis of Secrecy: On the Interpretation of Narrative* (Cambridge, MA: Harvard University Press, 1979), p. 35.

17 Ibid., p. 125.

18 Stephen Moore, *Literary Criticism and the Gospels: The Theoretical Challenge* (New Haven: Yale University Press, 1989), pp. 111, 124.

19 Kermode, *The Genesis of Secrecy*, p. 34.

20 Ibid., p. 47.

21 Ibid., p. 18.

22 Ibid.

23 Ibid., p. 19.

24 Ibid., p. 145.

25 Hans Frei, *The Eclipse of Biblical Narrative* (New Haven: Yale University Press, 1974), p. 1.

26 Hans Frei, 'Theology and the Interpretation of Narrative: Some Hermeneutical Considerations,' in *Theology and Narrative: Selected Essays* (ed. George Hunsinger and William Placher; Oxford: Oxford University Press, 1993), p. 102.

27 Ibid., p. 104.

28 Ibid., p. 108.

29 Frei, *The Eclipse*, p. 27.

30 Erich Auerbach, 'Figura,' in *Scenes from the Drama of European Literature* (ed. Wlad Godzich and Jochen Schulte-Sasse; Minneapolis: University of Minnesota Press, 1984 (originally published 1944)), p. 29.

31 Frei, *The Eclipse*, pp. 36–37.

32 Miroslav Volf, *Captive to the Word of God: Engaging the Scriptures for Contemporary Theological Reflection* (Cambridge: Eerdmans, 2010), p. 17.

33 Harold Bloom, *Where Shall Wisdom be Found?* (New York: Riverhead Books, 2004), p. 161.

34 Stephen Moore, *The Bible in Theory: Critical and Postcritical Essays* (Atlanta: Society of Biblical Literature, 2010), p. 357.

35 Moore and Sherwood, *The Invention of the Biblical Scholar*, p. 123.

36 Stanley Fish, 'One University under God?', *The Chronicle of Higher Education*, January 7th 2005: http://chronicle.com/article/One-University-Under-God-/45077/ (Accessed 1 December 2012).

37 Marie-Dominique Chenu, 'La littérature comme "lieu" de la théologie', *Revue des sciences philosophiques et théologiques* 53 (1969), pp. 76–77: quoted in Nicholas Boyle, *Sacred and Secular Scriptures: A Catholic Approach to Literature* (London: Darton, Longman and Todd, 2004), p. 4.

38 Karl-Josef Kuschel, *Born before All Time?* (London, SCM, 1992), p. 486.

Chapter Four

1 Miroslav Volf, *Captive to the Word of God* (Grand Rapids: Eerdmans, 2010), p. 14.

2 David Kelsey, *The Uses of Scripture in Recent Theology* (London: SCM, 1975), p. 2.

3 Ibid., p. 34.

4 Lionel Thornton, *The Dominion of Christ* (London: Dacre, 1952), p. 58.

5 Kelsey, *The Uses of Scripture*, p. 74.

6 Ibid., p. 81.

7 Article 2 of the Lausanne Covenant, 1974, www.lausanne.org/en/documents/lausanne-covenant.html (Accessed 3 December 2012).

8 John Stott, *Understanding the Bible* (Milton Keynes: Scripture Union; rev. edn, 2003), p. 149.

9 Ibid., p. 151–52.

10 Ibid., p. 145.

11 Wolfhart Pannenberg, *Systematic Theology* (vol. 1; trans. Geoffrey Bromiley; Edinburgh: T&T Clark, 1988), p. 232.

12 Wolfhart Pannenberg, *Systematic Theology* (vol. 2; Edinburgh: T&T Clark, 1994), p. 344.

13 Wolfhart Pannenberg, *Jesus – God and Man* (trans. Lewis Wilkins and Duane Priebe; London: SCM, 1968), pp. 89–91.

14 Pannenberg, *Systematic Theology*, p. 442.

15 Ibid., p. 55.

16 John Rogerson, *A Theology of the Old Testament* (London: SPCK, 2009), p. 18.

17 Rudolf Bultmann, *Theology of the New Testament:* quoted in Rogerson, *A Theology*, pp. 1–2.

18 Rogerson, *A Theology*, p. 18.

19 Ibid., p. 19.

20 Ibid., p. 174.

21 Ibid., p. 12.

22 Ibid., p. 174.

23 Ibid., p. 195.

24 Richard Niebuhr, *The Meaning of Revelation* (New York: Macmillan, 1941), p. 35.

25 George Lindbeck, 'The Bible as Realistic Narrative', *Journal of Ecumenical Studies*, 17(1) (1980), p. 84.

26 Ibid., p. 85.

27 George Lindbeck, 'Scripture, Community and Consensus', in *Biblical Interpretation in Crisis* (ed. Richard Neuhaus; Grand Rapids: Eerdmans, 1989), p. 211.

28 Gerard Loughlin, *Telling God's Story: Bible, Church and Narrative Theology* (Cambridge: Cambridge University Press, 1996), p. 37.

29 David Kelsey, *Eccentric Existence* (vol. 1; Louisville: Westminster John Knox, 2009), p. 123.

30 Ibid., p. 126.

31 Ibid., p. 129.

32 Brevard Childs, *Biblical Theology in Crisis* (Philadelphia: Westminster John Knox, 1970), p. 33.

33 Brevard Childs, *Introduction to the Old Testament as Scripture* (London: SCM Press, 1979), p. 79.

34 Childs, *Biblical Theology*, p. 211.

35 Ibid., p. 217.

36 Ibid., p. 219.

37 Walter Brueggemann, *Theology of the Old Testament: Testimony, Dispute, Advocacy* (Philadelphia: Fortress Press, 1997), p. 62.

38 Brevard Childs, *Biblical Theology of the Old and New Testaments: Theological Reflection on the Christian Bible* (London: SCM, 1992), pp. 442, 462, 587.

39 James Barr, 'Review of Brevard Childs', *Introduction to the Old Testament as Scripture*. JSOT 16 (1980), p. 13.

40 James Barr, *The Concept of Biblical Theology: An Old Testament Perspective* (London: SCM, 1999), p. 422.

41 Brueggemann, *Theology of the Old Testament*, p. 117.

42 Ibid., p. xvi.

43 Ibid., p. 121.

44 Ibid., pp. 230–31.

45 Ibid., p. 313.

46 Ibid., p. 359.

47 Ibid., p. 110.

48 Ibid., p. 83.

49 Mikhail M. Bakhtin, *Problems of Dostoevsky's Poetics* (trans. Caryl Emerson; Minneapolis: University of Minnesota Press, 1984), p. 6.

50 Ibid., p. 252.

51 Brueggemann, *Theology of the Old Testament*, p. 71.

52 Ibid., p. 64.

53 Ibid., p. 732.

54 Alasdair MacIntyre, *After Virtue: A Study in Moral Theory* (London: Duckworth, 1985), p. 206.

55 Hans-Georg Gadamer, *Truth and Method* (London: Continuum; Second rev. edn, 2003), p. 245.

56 Andrew Louth, *Discerning the Mystery* (Oxford, Clarendon, 1983), p. 96.

57 Henri de Lubac, *Mémoire sur l'occasion de mes écrits* (Paris: Cerf, 2006), p. 94.

58 Louth, *Discerning*, p. 94.

59 David Brown, *Tradition and Imagination: Revelation and Change* (Oxford: Oxford University Press, 1999), p. 7.

60 Ibid., p. 123.

61 Ibid., p. 59.

62 J'annine Jobling, *Feminist Biblical Interpretation in Theological Context: Restless Readings* (Aldershot: Ashgate, 2002), p. 86.

63 Elizabeth Schüssler Fiorenza, *In Memory of Her: A Feminist Theological Reconstruction of Christian Origins* (London: SCM, 1983), p. xiii.

64 Luce Irigaray, 'Equal to Whom?', in *The Essential Difference* (ed. Naomi Shor and Elizabeth Weed; Bloomington: Indiana University Press, 1994), p. 74.

65 Ibid.

66 Ibid., p. 76.

67 J. Cheryl Exum, 'The Ethics of Biblical Violence against Women', in *The Bible in Ethics* (ed. John Rogerson, Margaret Davies and Daniel Carroll; Sheffield: Sheffield Academic Press, 1995), pp. 248–71.

68 Ellen Davis, 'Critical Traditioning: Seeking an Inner Biblical Hermeneutic', in *The Art of Reading Scripture* (ed. Ellen Davis and Richard Hays; Grand Rapids: Eerdmanns, 2003), p. 164.

69 Nicholas Lash, 'Performing the Scriptures', in *Theology on the Way to Emmaus* (London: SCM, 1986), p. 37.

70 Ibid., p. 38.

71 Ibid., p. 46.

72 Frances Young, *The Art of Performance* (London: Darton, Longman and Todd, 1990), p. 162.

73 Samuel Wells, *Improvisation: The Drama of Christian Ethics* (London: SPCK, 2004), pp. 62–63.

74 Ibid., p. 65.

75 Miroslav Volf, *Captive to the Word of God* (Cambridge: Eerdmans, 2010), p. 20.

76 John Montag, 'Revelation: The False Legacy of Suárez', in *Radical Orthodoxy* (ed. John Milbank, Catherine Pickstock, Graham Ward; London: Routledge, 1999), p. 43.

77 Ibid., p. 57.

78 Herbert McCabe, *God Matters* (London: Continuum, 1987), p. 76.

79 Ibid., p. 77.

80 Karl Barth, *Church Dogmatics* (vol. 1.2; trans. G. Bromiley and T. Torrance; Edinburgh: T&T Clark, 1956), p. 501.

81 John Webster, *Holy Scripture: A Dogmatic Sketch* (Oxford: Oxford University Press, 2003), p. 23.

82 Donald Allchin, *Participation in God: A Forgotten Strand in Anglican Tradition* (London: Darton, Longman and Todd, 1988), p. 72.

83 Robert Jenson, *Systematic Theology* (vol. 2; Oxford: Oxford University Press, 1999), p. 276.

Chapter Five

1 Theodoret of Cyrus, *Commentary on Daniel*. Preface 1.1.

2 Sebastian Brock, *The Luminous Eye: The Spiritual World Vision of Ephrem the Syrian* (Kalamazoo: Cistercian Publications, 1992), p. 106.

3 Mitchell, *Paul*, p. 70.

4 Henri de Lubac, *Medieval Exegesis: The Four Senses of Scripture* (trans. Mark Sebanc; vol. 1; Edinburgh: T&T Clark, 1998), p. 76.

5 George Steiner, *Real Presences* (London: Faber and Faber, 1989), p. 49.

6 Kelsey, *The Uses of Scripture*, p. 111.

7 John Barton, *People of the Book? The Authority of the Bible in Christianity* (London: SPCK, 1988), pp. 9–10.

8 Ibid., p. 43.

9 Ibid., p. 44.

10 N. T. Wright, *Scripture and the Authority of God* (London: SPCK, 2005), p. 17.

11 Ibid.

12 Ibid., p. 22.

13 Ibid., p. 101.

14 Ibid., p. 23.

15 Jenson, *Systematic Theology*, p. 273.

16 Stephen Fowl, *Engaging Scripture* (Oxford: Blackwell, 1998), p. 2.

17 Ibid., p. 3.

18 Ibid.

19 Ibid., p. 8.

20 Ibid., p. 7.

21 Francis Watson, *Text, Church and World* (Edinburgh: T&T Clark, 1994), p. 3.

22 Ibid., p. 6.

23 Ibid., p. 231, *italics removed.*

24 Ibid., p. 236, *italics removed*.

25 Ibid., p. 240.

26 Philip Davies, *Whose Bible is it Anyway?* (London: T&T Clark, 2004), p. 14.

27 Christopher Rowland, 'An Open Letter to Francis Watson on *Text, Church and World*', *Scottish Journal of Theology*, 48 (1995), p. 508.

28 Ibid., p. 514.

29 Fowl, *Engaging*, p. 23.

30 As James Barr points out, attempts to argue on the basis of 2 Tim. 3.16 and 2 Pet. 3.16 that the Pauline letters were already classed as 'scripture' and that a New Testament canon was beginning to take shape at the time at which the later writings of the New Testament were being written are problematic for a number of reasons, principally, that there is still 'no *scriptural* evidence to decide what were the exact limits of the canon' (Barr, *Holy Scripture*, p. 25).

31 Joseph Ratzinger, *Milestones: Memoirs 1927 – 1977* (San Francisco: Ignatius Press, 1998), p. 127.

32 David Tracy, *Plurality and Ambiguity: Hermeneutics, Religion, Hope* (San Francisco: Harper San Francisco, 1987), pp. 18–19.

33 Eden, *Hermeneutics and the Rhetorical Tradition*, p. 58.

34 Augustine, *On Christian Teaching* 1.35.39

Chapter Six

1 John Cassian, *Conferences* 14.11 quoted by Henri de Lubac, *Scripture in the Tradition* (New York: Crossroad, 1968), p. 223.

2 Dale Martin, *Pedagogy of the Bible: An Analysis and Proposal* (Louisville: Westminster John Knox, 2008), p. 80.

3 Jean Leclercq, *The Love of Learning and the Desire for God* (New York: Fordham University Press, 1961), p. 71.

4 Martin, *Pedagogy of the Bible*, p. 101.

5 Ibid.

6 The relationship between criticism and imagination in the emergence of spiritual practices such as 'lectio divina' is explored in detail in Mary Carruthers, *The Craft of Thought* (Cambridge: Cambridge University Press, 2000).

7 Hadot, *Philosophy as a Way of Life*, p. 107.

8   Ibid., p. 264.

9   Jean Leclercq, 'Pour l'histoire de l'expression 'philosophie chrétienne," *Mélanges de Science Religieuse* 9 (1952), p. 221.

10 Hadot, *Philosophy as a Way of Life*, p. 83.

11 Philo, *Who is the Heir?* 253 and *Allegorical Interpretation* 3.18

12 Hadot, *Philosophy as a Way of Life*, pp. 126–40.

13 Rowan Williams, *Why Study the Past?* (London: Darton, Longman and Todd, 2005), p. 110.

FURTHER READING

Alter, Robert, *The Art of Biblical Narrative* (London: Allen and Unwin, 1981).

Alter, Robert and Frank Kermode (eds), *The Literary Guide to the Bible* (London: Collins, 1987).

Aquinas, Thomas, *Summa theologiae* (Cambridge: Cambridge University Press, 2006).

Auerbach, Erich, 'Figura'. In *Scenes from the Drama of European Literature* (ed. Wlad Godzich and Jochen Schulte-Sasse; Minneapolis: University of Minnesota Press, 1984 (originally published 1944)).

Barr, James, *The Bible in the Modern World* (London: SCM, 1973).

—, *The Scope and Authority of the Bible: Explorations in Theology 7* (London: SCM, 1980).

—, *Holy Scripture: Canon, Authority, Criticism* (Oxford: Oxford University Press, 1983).

—, *Biblical Faith and Natural Theology* (Oxford: Clarendon Press, 1993).

Barth, Karl, 'The Strange New World Within the Bible'. In *The Word of God and the Word of Man* (London: Hodder & Stoughton, 1928), pp. 28–50.

Barton, John, *People of the Book? The Authority of the Bible in Christianity* (London: SPCK, 1988).

—, *Holy Writings, Sacred Text: The Canon in Early Christianity* (London: Westminster John Knox, 1997).

—, *The Nature of Biblical Criticism* (London: Westminster John Knox, 2010).

Bauckham, Richard, *Jesus and the Eyewitnesses* (Grand Rapids: Eerdmans, 2008).

Bloom, Harold, *The Anxiety of Influence* (Oxford: Oxford University Press, 1997).

—, *Where Shall Wisdom be Found?* (New York: Riverhead Books, 2004).

Boff, Clodovis, *Theology and Praxis: Epistemological Foundations* (New York: Orbis, 1987).

Bousset, Wilhelm, *Kyrios Christos: A History of the Belief in Christ from the Beginnings of Christianity to Irenaeus* (English Translation: Nashville, Abingdon Press, 1970).

Boyle, Nicholas, *Sacred and Secular Scriptures: A Catholic Approach to Literature* (London: Darton, Longman and Todd, 2004).

Brett, Mark, *Biblical Criticism in Crisis? The Impact of the Canonical Approach on Old Testament Studies* (Cambridge: Cambridge University Press, 1991).

Brown, David, *Tradition and Imagination: Revelation and Change* (Oxford: Oxford University Press, 1999).

Brown, Raymond E., *The Birth of the Messiah: A Commentary on the Infancy Narratives in the Gospels of Matthew and Luke* (London: Chapman; New Updated Edition, 1993).

Brueggemann, Walter, *Theology of the Old Testament: Testimony, Dispute, Advocacy* (Philadelphia: Fortress Press, 1997).

—, *Disruptive Grace: Reflections on God, Scripture and the Church* (ed. Carolyn Sharp; Minneapolis: Fortress, 2011).

Bultmann, Rudolf, *Theology of the New Testament* (trans. Kendrick Grobel; 2 Vols; London: SCM, 1952–55).

—, 'Is Exegesis without presuppositions possible?'. In *Existence and Faith* (London: SCM, 1964), pp. 342–51.

Caird, George, *The Language and Imagery of the Bible* (London: Duckworth, 1980).

Carroll, Robert, *Wolf in the Sheepfold: The Bible as a Problem for Christianity* (London: SPCK, 1991).

Carruthers, Mary, *The Craft of Thought: Meditation, Rhetoric and the Making of Images, 400–1200* (Cambridge: Cambridge University Press, 2000).

Chalamet, Christophe, *Dialectical Theologians: Wilhelm Hermann, Karl Barth and Rudolf Bultmann* (Zurich: Theologischer Verlag, 2005).

Childs, Brevard, *Biblical Theology of the Old and New Testaments* (London: SCM, 1982).

Clines, David, Stephen Fowl and Stanley Porter (eds), *The Bible in Three Dimensions* (Sheffield: JSOT Press, 1990).

Coggins, Richard and Leslie Houlden (eds), *A Dictionary of Biblical Interpretation* (London: SCM, 1990).

Countryman, L. William, *Interpreting the Truth: Changing the Paradigm of Biblical Studies* (New York: Continuum, 2003).

Cummings, Brian, *The Literary Culture of the Reformation: Grammar and Grace* (Oxford: Oxford University Press, 2002).

Davies, Daniel, *Method and Metaphysics in Maimonides' Guide for the Perplexed* (New York: Oxford University Press, 2011).

Davies, Philip, *Whose Bible is it Anyway?* (London: T&T Clark, 2004).

Davis, Ellen and Richard Hays (eds), *The Art of Reading Scripture* (Grand Rapids: Eerdmanns, 2003).

Eden, Kathy, *Hermeneutics and the Rhetorical Tradition: Chapters in the Ancient Legacy and its Humanist Reception* (New Haven: Yale University Press, 1997).

Eichhorn, Albert, *The Lord's Supper in the New Testament* (English Translation: Leiden: Brill, 2008).

Exum, J. Cheryl and David Clines (eds), *The New Literary Criticism and the Hebrew Bible* (Sheffield: Almond Press, 1993).

Exum, J. Cheryl (ed.), *Retellings: The Bible in Literature, Music, Art and Film* (Leiden: Brill, 2007).

Fiorenza, Elizabeth Schüssler, *In Memory of Her: A Feminist Theological Reconstruction of Christian Origins* (London: SCM, 1983).

—, *Bread, Not Stone: The Challenge of Feminist Biblical Interpretation* (Boston: Beacon, 1984).

Fish, Stanley, *Is There a Text in this Class? The Authority of Interpretive Communities* (Cambridge, MA: Harvard University Press, 1980).

Fishbane, Michael, *Biblical Interpretation in Ancient Israel* (Oxford: Clarendon Press, 1985).

Fowl, Stephen (ed.), *The Theological Interpretation of Scripture: Classic and Contemporary Readers* (Oxford: Blackwell, 1997).

—, *Engaging Scripture* (Oxford: Blackwell, 1998).

—, *Theological Interpretation of Scripture* (Carlisle: Paternoster Publishing, 2010).

Frei, Hans, *The Eclipse of Biblical Narrative: A Study in Eighteenth and Nineteenth Century Hermeneutics* (New Haven: Yale University Press, 1974).

Gadamer, Hans-Georg, *Truth and Method* (London: Continuum; Second Revised Edition, 2003).

Gunkel, Hermann, *The Psalms: A Form-critical Introduction* (English Translation: Philadelphia, Fortress Press, 1967).

Gunton, Colin, *A Brief Theology of Revelation* (Edinburgh: T&T Clark, 1995).

Gutierrez, Gustavo, *A Theology of Liberation* (New York: Orbis, 1974).

Hadot, Pierre, *Philosophy as a Way of Life* (ed. Arnold I. Davison; trans. Michael Chase; Oxford: Blackwell, 1995).

Hauerwas, Stanley and Gregory Jones, *Why Narrative? Readings in Narrative Theology* (Eugene: Wipf & Stock, 1997).

Inwood, Michael, *Heidegger: A Very Short Introduction* (Oxford: Oxford University Press, 1997).

Jeanrond, Werner, *Theological Hermeneutics: Development and Significance* (London: SPCK, 1991).

Jenson, Robert, *Systematic Theology* (2 vols; Oxford: Oxford University Press, 1997–99).

Jobling, J'annine, *Feminist Biblical Interpretation in Theological Context: Restless Readings* (Aldershot: Ashgate, 2002).

Kelsey, David, *The Uses of Scripture in Recent Theology* (London: SCM, 1975).

Kelley, Shawn, *Racialising Jesus: Race, Ideology and the Formation of Modern Biblical Scholarship* (London: Routledge, 2002).

Kugel, James, *How to Read the Bible: A Guide to Scripture Then and Now* (London: Free Press, 2007).

LaCocque, Andrew and Paul Ricoeur, *Thinking Biblically: Exegetical and Hermeneutical Studies* (Chicago: Chicago University Press, 1998).

Lash, Nicholas, 'Performing the Scriptures'. In *Theology on the Way to Emmaus* (London: SCM, 1986), 37–46.

Leclercq, Jean, *The Love of Learning and the Desire for God* (trans. Catherine Misrahi; New York: Fordham University Press, 1961).

Lessing, G. E., 'On the Proof of the Spirit and of Power'. In *Lessing's Theological Writings* (ed. and trans. Henry Chadwick; Stanford, CA: Stanford University Press, 1956), pp. 51–56.

Levenson, Jon, *The Hebrew Bible, the Old Testament and Historical Criticism* (Louisville: Westminster John Knox, 1993).

Lubac, Henri de, *Scripture in the Tradition* (New York: Crossroad, 1968).

—, *Medieval Exegesis: The Four Senses of Scripture* (trans. Mark Sebanc; vol. 1; Edinburgh: T&T Clark, 1998).

Loughlin, Gerard, *Telling God's Story: Bible, Church and Narrative Theology* (Cambridge: Cambridge University Press, 1996)

Louth, Andrew, *Discerning the Mystery* (Oxford: Clarendon, 1983).

MacIntyre, Alasdair, *After Virtue: A Study in Moral Theory* (London: Duckworth, 1985).

Maimonides, Moses, *The Guide for the Perplexed* (trans. M. Friedländer; New York: Dover, 1956).

Martin, Dale, *Pedagogy of the Bible: An Analysis and Proposal* (Louisville: Westminster John Knox, 2008).

Mitchell, Margaret, *Paul, the Corinthians and the Birth of Christian Hermeneutics* (Cambridge: Cambridge University Press, 2010).

Moberly, Walter, *The Bible, Theology and Faith: A Study of Abraham and Jesus* (Cambridge: Cambridge University Press, 2000).

Montag, John, 'Revelation: The False Legacy of Suárez'. In John Milbank, Catherine Pickstock, Graham Ward (eds), *Radical Orthodoxy* (London: Routledge, 1999), pp. 38–63.

Moore, Stephen, *Literary Criticism and the Gospels: The Theoretical Challenge* (London: Yale University Press, 1989).

—, *The Bible in Theory: Critical and Postcritical Essays* (Atlanta: Society of Biblical Literature, 2010).

Morgan, Robert, with John Barton, *Biblical Interpretation* (Oxford: Oxford University Press, 1989).

Morgan, Robert, 'The Bible and Christian Theology'. In John Barton (ed.) *The Cambridge Companion to Biblical Interpretation* (Cambridge: Cambridge University Press, 1998).

Niebuhr, Richard, *The Meaning of Revelation* (New York: Macmillan, 1941)

Niehoff, Maren, *Jewish Exegesis and Homeric Scholarship in Alexandria* (Cambridge: Cambridge University Press, 2011).

Neill, Stephen, and N. T. Wright, *The Interpretation of the New Testament 1861–1986* (Oxford: Oxford University Press, 1988).

Pannenberg, Wolfhart, *Systematic Theology* (Vols 1–3; Edinburgh: T&T Clark, 1991–98).

Plantinga, Alvin, 'Two (or More) Kinds of Scripture Scholarship', *Modern Theology* 14 (1998), pp. 243–78.

Pyper, Hugh, *The Joy of Kierkegaard: Essays on Kierkegaard as a Biblical Reader* (Sheffield: Equinox, 2011).

Ratzinger, Joseph, *Jesus of Nazareth: From the Baptism in the Jordan to the Transfiguration* (London: Bloomsbury, 2007).

—, *Jesus of Nazareth: Holy Week – From the Entrance into Jerusalem to the Resurrection* (London: Bloomsbury, 2011).

Rhoads, David and Donald Michie, *Mark as Story: An Introduction to the Narrative of a Gospel* (Philadelphia: Fortress Press, 1982).

Rhoads, David, *Reading Mark, Engaging the Gospel* (Minneapolis: Fortress Press, 2004).

Ricoeur, Paul, *Essays on Biblical Interpretation* (trans. David Stewart and Charles Reagan; Philadelphia: Fortress Press, 1981).

Rogerson, John, *A Theology of the Old Testament* (London: SPCK, 2009).

Rowland, Christopher and Mark Corner, *Liberating Exegesis: The Challenge of Liberation Theology to Biblical Studies* (London: SPCK, 1990).

Rowland, Christopher and Jonathan Roberts, *The Bible for Sinners* (London: SPCK, 2008).

Sanders, Ed, *The Historical Figure of Jesus* (London: Penguin, 1993).

Sanders, James, *Torah and Canon* (Philadelphia: Fortress Press, 1972).

—, *Canon and Community: A Guide to Canonical Criticism* (Philadelphia: Fortress Press, 1984).

Sandys-Wunsch, John and Laurence Eldredge, 'J.P. Gabler and the Distinction between Biblical and Dogmatic Theology: Translation,

Commentary, and Discussion of his Originality', *Scottish Journal of Theology*, 33 (1980), No.2, pp. 133–58.

Schneiders, Sandra, *The Revelatory Text* (San Francisco: Harper, 1991).

Schweitzer, Albert, *The Quest of the Historical Jesus: A Critical Study of Its Progress from Reimarus to Wrede* (English Translation; London: A&C Black, 1954).

Sheehan, Jeremy, *The Enlightenment Bible: Translation, Scholarship, Culture* (Princeton: Princeton University Press, 2004).

Sherwood, Yvonne, *A Biblical Text and its Afterlives: The Survival of Jonah in Western Culture* (Cambridge: Cambridge University Press, 2001).

Sherwood, Yvonne and Stephen Moore, *The Invention of the Biblical Scholar: A Critical Manifesto* (Minneapolis: Fortress Press, 2011).

Simonetti, Manlio, *Biblical Interpretation in the Early Church* (Edinburgh: T&T Clark, 1994).

Steiner, George, *Real Presences* (London: Faber and Faber, 1989).

—, *No Passion Spent* (London: Faber and Faber, 1996).

Steinmetz, David C., 'The Superiority of Pre-Critical Exegesis'. In *The Theological Interpretation of Scripture: Classic and Contemporary Readings* (ed. Stephen E. Fowl; Oxford: Blackwell, 1997), pp. 26–38.

Stott, John, *Understanding the Bible* (Milton Keynes: Scripture Union; rev. edn, 2003).

Suarez, Francisco, 'Selected Texts from the Works of Francisco Suarez'. Trans. Sydney Penner. Available online from his website: www. sydneypenner.ca/suarez.shtml.

Sugirtharajah, Rasiah, *Voices from the Margin: Interpreting the Bible in the Third World* (London: SPCK, 1991).

Thiselton, Anthony, *New Horizons in Hermeneutics: The Theory and Practice of Transforming Bible Study* (London: Harper Collins, 1992).

Thornton, Lionel, *The Dominion of Christ* (Westminster: Dacre Press, 1952).

Tillich, Paul, *The Shaking of the Foundations* (Harmondsworth: Penguin, 1949).

Tracy, David, *Plurality and Ambiguity: Hermeneutics, Religion, Hope* (London: SCM, 1988).

Trible, Phyllis, *Texts of Terror* (Philadelphia: Fortress, 1984).

Troeltsch, Ernst, 'On the Historical and Dogmatic Methods in Theology' [1898] published in *Gesammelte Schriften* (vol. 2; Tubingen: Mohr Siebeck, 1913), pp. 728–53.

Volf, Miroslav, *Captive to the Word of God: Engaging the Scriptures for Contemporary Theological Reflection* (Cambridge: Eerdmans, 2010).

Walsh, Brian and Richard Middleton, *Truth is Stranger than it Used to Be: Biblical Faith in a Postmodern Age* (London: SPCK, 1995).

Warfield, Benjamin, *The Inspiration and Authority of the Bible* (Philadelphia: Presbyterian and Reformed Publishing Company, 1948).

Watson, Francis, *Text, Church and World: Biblical Interpretation in Theological Perspective* (Edinburgh: T&T Clark, 1994).

Webster, John, *Holy Scripture: A Dogmatic Sketch* (Cambridge: Cambridge University Press, 2003).

Wells, Samuel, *Improvisation: The Drama of Christian Ethics* (London: SPCK, 2004).

Williams, Rowan, 'The Discipline of Scripture'. In *On Christian Theology* (Oxford: Blackwell, 2000), pp. 44–59.

Wrede, William, 'The Task and Method of New Testament Theology So-called'. In Robert Morgan (ed.), *The Nature of New Testament Theology* (London: SCM, 1973), pp. 68–116.

Wright, George, *God who acts: Biblical Theology as Recital* (London: SCM Press, 1952).

Wright, N. T., *The New Testament and the People of God* (London: SPCK, 1992).

—, *Scripture and the Authority of God* (London: SPCK, 2005).

Young, Frances and David Ford, *Meaning and Truth in 2 Corinthians* (London: SPCK, 1987).

Young, Frances, *The Art of Performance* (London: Darton, Longman and Todd, 1990).

—, *Biblical Exegesis and the Formation of Christian Culture* (Cambridge: Cambridge University Press, 1997).

BIBLICAL REFERENCES

Old Testament

Genesis
1 9
1.27 114
3.16 7
9.25 7
22 6, 34–5, 125
37–8 75

Exodus
12.37f. 44
23.20 4
34.6–7 127

Leviticus
20.13 7

Numbers
13.16 87

Deuteronomy
4.9 113
25.17 113
26.5–9 98
34.5 6

Judges
19 139

1 Samuel
13.1 5
21.1–6 4

2 Samuel
9–24 76
11 76

1 Kings
1–2 76
15.5 76

Psalms
7 124

Song of Songs
8.4 77

Isaiah
6.1–13 150
40.3 4, 32
55.11 103

Ezekiel
1.15 13
1.16 14
1.20 15
11.19 14
16 143
23 143
36.26 14

Malachi
3.1 4, 32

Apocrypha

Ecclesiasticus
38.24 vii

2 Maccabees
12.43–6 153

New Testament

Matthew
1.1–16 32

5.17–18 103
19.21 2
27.25 7
28.18 159

Mark
1.2–3 32
2.26 4
3.21 6
4.11–12 82
11.12–14 7
13.14 35
14.9 140
14.14–15 5
16.8 64, 109

Luke
1.46–55 136
3.23–38 32
4.32 156
10.25–37 81
24.13–35 64, 99

John
1.10–11 53
1.18 104
4 139
8.39–40 159
10.34–5 97, 103
15.5–10 149
16.13 163
17.11 169
19.11 159
19.14–16 5
19.31 5
20.28 57
21.24–5 6, 28, 104

Acts
17.2b–3 29
17.6 30

Romans
1.16 103
1.27–8 7
5.12–21 61f.
13.1 159

13.13–14 1
14.1 2

1 Corinthians
1.21 103
2.5 45
2.13 106
6.9–10 7
13.12 109
14.34–5 153
15.10–11 108

2 Corinthians
3.6 11, 14, 152
4.6 11
12.19 172
13.14 149

Galatians
4.24 11

Ephesians
1.17–18 103
3.10 103
3.18 103
5.22–33 7, 136
6.5–9 7

Colossians
3.22–4.1 7, 136

1 Timothy
2.11–15 7

2 Timothy
3.16 97, 103

Hebrews
1.1–2 159

2 Peter
1.19–21 97, 103

1 John
4.7–12 180

Jude
3 103

SUBJECT INDEX

Albright, William 110
Alexandria 4, 14, 31, 34–6, 51
allegory 16, 36, 77, 85–9, 132–4
Alter, Robert 71–6
Antioch 35–6
Antony of Egypt 2
Apocrypha 5, 153
apostolicity 28–31, 57, 62–5,
    167–9
Aquinas, Thomas 3, 18, 38,
    43, 147
Arianism 12
Aristotle 10, 17–18, 34–5
Assmann, Jan 112–13
Athanasius 181
atheism 7, 70, 107
Auerbach, Erich 84, 87–9, 117
Augustine of Hippo 1–4, 7–9,
    12–13, 16, 18, 21, 23, 25–6,
    36–7, 40, 43, 61–3, 68, 81, 86,
    169, 172–3
authority of scripture 21–3,
    103–6, 123–4, 154–60

Bakhtin, Mikhail 129
Barr, James 52–3, 98, 119, 124–5
Barth, Karl 20, 99–100,
    116, 148–9
Barton, John 156–9
Bartsch, Hans-Werner 97–8
Beckett, Samuel 114
Bede 68
Biblical Archaeology 110–11
Biblical Theology Movement
    97–8, 120–1
Biblicism 155–9

Blondel, Maurice 133
Bloom, Harold 90
Bockmuehl, Markus 57
Boff, Clodovis 137–8
Bousset, Wilhelm 48
Boyarin, Daniel 163
Brett, Mark 119
Brown, David 134–5
Brown, Raymond 59–62
Brueggemann, Walter
    123–32, 153
Bultmann, Rudolf 51–4, 101, 111

Calvin, John 16, 87, 155
Calvinism 97, 123
canon 5, 27–31, 50–1
Canonical approach 119–26
Cardenal, Ernesto 137
Cassian, John 175, 180
Catholic Epistles 36
catholicity 93–4, 164–9
Celsus 31–4, 37, 45, 56
Chatman, Seymour 79
Chenu, Marie-Dominique
    92–3, 168
Childs, Brevard 119–26, 129, 162
Christology 21, 36, 59, 99–100,
    104, 108, 130
Chrysostom, John 36, 68
Church 151–6, 160–73
Clines, David 75, 89
composition criticism 82
conflict 169–73
Congar, Yves 92, 133
consensus 169–73
contextual approaches 135–43

conversation 154–5, 169–73
Courcelle, Pierre 25
critical realism 55–6
criticism 50–65, 176–80
culture 90–4
Cummings, Brian 40
Cyril of Jerusalem 168

Daniélou, Jean 92
Darwin, Charles 71
Davies, Philip 163
Davis, Ellen 143
Dawkins, Richard 6
deconstruction 72, 74,
    90–1, 141
Dei Verbum 166
demythologization 101
Derrida, Jacques 91
development of doctrine
    57–62, 131–5
devotional reading 160, 176–9
dialogical 128–9, 153
dialogue, interfaith 162–3
Dilthey, Wilhelm 131
discipleship 140–1, 145–6, 180
Dostoevsky, Fyodor 129

Ehrman, Bart 104, 134
Eichhorn, Albert 48
Eichrodt, Walther 120
Enlightenment, the 4, 21–3, 42,
    56, 84, 115
Ephrem the Syrian 151–2
epistemology 56–7, 115–17
Erasmus 30, 38–40
eschatology 107–9
Essays and Reviews 69–70, 92
eucharist 141, 144, 161
Eusebius of Caesarea 18, 32–3,
    37, 51, 65
evangelical 102–3
existentialism 53, 100–1
Exum, Cheryl 77, 84, 142–3

feminist theology 72, 78,
    135–42, 170
fiction 32
Figura 87
figural reading 21, 85–90, 117
Fiorenza, Elizabeth
    Schussler 140–2, 152
Fish, Stanley 78, 82, 91–2,
    96, 160
Fishbane, Michael 34
Fitzmyer, Joseph 59, 61–3
form criticism 51–2, 74, 120
Fowl, Stephen 161–2, 165
Frei, Hans 84–90, 92,
    115–17, 119
fundamentalism 156
fusion of horizons 131

Gabler, Johann Philipp 44, 46–9
Gadamer, Hans-Georg 96,
    131–5, 160
Glossa ordinaria 38
Gnosticism 27–8, 101
Gregory, Pope 13–16
Gunkel, Hermann 48
Gunn, David 76–7
Gutierrez, Gustavo 138

Hadot, Pierre 25, 178–80
Hadrian 67–9, 71
Halbwachs, Maurice 112
Hanson, Richard 34
Hauerwas, Stanley 115
Heidegger, Martin 53
Heraclitus 10, 181
hermeneutics 7, 14, 20, 22,
    37, 59, 81, 96, 126, 131–2,
    135, 138, 142, 144, 146, 160,
    164, 175–7
Herodotus 33
Hippocrates 10
historical approaches 25–65,
    106–10, 176–9

History of Religions School 49,
51, 99, 108, 120, 140–1
Homer 10, 34, 181
homosexuality 7, 164

ideology 21–2, 52, 55, 64, 72, 95,
135–9, 141–2, 171
idolatry 149, 160
imagination 134–5, 176–80
improvization 144–6
incarnation 31, 53, 57–9, 93, 142,
149, 159
inerrancy 41, 85, 104, 156
infallibility 103, 155–6, 158
inspiration 69–70, 95–9, 102–6,
147–50, 154–60
Irenaeus of Lyons 27–31, 50–1,
156–8, 161, 167
Irigaray, Luce 141–2
Islam 163
Israel 11, 29–30, 77, 106–7,
110–11, 120, 127–30

Jauss, Hans 96
Jenson, Robert 150, 160
Jesus see Quest of the historical
Jesus
Josephus 34–5
Jowett, Benjamin 69–71,
73, 91–2
Judaism 124, 140–1, 163

Kelsey, David 96–7, 100–1,
115–16, 118–19, 152–3, 157
Kermode, Frank 71–3, 80–9
Kierkegaard, Søren 3, 6, 19–20
Kuschel, Karl-Josef 94

Lamberton, Robert 10
Lash, Nicholas 143–5
Lausanne Covenant 102–3, 145
Leclercq, Jean 177–8
Lectio divina 176–7

Lessing, Gotthold Ephraim 44–6,
48, 51, 54, 58–9, 89, 109
Lévi-Strauss, Claude 113
Libanius 36
Liberation theology 136–9, 142
Lindbeck, George 115–17, 119
literal sense 12, 14, 16–17, 36, 39,
77, 84–90, 152
literary approaches 21–3,
67–94, 116–17, 128–30, 138–9,
162–3, 176–7
liturgy 116, 144, 177
Louth, Andrew 132–5
Loyola, Ignatius 160, 176, 179
Lubac, Henri de 92, 132–3, 152
Luther, Martin 3, 16, 38, 40, 87,
132, 154–5, 165

McCabe, Herbert 148
MacIntyre, Alasdair 117, 131,
133–4
magisterium 60, 155
Maimonides 17–18, 20, 77
Marcion 28
Martin, Dale 176–9
Marxism 137
Masoretic text 5
maximalist and minimalist 111
Medellin 136–7
memory 100–15
metanarrative 119
metaphor 17, 26, 67, 77, 97, 127,
142, 145, 171, 173
metaphysics 17–18, 52
Michie, Donald 78–80
Mitchell, Margaret 14, 152, 172
Moberly, Walter 119, 125
modernity 84, 117, 131, 147
Momigliano, Arnaldo 33
monasticism 2, 67–8, 176, 178
Montag, John 147
Moore, Stephen 78–82, 90–1
Morgan, Robert 141

Murphy, Francesca 117
myth 26, 101

narrative 84–90, 115–17
narrative criticism 78–80
New criticism 74, 121
Newman, John Henry 133
Nicene Creed 167, 169, 176
Niebuhr, Richard 115
Niehoff, Maren 34–5

objectivity 21, 95–6, 179
obscurantism 18
obscurity of scripture 9–21
Origen 4, 14, 31–4, 36–7, 45, 51, 65, 71
original sin 61–3

Pannenberg, Wolfhart 106–10, 114–15
Papias 28
parables 81–2, 86
participation 15–17, 43, 149–50, 160, 168
Passover 5, 88, 113
patriarchy 136–42
Peirce, Charles 117
performance 143–8
Philo 34–5, 178
philosophy 3, 10, 17–19, 31–2, 178–80
Plato 10, 71
Platonism 18, 31
Plotinus 9
poetry 73–8
Polycarp 28
Porphyry 32–3, 37, 56
positivism 22, 55, 106, 130
postcolonialism 72, 91, 95
postliberal theology 115–17, 135
postmodernism 55–6, 116–17
poststructuralism 80, 82, 90, 94
praxis 137

prayer 15, 91, 121–2, 153, 160, 169
proof 102–6
Pyper, Hugh 19

Quest of the historical Jesus 51, 54, 59, 75, 81, 107, 138

racism 167
Rad, Gerhard von 98, 120, 138
Rahner, Karl 166
Ratzinger, Joseph 57–9, 166
reason 13–18, 42–50, 146–50
reception history 5, 78, 91, 96
redaction criticism 74, 79–80, 82, 138
Reformation 4, 16, 38–40, 43, 132, 154–5, 165–6
Reimarus, Hermann Samuel 44–5
resistance 135–43
Ressourcement 92, 133
resurrection 55–7, 63–4, 107–9
retrieval, hermeneutics of 135, 136
revelation 43–4, 106–10, 146–50
Rhoads, David 78–80
Ricoeur, Paul 126, 135
Rogerson, John 111–15
Rowland, Christopher 137, 164, 167
Ruether, Rosemary Radford 139–40
Russell, Bertrand 7

salvation history 98–9
sanctification 157–8
Sanders, Ed 107
Schleiermacher, Friedrich 131
Schweitzer, Albert 51
Scriptural reasoning 163
Septuagint 5, 124
sexism 167, 170
Sheehan, Jeremy 41

Sherwood, Yvonne 80, 91
social-scientific
  approaches 100–15
Socrates 7
sola scriptura 38, 154, 165
Solentiname 137
source criticism 74–6
spiritual exercises 13–14, 82–3,
  86–7, 176–80
Steiner, George 22, 152, 158
Story *see* narrative
Stott, John 103–6, 152
Suárez, Francisco 147
supersessionism 16
suspicion, hermeneutics of 135–6

Tertullian 87
testimony 26–31, 44–6, 57–65,
  104–5, 125–36
Theodore of Mopsuestia 36, 83
Theodoret of Cyrrhus 151–2, 173
Thornton, Lionel 100–1
Thucydides 33
Tiberius 31
Tillich, Paul 100–1
tradition 27–30, 36–41, 59–64,
  131–5, 154–5, 165–6
Trent, Council of 61, 154–5

Trible, Phyllis 139
Troeltsch, Ernst 49
Tyndale, William 4, 40–1
typological 85, 87, 100, 113, 117,
  125, 133

Valentinus 17–28
Verbum Dei 166
Vermes, Geza 59
vernacular 39–42, 155
virginal conception 59–60,
  62–3
Volf, Miroslav 95
Vulgate 40

Watson, Francis 161–5, 167
Webster, John 148–9
Williams, Rowan 179
Wirkungsgeschichte 132, 135
Wittenberg 38
Wittgenstein, Ludwig 3, 117
worship 146, 148, 160–1, 177
Wrede, William 44, 48–50
Wright, George Ernest
  98, 110–11
Wright, Tom 54–7, 118, 158–60

Young, Frances 36, 144–5